Transforming Politics,
Transforming America

Race, Ethnicity, and Politics
Luis Ricardo Fraga and Paula D. McClain, *Editors*

Transforming Politics, Transforming America

The Political and Civic Incorporation of Immigrants in the United States

Edited by Taeku Lee, S. Karthick Ramakrishnan, and Ricardo Ramírez

University of Virginia Press

Charlottesville and London

University of Virginia Press
© 2006 by the Rector and Visitors of the University of Virginia
All rights reserved
Printed in the United States of America on acid-free paper
First published 2006

9 8 7 6 5 4 3 2 1

Library of Congress Cataloging-in-Publication Data

Transforming politics, transforming America : the political and civic incorporation of immigrants in the United States / edited by Taeku Lee, S. Karthick Ramakrishnan, and Ricardo Ramírez.
    p.   cm. — (Race, ethnicity, and politics)
  Based on a conference on "A Nation of Immigrants: Ethnic Identity and Political Incorporation" held in May 2003 in Berkeley, Calif.
  Includes bibliographical references and index.
  ISBN 0-8139-2545-2 (cloth : alk. paper)
  1. Immigrants—United States—Political activity—Congresses. I. Lee, Taeku.
II. Ramakrishnan, S. Karthick (Subramanian Karthick), 1975– III. Ramírez, Ricardo, 1973– IV. Series.
JV6477.T73 2006
323'.0420869120973—dc22

2005033301

To Shirley, Brinda, and Lupe

Contents

Acknowledgments

This volume started as a series of casual conversations between Bruce Cain, Jack Citrin, and the three of us in the fall of 2002. These riffs eventually harmonized into a few convergent themes about the state of political science research on immigration and ethnic politics in the United States. First, political science lagged far behind sociology and economics in bringing its attention to bear on the dramatic post-1965 wave of immigration to the United States and its implication for established understandings of political behavior. Second, this gap was starting to be filled by an emerging body of research, using new datasets and suggestive of new theoretical approaches.

From these themes emerged a consensus to convene a meeting of political scientists doing what we agreed was important and innovative new work on immigrant politics. With generous support from the University of California's Institute of Governmental Studies (IGS), we convened a conference, "A Nation of Immigrants: Ethnic Identity and Political Incorporation," over two sun-kissed days in Berkeley in early May 2003. In addition to the contributors to this volume, participants at the conference included Dennis Chong, Rodney Hero, Amaney Jamal, Pei-te Lien, Reuel Rogers, Leland Saito, David Sears, Carole Uhlaner, and Carolyn Wong. A number of other invited scholars expressed interest and enthusiasm in attending but were otherwise unable to make our meeting. The convening was replete with constructive exchange of each other's research and a natural setting for some fruitful stock taking and discussions of agenda setting.

One of the postscripts to the conference—in addition to the usual largesse of bonhomie and litany of ideas and plans for future studies and data gathering efforts—is this edited volume. This volume brings together a select number of essays from the initial IGS convening and offers in one volume a wide-ranging examination by political scientists of immigrants in the contemporary politics of the United States.

In making this volume possible, we have accumulated many debts. A heap of thanks is owed to Dick Holway for championing this volume and ensuring its timely publication, and to the University of Virginia Press's series editors Paula McClain and Luis Fraga for seeing the value of this project and providing guidance through various reviews. We are also grateful to Marc Levin at IGS for keeping the conference organized and ensuring that papers were prepared and disseminated in a timely manner. We also thank Kristel Bou-Lahoud, Connie Hsu, Tiffany Ko, and Arezo Yazd for their expert research assistance on this volume.

Finally, this work would not have been possible without the aid of our respective homes, personal and professional. We thank the University of California at Berkeley, the Public Policy Institute of California, the University of California at Riverside, and the University of Southern California for their institutional support of this project. We further thank our respective partners, Shirley, Brinda, and Lupe—to whom this volume is lovingly dedicated—for their indulgence, inspiration, and irremunerable willingness to incorporate our immigrant lives into their own.

Transforming Politics,
Transforming America

Introduction

Taeku Lee, S. Karthick Ramakrishnan, and Ricardo Ramírez

Why should the Palatine boors be suffered to swarm into our
settlement, and, by herding together, establish their language and
manners, to the exclusion of ours? Why should Pennsylvania,
founded by the English, become a colony of aliens, who will
shortly be so numerous as to Germanize us, instead of our An-
glifying them, and will never adopt our language or customs any
more than they can acquire our complexion?
　　　　　　　—Benjamin Franklin, "Observations Concerning the
　　　　　　　Increase of Mankind, Peopling of Countries, etc."

What then is the American, this new man? . . . He is an American,
who, leaving behind him all his ancient prejudices and manners,
receives new ones from the new mode of life he has embraced, the
new government he obeys, and the new rank he holds. He has become an American by being received in the broad lap of our great
Alma Mater. Here individuals of all races are melted into a new
race of man, whose labors and posterity will one day cause great
changes in the world.
　　　　　　　　　　—Hector St. John de Crèvecoeur,
　　　　　　　　　　Letters from an American Farmer

The idea of America as a "nation of immigrants" harkens to well before the country's founding, with thousands of settlers and slaves
pouring into the Colonies from England, continental Europe, and Africa. As the epigraphs from Franklin and Crèvecoeur suggest, there
has been little consensus throughout our history on the consequences
of this idea of a nation of immigrants. The concept has often embod-
ied competing visions of the desirability of immigration and its likely

consequences for civic and political life in the United States. Crève-coeur's *Letters from an American Farmer* (1782) at the close of the eighteenth century presents an optimistic picture of assimilation and amalgamation, with immigrants coming to the "great American asylum" to shed their skin and their customs and transform into a "new race of man." Franklin's "Observations Concerning the Increase of Mankind," (Ziff 1959) by contrast, cautions that immigration would balkanize the New World rather than assimilating into the established Anglo culture or even amalgamating with existing settlers to create a new race of Americans. The immigration of Germans to Pennsylvania was seen by Franklin as an excessive incursion that tarnished the "complexion" of America, a threat similar to that posed by the forced migration of Africans to the New World.

These debates over immigration and its likely impact on civic and political life in the United States have continued through each successive wave of immigration—from German and Irish immigrants of the 1800s to later arrivals from Italy, Eastern Europe, Mexico, China, and Japan. Immigration was a particularly salient issue in the early twentieth century, as hundreds of thousands reached American shores and the foreign born accounted for more than one in seven residents (figure 1). Concerns grew during this era about the civic and political incorporation of the foreign born and their native-born children. These concerns found expression in various political campaign speeches, such as Theodore Roosevelt's declaration in 1915 that there was no room in this country for "hyphenated Americans."[1] They also found expression in various legislative measures such as the Immigration Act of 1924, which banned immigration from most Asian countries and limited the entry of immigrants from Eastern and Southern Europe. With the onset of the Great Depression and World War II, immigration levels dropped drastically and so did concerns about the civic and political incorporation of immigrants.[2]

The 1965 Hart-Cellar Act amendments to the Immigration and Nationality Act of 1952 have led to a profound transformation in immigration that has rekindled debates about the economic, social, civic, and political adaptation and incorporation of immigrants into the United States. In sheer volume, we are witnessing the largest influx of immigrants since the early twentieth century. According to Census Bureau statistics, immigrants and their children compose close to one in four Americans today, with more than 34 million foreign-born and almost 32 million second-generation immigrants in the United States in 2002 (U.S. Census Bureau 2002). These numbers compare to 9.6 million foreign-born residents and 24 million second-generation immi-

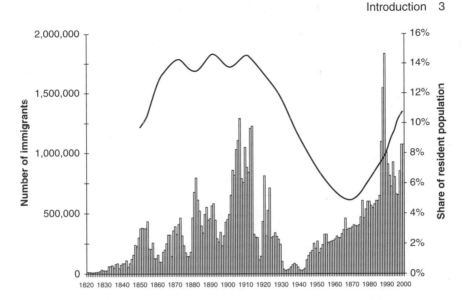

Figure 1 Trends in immigration and the immigrant share of the U.S. population, 1821–2001
Sources: USCIS; Census Bureau.
Note: The foreign-born share of the resident population is based on the decennial census starting in 1850, and intercensal estimates are based on an assumption of linear change between one census and the next.

grants in 1970 (Gibson and Lennon 1999). In addition to the upsurge in the foreign born, this wave of immigration has also produced a sea change in the racial and ethnic composition of this nation. Contemporary immigrants come from different shores than the earlier immigrants from Europe, arriving instead from Asia, the Caribbean, and Latin America. Up until the first decade of the twentieth century, about 90 percent of new migrants to the United States set sail from European shores. By the 1980s, this proportion had dwindled to about 12 percent, with almost 85 percent of new migrants coming from Asia and the Americas (U.S. Immigration and Naturalization Service 2002).

These immigrant-induced demographic changes are likely to continue in the foreseeable future. In the latest 2000 decennial census, Latinos emerged as the largest nonwhite minority in the United States (U.S. Census Bureau 2001). Moreover, according to the Census Bureau, America will become a "majority-minority" nation sometime in the middle of this century, when white Americans are projected to fall below 50 percent of the U.S. adult population. This majority-minority status already describes the demographics of New Mexico, Hawaii, and California, as well as numerous cities throughout the nation. Emblematic of these future trends, according to a *Washington*

Post poll in 1994, Americans on average already perceive whites to be only about 50 percent of the U.S. adult population (Brodie 1995).

These sweeping demographic changes, moreover, are occurring in the midst of equally far-reaching changes in the way we categorize and classify people (see Prewitt in this volume). Starting with the shift from enumerator observation in the U.S. Censuses to respondent self-identification in the 1960 Census, we have seen a succession of dramatic changes in our system of ethnoracial classification, with the introduction of a separate "Hispanic" ethnic identifier in 1980, a proliferation of Asian, Pacific Islander, American Indian, Native Hawaiian, Alaska Native categories in 1980 and 1990, and, in the most recent decennial census, the option of choosing more than one among these categories. These changes both reflect and contribute to the multiplicity and hybridity of identities defined by race, ethnicity, and national origin, not to mention the critical intersections of these boundaries with other identities defined by gender, class, sexual orientation, religion, region, and the like.

As Crèvecoeur observed, this new face of America portends "great changes in the world," especially in the realm of race relations and ethnic politics. To a significant extent, we are already witness to these changes. The emergence of Latinos and Asians has already affected congressional apportionment, electoral contests, policy debates, and daily social and economic relations at the state and local levels. In Los Angeles, this new politics has entailed a shift in electoral cleavages from one of racial polarization along black-white lines as captured by Tom Bradley's attempts—unsuccessful, then successful—to unseat Sam Yorty, to one of Asian and Latino challenges to the status quo with Michael Woo's unsuccessful campaign against Richard Riordan, and Antonio Villaraigosa's unsuccessful, then successful, campaigns against James Hahn. Los Angeles, too, saw the potentially incendiary effects of the new racial order in the United States in the 1992 urban riots in the aftermath of the Rodney King verdict—a verdict adjudicated by an all-white jury in Simi Valley, California, that was perceived by many black residents as a vindication of police brutality and that led to what many have referred to as the nation's first multiracial urban uprising.

At the statewide level, the rising tide of anti-immigrant sentiments has been organized and mobilized in California through citizen initiatives, as evidenced by the overwhelming success of Proposition 63 in 1986 (which recognized English as the official language of the state), Proposition 187 in 1994 (which sought to deny health, education, and social service benefits to undocumented immigrants and their children), Proposition 209 in 1996 (which made illegal the use of race, sex, color, ethnicity, or national origin as a consideration in any decisions of public employment, public education, or public contracting), and Proposition 227 in 1998 (which effectively abolished bilingual education in California). In fact, the politics of race and immigration in California have so transcended and transformed the conventional markers of party politics and liberal-conservative ideology that the October 2003 special election saw the triumphant Republican candidate Arnold Schwarzenegger claim the mantle of the immigrant candidate at the same time that a citizen initiative (Proposition 54), spearheaded by a conservative African American, Ward Connerly, sought to bar state and local governments from collecting information on race, ethnicity, color, and national origin. Interestingly, the prior pattern of a white majority voting in large measure as an electoral bloc to pass a citizen initiative that disproportionately burdens nonwhite communities did not repeat itself with Proposition 54.

While California is the most commonly cited setting for emerging trends in immigrant politics, the changing tides are not isolated to the Golden State. In statewide politics elsewhere, the multiracial and multiethnic bases of electoral competition span the nation from the successful gubernatorial bids of Gary Locke in Washington and Bill Richardson in New Mexico to the unsuccessful bids of Bobby Jindal in Louisiana and Tony Sanchez in Texas. There are even signs of the political maturation of Asian and Latinos on the national level, with the election of representatives such as David Wu (Oregon-D), Ileana Ros-Lehtinen (Florida-R), and Bobby Jindal (Louisiana-R). The presence of immigrants has also been felt in the executive branch, with Mel Martinez, a Cuban immigrant; Elaine Chao, an immigrant from Taiwan; Rosario Marin, a Mexican immigrant; and Norman Mineta, a second-generation Japanese immigrant, serving in George W. Bush's cabinet. In fact, given President Bush's razor-thin margin of victory in Florida in 2000, the plausible (if extravagant) claim might be made that the disproportionately Republican partisanship of Cuban Americans was a decisive factor in the first Bush victory and solidified his gains in the second.

In addition, the aftershocks of 9/11 have galvanized efforts to further close America's borders, both literally and figuratively. The Department of Homeland Security placed more onerous tracking and identifying requirements on foreign students in the United States and implemented a program in 2002 (since discontinued) that required immigrants from predominantly Muslim countries to register with the U.S. Bureau of Immigration and Customs Enforcement. This restrictionist trend following the 9/11 attacks was reflected not only in government policy but also in public attitudes and opinions. A November 2001 National Public Radio poll, for instance, found that, while 75 percent of the American public opposed racial profiling in general, fully 66 percent supported such practices for persons of Arab or Middle Eastern descent. A majority (56 percent) of respondents agreed that "non-citizens living legally in or visiting the United States . . . should not have the same legal rights as citizens."

Moreover, respondents were largely in favor of barring from certain activities "someone who says that terrorism is the fault of how our country behaves in the world" (Rosenbaum et al. 2001) Specifically, almost two in three Americans would limit that person's ability to teach in public schools (64 percent) and to work in government (63 percent), and more than a third (38 percent) would even limit that person's right to free speech. These findings are even more incisive when juxtaposed with a New California Media poll in which a large majority of Latinos, Middle Easterners, and Asian Americans agreed that "the United States has too much influence around the world," characterizing a current political milieu with little room for critical patriotism and free exchange of opinions (September 5, 2002).

Clearly, widespread apprehension exists today about the consequences of immigration for civic and political life in the United States. Such anxieties, moreover, are not isolated to the uneducated hoi polloi, but find voice among elite intellectuals like Harvard University's Samuel Huntington, who asks:

> Will the de-Westernization of the United States, if it occurs, also mean its de-Americanization? If it does and Americans cease to adhere to their liberal democratic and European-rooted political ideology, the United States as we have known it will cease to exist and will follow the other ideologically defined superpower [referring to the former Soviet Union] onto the ash heap of history. (1993, 188)

More recently, Huntington has aimed his alarmism more narrowly toward Latino immigrants, arguing that "[i]n this new era, the single most immediate and most serious challenge to America's traditional identity comes from the immense and continuing immigration from Latin America, especially from Mexico" (2004a, 31).[3] Huntington concludes: "There is no Americano dream. There is only the American dream created by an Anglo-Protestant society. Mexican Americans will share in that dream and in that society only if they dream in English" (41).

There is, in sum, no shortage of forecasts—sunlit or dire—on where the prevailing winds of such demographic change will lead. Yet, the sum total of this capacious body of work as a set of systematic, carefully researched, evidence-based research on the political future of Asian Americans and Latinos remains nebulous. While sociologists have developed a rich literature on Latino and Asian American acculturation (vis-à-vis debates about assimilation, ethnogenesis, racial stereotyping, second-generation immigrants), political science lags considerably behind.[4] Beyond the sheer paucity of published works and relevant datasets, political scientists have largely examined Latinos and Asian Americans either in isolation (i.e., without comparing groups or taking an explicitly multiracial context) or by using research questions, conceptual frameworks, and methodological tools that have evolved from the study of black-white relations in the United States.

Thus, the focus of political science research on Asian Americans and Latinos has been almost exclusively aimed at narrowly conceived questions about partisanship acquisition, political participation, and political coalition formation. With partisanship, the primary question has been whether Latinos and Asians will predominantly identify with the Democratic Party, as African Americans have since the civil rights era, or whether they will split more evenly between parties along sectarian issue preferences. With political participation, the primary question has been whether racial group consciousness will be the primary engine of Latino and Asian political behavior, as it has been for African Americans, or whether the story will highlight the importance of socioeconomic status and political mobilization by the Democratic and Republican parties. And with political coalitions, the primary question has been whether Latinos and Asians will form multiracial coalitions with African Americans, pan-ethnic coalitions across constituent ethnic groups, or whether racial and ethnic markers will recede in significance and cede to ideological, issue-specific, or context-specific determinants of intergroup conflict and cooperation.

While these are key questions to ask, other crucial dimensions of immigrant ethnic politics have come to be overlooked or discounted. How well do existing social and political categories—around citizenship, race, ethnicity, and partisanship—fit the experiences and circumstances of Asian and Latino immigrants to the United States? In what ways are the public opinions of racial and ethnic groups similar, different, and interdependent? How well do the experiences of Asians and Latinos fit with conventional theories—assimilationism (straight-line or segmented), pluralism, internal colonialism, separatism, and the like—that have been developed to explain the experiences of white ethnic immigrant communities or African Americans? What patterns of interracial contact—where we live, where we work, whose company we keep as friends and intimate partners, and whom we randomly encounter in the streets—characterize the lives of Asians, Latinos, and other immigrant groups?

This book presents a first attempt at a comprehensive, evidence-based examination of immigrants in the landscape of contemporary politics in the United States. Its contributors tackle some fundamental questions relating to immigrants and their political participation, such as what meaning citizenship holds, whether existing systems of ethno-racial classification and prevailing understandings of group identity are politically relevant, and whether traditional patterns of mobilization, participation, and political assimilation apply to these groups. For a long time, such questions have been relatively neglected in scholarship on immigration in the United States. This volume brings together a collection of the newest research by political scientists and sociologists, with an emphasis on research that brings innovative theory, quantitative methods, and systematic data to bear on the above questions. Its central aim is to provoke political scientists and immigration scholars to consider the consequences of these immigrant-driven demographic changes for contemporary politics of the United States as well as for the questions, categories, and conceptual frameworks we use to study race relations and ethnic politics.

The contributors to this volume are a distinguished set of social scientists working on the issues of race, immigration, and political behavior. They have been asked to engage their research areas through historical analysis, discussion of contemporary controversies, and consideration of possible trajectories in the future. While many of the essays tend toward quantitative empirical analyses of participation and incorporation, several rely on historical and institutional approaches to the issue.

The volume is organized into four parts. The first section delves into the fundamentals of measurement—what are the implications of immigration for our measurement of race and ethnicity and what are the consequences of existing approaches to such identity categories for political behavior. The lead essay, by Kenneth Prewitt, former director of the U.S. Census Bureau, introduces us to our current ways of thinking about race and ethnicity by charting the long history of ethnoracial categorization in the United States. As Prewitt notes, the prevailing five-part scheme of "white, black, brown, yellow, and red" is now giving way to a much more complex mosaic of classification, with potentially profound implications for the shape of American politics to come. Jane Junn follows Prewitt by striking a conspicuously cautious and contrarian note about the destiny of demography. Unlike others who rush to dire prognostications of "race wars" and the balkanization of American national identity, Junn insists on first interrogating the slippery steps from ethnic and racial categories to group consciousness, and from group consciousness to political action. By clarifying what is assumed and what is at stake—both empirically and normatively—Junn sets the stage for the more careful consideration of the political significance of the demographic transformation in the United States today.

In the second part of the volume, several scholars examine the ambiguous boundaries that new immigrants navigate between individuals and nation-states—what is at stake in juridico-legal definitions of citizenship and whether transnational ties to one's home country politics inhibits or potentiates the political incorporation and activation of immigrants in the United States. Lisa García Bedolla examines how current policies regarding naturalization affect the political and civic life of immigrants in the United States. She calls for a more inclusive policy of American citizenship, premised on a clear notion of the role of the state as well as the rights and responsibilities of immigrants. Next, Cara Wong and Grace Cho discuss the relatively unexplored relationship between citizenship and military service. While we mostly assume that obligations to serve the nation follow from citizenship, Wong and Cho note that the converse—obtaining citizenship through the fulfillment of one's responsibility to the state in the form of military service—is a long-standing practice in the United States, one that is made poignant and prominent by the restrictionism of U.S. immigration policy and continued use of foreign-born soldiers in U.S. interventions around the world.

The two remaining essays in this section examine dual citizenship status and its implications for political participation within the United States and beyond. Bruce Cain and Brendan Doherty take on the focused question of whether citizenship in two countries burdens one's participation in the United States. The authors argue that there are opportunity costs to participating in multiple contexts, and bring their analysis of a recent *Washington Post* survey of Latinos (as well as secondary evidence from studies of Asian and Caribbean immigrants) to bolster this claim. Louis DeSipio considers the other face of dual citizenship: whether it affects the politics of immigrants' home countries? DeSipio examines this complex relationship of immigrant participation in the politics of the homeland by carefully weighing the evidence from a 2002 Tomás Rivera Policy Institute survey of Latino immigrants.

The third section of our volume examines whether and how institutions serve as a focal influence on the political activation and mobilization of new immigrants. Zoltan Hajnal and Taeku Lee examine the contemporary relationship between immigration-based groups and the American two-party system—whether individuals come to identify with a particular political party and, if so, which party they identify with and why they do so. The authors argue that traditional accounts of party identification—premised on socialization within the United States and the "linear" measurement of partisanship—is especially ill-suited to understanding how Asian Americans and Latinos identify with political parties. In this study, the authors use data from the Latino National Political Survey and the Pilot National Asian American Politics Study to support their insistence on a new, more broadly generalizeable account of party identification. Next, Ricardo Ramírez and Janelle Wong examine the role of elites in mobilizing immigrants to participate in U.S. elections. Using innovative voter mobilization experiments of Asians and Latinos in Southern California from 2002, they compare the obstacles and mobilization strategies of partisan and nonpartisan elites and focus on the consequences of such strategies on the actual turnout of immigrants on election day.

The final part of the book looks ahead to the future of immigrant incorporation in the United States. John Mollenkopf and his colleagues on the New York Second Generation Project (Jennifer Holdaway, Philip Kasinitz, and Mary Waters) lead this section with a study of attitudes toward government and politics among first- and second-generation immigrants in the New York metropolitan area. They find considerable variations in the political trajectories of immigrants from different regions of the world and argue that the dynamics under way in New York serve as a portent for the future of immigrant politics in the United States. Tatishe Nteta examines the issue of intergroup relations more directly to address the question of how differentiation from blacks varies between the foreign born and the native born. Using data from the Multi-City Survey of Urban Inequality, Nteta points out that foreign-born Latinos and Asian Americans are more likely than their native-born counterparts to hold negative stereotypes of African Americans. Furthermore, he argues that the traditional models of tolerance based on educational attainment and racial contact do little to explain racial differentiation among immigrants. Instead, factors related to immigrant adaptation, such as length of stay in the United States and English proficiency, play a more significant role, pointing to the possibility that these stereotypes may diminish over time.

What the future portends also receives scholarly attention from Kathryn Pearson and Jack Citrin, who examine whether the "straight-line" assimilation model is relevant to the attitudes and experiences of Asian and Latino immigrants. Using both national-level and California-specific data, the authors present a mixed picture, showing that the adaptation process often involves the creation of separate ethnic identities as opposed to identification with the ideal of a unified "melting pot." In the last essay of the section, Karthick Ramakrishnan examines differences in civic volunteerism across racial groups and immigrant generations. Using data from the Current Population Survey, Ramakrishnan shows that immigrant-related factors play a stronger role than race in shaping civic participation and that group inequalities in civic volunteerism mirror those found for formal political participation, suggesting that persistent biases are likely in who participates in our political and civic institutions in the years to come. Finally, the volume concludes with some thoughts regarding future directions in the study of immigrant politics and recommendations on ways to give immigrants greater voice in the political process.

The study of immigrant incorporation inevitably involves a multitude of terms. Some are based on legal and administrative protocols, others are regenerated in our habits of the mind and tongue, while still others arise in response to trends and transformations in society, politics, and scholarship. Language not only has the ability to define and frame the way we think about an issue with great clarity, but also the power to mystify, muddle, and complicate. Given the various meanings and usages associated with terms related to immigrant incorporation, we conclude this introduction with a few words about the terms and concepts used in this volume.

First, the federal government differentiates the *foreign born* into various types: (1) children of U.S. citizens born abroad who still are considered U.S. citizens by birth, (2) naturalized citizens who have been sworn in as U.S. citizens, (3) legal immigrants who are eligible to live in the United States on a permanent basis, (4) refugees and those

given asylum who are allowed to stay in the country to avoid persecution in their home countries, (5) nonimmigrants who are authorized to
stay in the country on a temporary basis, and (6) illegal aliens (or unauthorized or undocumented immigrants) who are not eligible to enter or remain in the country. In the fiscal year ending September 2002,
the Department of Homeland Security reported over 600,000 naturalizations, about 1 million immigrants, 44,000 refugees and people
granted asylum, and nearly 28 million nonimmigrants (U.S. Department of Homeland Security 2004). No estimate of illegal immigrants
was given, but the estimated total population of undocumented immigrants in 2004 was 10.3 million (Passel 2005).

Within these categories, there are further classifications. Legal immigrants can obtain permanent residence in the United States based
on sponsorship by a family member or employer, adjustment of status
from being a refugee or asylum grantee, or special considerations such
as "diversity programs" that favor those entering from countries that
are underrepresented among contemporary immigrants. Refugees are
those persons who emigrate to the United States as a result of immi-
nent persecution in their home countries; asylum grantees are those
persons already living in the United States and who face likely persecution if returned to their home countries. Over 85 percent of the nonimmigrants recorded by the Department of Homeland Security are
temporary visitors on vacation or business, while students and temporary workers and their spouses account for most of the remainder.
Finally, unauthorized immigrants (also referred to as undocumented
or illegal immigrants) can be those who enter the country illegally to
work or to be reunited with family members, those who overstay their
nonimmigrant visas, and those who remain in the United States despite having their asylum cases denied.

A second important categorical distinction is by *nativity* and *generation.* The term "first-generation" immigrant is used to refer to those
persons born outside the United States. A commonly used differentiation is between those who immigrate as teenagers or older ("Generation 1.0") and those who arrive before their teenage years ("Generation 1.5").[5] "Native born" is used to refer to those persons born in the
United States. Among the native born, "second-generation" is used to
define those persons born in the United States to at least one foreign-
born parent, and some even differentiate the second generation further
into those with two foreign-born parents ("Generation 2.0") and those
with one native-born parent and one foreign-born parent ("Genera-

tion 2.5").[6] Finally, "third generation (and higher)" refers to those persons born in the United States to U.S.-born parents.

As we noted at the outset of this introduction, one of the distinguishing characteristics of the current "wave" of immigration to the United States is the disproportionate number of persons from Asia and Latin America, in contrast to earlier waves dominated by migrants from Europe. As a result, the concepts of *race* and *ethnicity* are commonly used as markers of the current influx of immigrants. The most prevalent distinction between the two terms is that race marks processes of external ascription and internal identification by putatively indelible, and often biologically based, traits such as a person's skin color and phenotype. Ethnicity, by contrast, is commonly used to mark the processes of external ascription and internal identification by ostensibly nonbiologically based traits such as language and dialect, religion, culture, national origin, and so on. The distinction between the two is admittedly somewhat arbitrary and quite pointedly the result of political contestation and bureaucratic categorization, rather than external realities. For one thing, groups that have previously been considered to be "racial" (such as the Greeks, Irish, and Italians at the turn of the twentieth century) are now viewed uncontroversially as being "ethnic." Today, we see the murky boundaries between these two concepts even in the categorization of race and ethnicity in the decennial census: persons of European origin are lumped together under the monoracial category of "white," while persons who identify with the categories of "Asian Indian," "Chinese," "Filipino," "Japanese," "Korean," "Vietnamese," and even "Other Asian" are conferred the status of a separate race (Asian), and persons of Latin American descent are alone in having a separate measure of "ethnicity."

The terms we use to describe particular racially and ethnically defined communities are equally contested. In this volume, the contributors use variants of the terms used to characterize the revised "Directive 15" categories of race and ethnicity (Office of Management and Budget, 1997). In practical terms, this means the interchangeable use of the terms "Anglo" and "white" to describe persons of European origin; "African American" and "black" to describe persons of African origin; "Latino" and "Hispanic" to describe persons of Latin American origin; "Asian" and "Asian American" to describe persons with origins from the Far East, Southeast Asia, or South Asia.[7]

Finally, many terms refer to the influence of American society on immigrants and the response of immigrants to these societal influences. Several of these refer to how immigrants adapt to life in the United States, with sharp disagreements over what constitutes the nature of American society and whether immigrants gain equal entry into all social and political strata in the United States. The front lines of this debate are marked by the question of whether new immigrants engender greater heterogeneity or homogeneity in the United States. Those who see greater heterogeneity resulting from immigration generally advocate one of three distinct theories—*internal colonialism, balkanization,* or *pluralism*—all of which foresee persistent racial and ethnic differences throughout the process of immigrant adaptation. For internal colonialists, this differentiation is defined by the power and the will of entrenched groups to maintain their dominance and subjugate new immigrant groups to the margins of social, economic, and political life. Those who refer to greater balkanization see increasing heterogeneity as a strain on the social and political order with adverse consequences for the native-born population. Pluralists, however, see few negative consequences to the greater heterogeneity brought about by immigrants in the United States. Rather than viewing identities as "either/or" choices, pluralists tend to advocate "both/and" between a single, universal "American" identity and multiple, particularistic ethnic identities.

Finally, advocates of *assimilation* theory emphasize the blending of immigrants into the practices, norms, and ideologies of the host society. In many instances, the term assimilation is used in reference to the absorption of cultural differences ("acculturation"); in other cases, they refer to such changes as health outcomes and socioeconomic status. Often, there is disagreement over what constitutes an appropriate reference point—whether, as in Huntington's case, the essential character of American society is "Anglo-Protestant," or, as in Crèvecoeur's case, a sui generis American culture arises in the New World, or, as in yet other cases, whether the notion of American culture itself is fluid and shifting, in part from the continuous contribution of new waves of immigrants. Similar debates occur for noncultural aspects of immigrant assimilation—over what constitutes a relevant touchstone for examining outcomes such as fertility, residential segregation, educational attainment, and earnings.

Related to the common confusion around the usage of the term assimilation is the similar lack of clarity on the use of *political incorporation.* The challenge lies in the absence of a widely agreed definition of or method of measuring "political incorporation." Instead, political incorporation often serves as the umbrella term when discussing a range of political activities, institutional behaviors, and measures of civic engagement. Moreover, the often-cited framework for assessing political incorporation provided by Rufus Browning, Dale Rogers Marshal, and David Tabb (1984) emphasizes the realm of formal politics, to the neglect of often-critical informal spheres of political life. This limitation is especially acute for immigration-based groups, whose full access to spheres of formal, institutionalized politics is often limited by citizenship status. Yet another problem with existing frameworks for assessing political incorporation is the expectation that incorporation is linear, echoing the linearity of classical assimilation theory.

As the essays in this volume show, the core notion of what constitutes immigrant political incorporation needs to move well beyond the narrow construction of voter turnout, ethnic officeholding, and policy benefits (see also Fraga and Ramírez 2003). Indeed, political incorporation does not prefigure a particular set of outcomes but rather encompasses various processes that relate to how immigrants gain political voice in the United States or find their political opportunities constrained. This expanded notion of political incorporation as a set of processes includes ethnoracial classification and operationalization, military service, citizenship definitions and enforcement, how parties shape immigrant identification to politics, how parties and other political groups target and mobilize immigrants, and how civic and transnational ties and institutions connect immigrants to politics or serve as alternative avenues for participation and engagement. For some groups, these processes may operate in a relatively independent manner, while for other groups, developments in one aspect of political incorporation may lead to advancements in other aspects of incorporation. Processes of political incorporation are also likely to vary, depending on the immigrant group and factors unique to particular local contexts and particular historical moments.

A final note before we proceed to the heart of this volume regards who is driving this immigration-based transformation of politics within and outside the United States. For the most part, the contributors to this volume focus their analyses and arguments on two pan-ethnically defined groups among the many possible configurations of immigrants in the United States—Latinos and Asian Americans. There are (at least) two sources of this limitation. First, with the exception of a handful of mostly media or interest-group polls, there are few publicly available survey data on Arab, Afro-Caribbean, African, and other immigrants. This results, in part, from the fact that Asian Americans and Latinos constitute the most numerous groups at the national level. We hope that the empirical findings and theoretical contributions from this volume can provide the stage for further exploration among these other immigrant populations. As the following essays attest, immigrants are transforming the American polity in myriad ways, and the continued growth and diversification of the foreign-born population will require renewed efforts to understand the implications for political theory and practice in the United States.

Notes

1. From a speech before the Knights of Columbus, October 12, 1915.

2. For a more complete and detailed history of immigration, see Chan (1991), Gutiérrez (1995), Portes and Rumbaut (1996), Gonzalez (2000), and Dinnerstein and Reimers (1999).

3. Huntington's most recent missive in *Foreign Policy* received an almost instantaneous and sharply critical response from immigration scholars, Latino clergy and civil rights leadership, and others.

4. To mention just a few works in this literature, see Alba and Nee (2003), Bean and Stevens (2003), Bobo (2000), Espiritu (1992), Portes and Rumbaut (1996, 2001), Portes and Zhou (1993), Waldinger (2001), and Waters (1990, 1999).

5. See Rumbaut and Ima (1988).

6. See Ramakrishnan (2004).

7. Those with Middle Eastern or Arab origins have largely self-identified as white in past U.S. censuses. Efforts to advocate for a separate category for Arab Americans have been dampened following the targeting of Arab Americans after 9/11 (Latif 2003).

Part 1

The Fundamentals of Measurement

Immigrants and the Changing Categories of Race

Kenneth Prewitt

The study of immigration has its distinct vocabulary—incorporation, assimilation, mobilization, coalitions, conflict, identity, and so forth. The terms in play touch on the broad question of whether ethnic and racial boundaries are being hardened or blurred, and to what extent the recent immigrant flows contribute to some mixture of these outcomes. The small contribution I offer is the reminder that the boundaries themselves, or at least their accessibility to research, rest on the way in which official statistics label population groups—starting even with the labels foreign born and native born.

Subdividing the population is as old as census taking itself. Numbers, the fourth book of the Hebrew Bible, has Yahweh instructing Moses: "Take ye the sum of all the congregation of the children of Israel, after their families, with the number of their names, every male . . . from twenty years old and upward." Here the key categories are male/female and under/over twenty. The intent, of course, was to know how many of the Israelites are "able to go forth to war." A census is never just a count; it is always also a series of classifications selected to serve policy decisions.

America's earliest national census in 1790 rested, first, on a geographical classification—needed, of course, to allocate seats in the new Congress proportionate to population size. This census also divided the population by civil status: taxed and untaxed, free and slave. These civil status categories generated a racial classification that separated those of European descent from those of African descent and from Native Americans. The earliest censuses did not even bother to distinguish between native born and foreign born.

The nation's first racial classification carried a lot of policy and political weight. Including slaves in the census counts, even at three-fifths, rewarded the South with approximately a dozen more congressional seats and votes in the Electoral College than a count limited to its white population would have provided. This population bonus was among the several compromises struck with the slave-owning states to secure ratification of the new federal constitution. It had immense consequences. Known by historians as the "slave power," the bonus in the Electoral College put Thomas Jefferson in the White House, and then his Virginian compatriots, James Madison and James Monroe. As Gary Wills documents in detail, a steady stream of pro-slavery (and anti-Indian) acts by Congress can be traced to the "extra" congressional seats awarded to the Southern states by the three-fifths clause (Wills 2003).

It is instructive to compare the ease with which a racial classification was introduced into our statistical system with the resistance resulting from an occupational classification. In preparing for the nation's first decennial census, James Madison proposed a question to classify America's working population into agriculture, commerce, or manufacturing (Cohen 1982).[1] The new Congress rebuffed his initiative, registering both a technical and a philosophical objection. Technically, said the congressional opponents, the categories were imprecise, because, after all, the same person could fall into all three sectors—being a farmer who manufactured nails on the side and traded those he did not need to a neighboring farmer who made ax handles. More philosophically, Madison's critics held that an occupational classification would admit to, and perhaps even excite, differing economic interests. This very possibility challenged eighteenth-century thought that took society to be a harmonious whole, and viewed the task of governing as that of divining a common good rather than that of managing conflicting interests. The harmonious whole that was blind to occupational differences was not, of course, color-blind. In the color-coded language that becomes prominent in the nineteenth century, the earliest census separates the black, red, and white population groups.

I take from the 1790 census a larger lesson. To divide the population into its several race groups was unquestioned. The categories could change, but not the need for the classification itself (see, e.g., Nobles 2000). In 1820 "free colored persons" was added to the census form (as, by the way, was Madison's occupation question). After the Civil War, interest in shades of color led the census to classify people as mulatto, quadroon, and octoroon, motivated by a race science that viewed race mixing as detrimental to the moral fiber of the nation itself. New immigrant groups began to appear in census categories around the same time. Chinese and Japanese were counted in

1890. Later, in 1920, Filipinos, Koreans, and Hindus appeared on the census form. Before 1930, Mexicans were counted as white, but in 1930 were separately counted as a race. This was quickly dropped when the government of Mexico complained, and Mexicans remained "white" until the category Hispanic origin appeared in the 1980 census (and has remained in every census since), though as I note in more detail below, labeled an ethnic rather than racial group.[2] Following statehood for Hawaii, Hawaiian and part-Hawaiian appear on the 1960 census form, though statehood for Alaska did not generate a specific category for Aleut and Eskimo until 1980.

America's changing demography is traced to both immigration and imperialism, the latter resting on purchase as well as conquest. The Louisiana Purchase brought Creoles into America's population. The purchase of the Russian colony of Alaska in 1867 added the Inuit, the Kodiak, and other Alaskan natives. The Mexican-American War in midcentury added the nation's first large Mexican population. The Spanish-American War later in the century added Puerto Rico, other Caribbean islands, and their peoples, as well as Guam and the Philippines. When Hawaii was annexed in 1898, its native Pacific Islander population fell under American rule. Although population increases that resulted from conquest and purchase were relatively small, they added substantially to the country's racial diversity, completing David Hollinger's "racial pentagon" (1995) by adding brown and yellow to the eighteenth-century population base of white, black, and red.

The nineteenth- and early twentieth-century immigration story is less about race than about national origin and religion, though these traits were often "racialized" as in the swarthy southern Europeans or the Jewish race. The well-known story is how a permissive immigration policy that brought workers to a growing economy was combined with civic exclusion, denial of citizenship, and limited rights (Smith 1997, Zolberg 2005). And when people with nativist tendencies in American political life worried that the internal borders were not holding, permissive immigration was brought to a sharp and sudden halt (Chan 1991, Hing 1993). The restrictive 1924 legislation drew specifically on the census to set limits that effectively denied entry to those national origin groups that had dominated immigration flows for the previous half century (Anderson 1988).

From the founding period through the Second World War, racial classification in our official statistical system interacted with two politically related policy narratives. One, the three-fifths clause, entrenched slaveholding interests until the Civil War, and then, even as three-fifths gave way to a full count of African Americans, entrenched a Jim Crow society and continued disproportionate power for the South in Congress and the Electoral College. The census made room for Southern blacks, but voting rolls and polling booths did not (Keyssar 2000). The second policy narrative is the racially constructed policy that excluded Asians, Mexicans, Hawaiians, Puerto Ricans, and other minorities from civic life, and then, with the Immigration Act of 1924, sought to wind the demographic clock back to Anglo dominance (Haney Lopez 1996). These policy narratives eventually gave way to a liberalization of immigration and a reopening of America's gates with the Immigration and Nationality (McCarran-Walter) Act of 1952 —which lifted the ban on immigration set by the 1924 Act, but kept stringent quotas on immigrants from particular sending countries (e.g., the limit on Japanese immigrants was set at 128 persons per year)—and the 1965 Hart-Cellar Act amendments to the 1952 legislation, which effectively ended the discriminatory national origin-based quota system.

If state-sanctioned discrimination is the central policy narrative linked to racial classification for more than a century and a half, the 1960s ended it only in part. Discrimination was to end, but not classification itself or its tight coupling to national policy. That is, the long period that precedes the civil rights legislation of the 1960s and the shorter period that immediately follows it rest on two propositions: First, that there should be a racial classification system that assigns every American to one and only one of a small number of discrete ethnoracial groups. The second proposition is that this racial classification system should be designed to serve public policy purposes. Where earlier policies had been discriminatory, new civil rights policies were intended to right those wrongs and benefit groups that had been "historically discriminated against." Belonging to a racial minority becomes a basis from which to assert civic rights. In this task, statistical proportionality became a much-deployed legal and administrative tool. Soon, the nation was enmeshed in a new form of politics. Equal opportunity becomes proportional representation. Disparate impact gains an important place in legal reasoning. Institutional racism enters the political vocabulary. Individual rights came to share political space with group rights.

Accompanying this shift in vocabulary and focus was a broadened understanding of civil rights, which was quickly adjudged to be about more than redressing the legacy of slavery. It was about all "groups historically discriminated against"—including, especially, Native Americans, Hispanics, and Asians. Civil rights became minority rights, and references to black-white were supplanted by references to people of color. Even this was too narrow a construction. The minority rights revolution came to encompass other groups historically discriminated against, in particular, women and the disabled (Skrentny 2002).

Statistical proportionality was central to this steady broadening of the civil rights agenda. Through legislation like the Civil Rights Act of 1964 and the Voting Rights Act of 1965 and the subsequent Supreme Court interpretations of these laws, the discriminatory and exclusionary nature of society came to be determined by examining whether certain groups were statistically underrepresented in colleges and universities, in the better jobs, in winning government contracts, in home mortgages, and in elected office. Underrepresentation was accepted as an indicator of denied social justice.

The census racial classification system that gave rise to concepts of underrepresentation and to statistical proportionality as a juridical and administrative tool had a small number of discrete categories—white, black, Indian, Asian and, as an ethnic category, Hispanic. But with the census classification scheme steadily accumulating more policy weight, the categories themselves could hardly be left to chance. The "politics of classification" changed, drawing fresh energy from multicultural identity politics. These politics brought many advocacy groups to issues that had generally been the preserve of statistical agencies (Anderson 1988, Espiritu 1992, Nobles 2000).

Fueling these politics is a broad public question. Why do we have an official ethnoracial classification? For much of American history, the answer was self-evident: the classification helped in the design and implementation of discriminatory and exclusionist policies. When these policies were radically challenged and eventually dismantled, the policy use of classification remained in place. Except now it was historical wrongs and ongoing discrimination that were made tractable to policy intervention.

Recent developments have begun to confuse this basic understanding of the policy function of ethnoracial classification. Today the country has a less sure or agreed-upon answer to why we preserve the racial classification system, at least in its current broad outline, which essentially carries forward race categories that date to the seventeenth century. There are many reasons for why we are on shakier grounds at present. Here I take up two: immigration and multiracialism.

Immigration

It should be stressed at the outset that at various moments in American history, new immigrant groups fit uneasily into the prevailing color-denominated racial classification. In the late nineteenth century, Southern European Catholics and Central European Jews, though in different ways, fiercely resisted being "racialized" and thereby prevented from joining the dominant white group. Our attention, however, is with the present period, starting with the Hart-Cellar Act in 1965 that removed national origin-based quotas and introduced, instead, family reunification, political refugee status, and skill-based criteria as the controlling factors in immigration policy. The late twentieth-century immigration surge led to shifts in the regions of the world sending immigrants to the United States. Asians and Latinos arrived in large numbers, patterns that show no signs of reversal. The current immigration flows—to the United States and elsewhere—bring immigrants who are culturally, linguistically, ethnically, and religiously unlike the populations of the receiving countries.

The post-1965 wave of immigration challenges an ethnoracial classification designed for the midcentury demographic makeup of the country. Policymakers and statisticians are today being pressed by ethnic lobbies, demographers, and indeed common sense to provide data that allow for meaningful generalization about America's much more diverse population. There is now an active, self-conscious politics of how the country should sort and classify.

For example, the Census Bureau presently has five racial and ethnic advisory committees, representing groups historically discriminated against: African Americans, Asians, Hispanics, Native Hawaiians and Pacific Islanders, and Native Americans. Do immigrants from the Middle East, Central Asia, and Islamic Africa have to find their way into this preexisting structure or argue for their own committees? If the latter, how many such committees should the Census Bureau appoint? Today's immigrants, or their leaders, take for granted that categories will not be determined by distant government agencies but will result from advocacy and agitation.

We got a taste of this in the period leading up to the 2000 census, when the government initiated a review of the standards for collecting information on race and ethnicity announced in 1977. Those standards, issued by the Office of Management and Budget (OMB) as Statistical Policy Directive No. 15, instructed all federal agencies to collect and report race and ethnic data in five categories: American Indian or Alaskan Native; Asian or Pacific Islander; black; white; and Hispanic, with the first four called races and Hispanic called an ethnic group.

These standards were examined again in the 1990s. Two major changes were made. First, responding to research that documented differences between Native Hawaiian/Pacific Islanders and the Asian category to which they had been assigned, as well as to advocacy by a persuasive senator from Hawaii, the federal office responsible for statistical policy allowed Native Hawaiian/Pacific Islanders to become a separate racial group (Wallman 1998). Other groups—Arabs, Creoles, and Cape Verdeans, particularly—presented arguments for why they, too, should get their own category. Though none of these efforts were eventually successful, the Arab case was the one most closely considered. The inability of this group to decide whether Arab or Middle Easterner was the best label, and how geographically to define the Middle East, made it difficult for OMB to be responsive. Advocacy groups indicated at the time that they would continue to press for a separate category, but the aftermath of 9/11 and the subsequent stereotyping of Arab Americans may complicate these efforts. The new standard also made it clearer that the population was to have two primary "ethnic" groups: "Hispanic or Latino" and "Not Hispanic or Latino" (*Federal Register* 1997, Snipp 2003).

The changes introduced in 1997 did not, however, resolve the larger issue: how well do the present race categories accommodate the great demographic diversity introduced by four decades of immigrants coming to the United States from every world region. Consider recent immigrants from Africa. The cultural, linguistic, religious, and even color differences between, for example, Islamic Somalis and sixth-generation descendents of Bantu slaves from Africa's Gold Coast are great indeed. Yet these Somalis, as well as Ethiopians, Sudanese, Senegalese, and others, have no place in official statistics to go except to the black African American category. Similar points can be made about Northern Africans, except in this case they are treated as white in the official statistics. If in the 1990s, Arabs, Creoles and Cape Verdeans complained of a mismatch with official statistical categories, diasporic Africans are likely to offer similar complaints in the decades ahead. We return below to the complications that late twentieth-century immigration introduces into our classification system, but first we turn to the second major change introduced in 1997.

Multiracialism

The most noticed change in the 2000 census was, of course, the multiple-race option. The revision of OMB Directive 15 that was announced in the October 1997 *Federal Register* introduced the "Mark one or more" provision in connection with the race categories. This change allows respondents to indicate their heritage as they select one or more of the five primary race groupings. As a result, rather than the previous scheme of five racial categories and two ethnic categories, there were now 63 possible combinations of "Mark one or more" among the race categories and 126 possible combinations when race is cross-tabulated with the Hispanic/non-Hispanic distinction (Snipp 2003).[3]

The multiple-race option was not heavily used in the 2000 census (2.4 percent of the population), and agencies that enforce nondiscriminatory laws accommodated the expanding number of racial categories by devising collapsing rules. No major disruptions in political/administrative conditions occurred. The short-term public and political response to the multiple-race option does not, I suggest, adequately predict what is in store for the United States. Self-identification as multiracial will increase, partly as a result of social legitimation, especially among the young, but also resulting from increasing rates of marriage across racial lines. Beyond this, there will be continuing pressure to expand the number of primary groups in the classification system (Perlmann and Waters 2002).

I suggested earlier that there was a generally agreed-upon answer to the basic question: Why does the nation classify by race and ethnicity? Because the classification facilitates policymaking. Since the 1960s, the policies that have drawn most heavily on racial classification have, of course, been those associated with voting rights, affirmative action, and related social justice measures.

Those who advocated for the multiple-race option, and for expanding ethnoracial categories more generally, start from a different place. For them, the categories are less about social justice than social identity. If this makes the classification less useful, or perhaps even useless, for race-sensitive policies, that is the price to pay for the right to be recognized for who one is (Mezey 2003).

In 1997 congressional hearings reviewing whether to introduce a multirace option, the opposing positions were clear. Traditional civil rights organizations argued against a multirace option, stressing the responsibility of government to police discrimination. The NAACP held that the "creation of a separate multiracial classification might disaggregate the apparent numbers of members of discrete minority groups, diluting benefits to which they are entitled as a protected class under civil rights laws and under the Constitution itself" (U.S. Government Printing Office 1998, 578). A Latino spokesperson noted that, though identity claims "resonate with the Latino community, we understand that the purpose of the census is both to enforce and implement the law, and inform lawmakers about the distinct needs of special historically disadvantaged populations" (U.S. Government Printing Office 1998, 318).

The advocates for multiracialism countered that to force them into a box that did not reflect their true identity was to deny them their civil rights. The counterargument, as voiced by the Association of Multiethnic Americans, was explicit: "We want choice in the matter. We want choice in the matter of who we are, just like any other community. We are not saying that we are a solution to civil rights laws or civil rights injustices of the past." It is ironic, the testimony continued, that "our people are being asked to correct by virtue of how we define ourselves all of the past injustices [toward] other groups of people" (U.S. Government Printing Office 1998, 389). In this testimony, and the advocacy movement it represented, the purpose of ethnoracial classification extends beyond its use in the enforcement of public policies. Official statistics are a site for choice, expression, and identity. As Jennifer Hochschild observes, it is ironic that the Census Bureau, widely perceived to be a stodgy data collection agency, is acting as a leading force for deconstruction (Hochschild 2002).

We begin to see ways in which the immigrant flows and the new multirace option might combine to further destabilize the current classification system. Much will depend on how different immigrant groups position themselves in the arguments that opposed "enforcement of antidiscrimination laws" against "expression of social identity." On the one hand, immigrants are likely to experience discrimination. President Bill Clinton's "Initiative on Race" offers the following argument: New immigrants from Southeast Asia "continue to feel the legacy of discriminatory laws against Asian Pacific Americans because they continue to be perceived and treated as foreigners" (Franklin 1998, 43). If discrimination is the issue, we might expect new immigrant groups to side with those African Americans and Hispanics who believe, reasonably so, that a small number of discrete categories in the classification system is needed for enforcement purposes.

On the other hand, some new immigrant groups, Asians in particular, are marrying across racial lines at rates that far exceed those of African Americans and Hispanics (Lee and Fernandez 1998, Rosenfeld 2002, Lee and Bean 2004). This will likely draw them, or their children, to the "mark one or more" option, and will align them with the advocates insisting that the purpose of categories is to offer choice and expression.

Hispanics present yet a further complication. As an officially designated ethnic group, they can be of any race—when race, in the statistical system, is limited to the five primary groups noted above. What actually happened in the 2000 census strongly suggests that a large number of Hispanics, as many as fifteen million, do not see themselves as fitting into one of those five groups (Grieco and Cassidy 2001, Rodriguez 2002). The census form allowed for "Other" as a sixth option in the race question.[4] Hispanic respondents account for 97 percent of those who used the "Other" option, and the proportion of all Hispanics who selected it was 47 percent in 2000. This group essentially opted out of choices presented by the primary race classification and declared themselves to be their own race group (Haney Lopez 2005). That these patterns cannot be attributed to confusion on the part of Hispanics is suggested by independent survey data. When 3000 Hispanics were asked in a 2002 survey what race they considered themselves to be, 46 percent responded that they were Hispanic or Latino—even though this was not one of the options presented (Brodie et al. 2002).

What we have, then, is a far-from-settled classification system, at least from the perspective of the fastest growing segment of America's population—its recent immigrants. There are two other, perhaps smaller, perhaps not, chapters to the story—the political movement to end racial classification altogether and the arrival of the diversity rhetoric. I discuss each briefly.

End Racial Measurement

A statewide California ballot initiative, Proposition 54 (officially termed the "Classification by Race, Ethnicity, Color, and National Origin" initiative, but popularly known as the "Racial Privacy Initiative"), in the fall of 2004, declared that "[t]he state [including all political subdivisions or governmental instrumentalities] shall not classify any individual by race, ethnicity, color or national origin in the operation of public education, public contracting, or public employment." Spearheaded by University of California regent Ward Connerly (who also led the successful effort to eliminate affirmative action programs in public-sector employment and education with Proposition 209), Proposition 54 met with significant opposition, and despite drawing three million voters, was easily defeated. Its supporters have promised to push ahead, perhaps next in Michigan.

Our interest here is less the fate of this particular referendum than in the sentiment it reflects. Many Americans, and not just those who would end racial measurement in order to end affirmative action or other race-sensitive practices, are uncomfortable with ethnoracial classification. They would like it to go away, or, at least, play a less-prominent role in American life. It is difficult to gauge how widespread or deep this sentiment is, particularly among recent immigrant groups—though, at least in California, racial minorities voted strongly against the Racial Privacy Initiative.

The Diversity Agenda

The diversity vocabulary, now widespread in higher education and corporate America, can be viewed as the end point of a half-century process that steadily broadened the civil rights language, which, as noted, starts with a focus on slave descendents, is broadened to encompass people of color, and then again to all groups historically discriminated against, and on to any group experiencing discrimination, and finally to the generalized notion of any group underserved or underrepresented. Diversity is the natural next step.

Consider first how the term "diversity" is used in higher education. Claims to diversity invariably start with reference to groups historically discriminated against. But higher education does not stop at this point. The diversity initiative is about much more than compensating for patterns of historic discrimination.

Universities claim they are diverse because they attract students from every state in the nation and, even better, from many foreign countries. Claims to diversity reference multiple religions on campus or students of differing social class backgrounds. Diversity statements often take note of lifestyles and sexual orientation. Many move beyond demographic traits altogether and stress how different intellectual persuasions can be (or should be) found on campus. At Rutgers, to take only one example, diversity "encompasses race, ethnicity, culture, social class, national origin, gender, age, religious beliefs, sexual orientation, mental ability and physical ability." The rationale for diversity is less focused on social justice than on the pedagogic argument that it improves the educational experience for all students on campus. At Harvard, for example, diversity "develops the kind of understanding that can only come when we are willing to test our ideas and arguments in the company of people with very different perspectives."

Diversity is broadly construed by corporate America as well. General Motors notes that "diversity includes race and gender as well as the broader aspects of age, education level, family status, language, military status, physical abilities, religion, sexual orientation, union representation, and years of service." At DuPont, "When employees offer their own diverse insights and cultural sensitivities, they open new customer bases and market opportunities." Here the rationale is gains in profit or productivity.

The diversity language interests here for what it says about the statistical underpinnings of affirmative action efforts. In 2004 the Supreme Court ruled in *Grutter v. Bollinger* (123 S. Ct. 2325, 2341 [2003]) that universities can apply various criteria in constituting their student bodies. But this ruling left little room for the application of statistics in determining how many of which groups will constitute diversity. This is probably a good thing. Taking the term diversity at face value—which would imply measuring, perhaps, the dozens if not hundreds of different cultures, language groups, and nationalities represented in American society—runs into the small "n" problem rather quickly. The University of Michigan lawyers defending diversity before the Supreme Court emphasized the importance of "critical mass," but they were careful not to put a numeric value to it. Diversity, they suggested, is a matter of judgment rather than measurement—a "know it when you see it" defense.

If this position can be sustained, applying a diversity rationale when assembling an entering college class or a workforce or an army will simply sidestep measurement and will not seriously impact racial classification. If, however, there were an attempt to bring statistics to diversity arguments, categories would proliferate well beyond the capacity of measurement. The effort would collapse, with unforeseeable consequences for racial classification. It is simply too early to know how diversity considerations will work their way through the institutions of America and whether immigrant groups will latch onto the diversity rhetoric as a way to claim places in education or the job market.

Conclusions

The ethnoracial classification system that currently underpins official statistics in the United States is unstable and will undergo additional changes. Elsewhere I have argued that the distinction between race and ethnicity as used in official statistics is itself suspect (Prewitt 2005). This argument gains even more force when considering the great diversity of national origin, linguistic, and religious groups that have made their way to American shores since immigration policy was liberalized in 1965. Certainly the presumption that there are only two ethnic groups in the United States—Hispanic and Non/Hispanic—makes little sense. Nor should we expect every recently arrived group to feel comfortable in one of the preexisting five primary race groups. So what gets added, by what criteria, and in response to what political pressure? Hovering over these issues is the broader question of the purpose to be served by the classification system: enforcement or affirmation? Perhaps there is a way to realize both of these functions. I have suggested elsewhere a way to preserve the enforcement purpose with one question on the census form, and yet respond to the demands for affirmation and identity expression through another question on the form (Prewitt 2005). Whether that is practical remains to be tested.

The only certainty I see in the future of racial classification is a politics that includes a much more active role by recent immigrants, especially by Hispanics and Asians, than has historically been the case. This is not to say that how to incorporate immigrants into preexisting classification is a new consideration in statistical policy. It is not, but compared to the nineteenth and early twentieth century, the politics today are much more open. Who "owns" the racial classification system? No one and everyone is probably the answer, and immigration scholars will need to be attentive to how different groups politically position themselves as the classification system again comes under review.

Notes

1. For a discussion of Madison's failed proposal, see Cohen 1982, pp. 159–64.

2. The politics behind this decision were intense, as reflected in U. S. Commission on Civil Rights report, *Counting the Forgotten* (1974).

3. The OMB discussion indicates that "mark one or more" might also be appropriate for the ethnic question, but that insufficient research had been conducted to justify that change in time for the census in 2000.

4. The "Other" option was on earlier censuses to accommodate multiple-race respondents, but was not removed from the form in 2000, even though multiple-race was now accommodated by the "mark one or more" option.

Mobilizing Group Consciousness
When Does Ethnicity Have Political Consequences?

Jane Junn

On any weekend between early spring and late fall in New York City, a celebration of identity marching on Fifth or Madison Avenues can be witnessed. "Kiss Me I'm Irish" buttons mark the beginning of the season of the mass display of group identification at the most venerable of parades on St. Patrick's Day. Italians, another of the earlier immigrant groups to New York, hold two large public celebrations, the Columbus Day parade and a stationary festival in Little Italy at the Feast of St. Anthony. Newer immigrant groups have followed suit with their own commemorations, including Puerto Rican Day—the largest of the Latino celebrations with tens of thousands of marchers and spectators—the Cuban Day parade, the Dominican Day parade, and the Celebration of Caribbean Culture. Asian immigrant groups publicly mark their ethnic identities with the Chinese New Year celebration in lower Manhattan, Philippine Independence Day Parade and Festival, Korean Day, Pakistani American Independence Day, and the India Day parade among them. There is no pan-Asian parade, and while a Hispanic Day parade was held several years ago, pan-Latino celebrations have occurred only sporadically since then.

While New York City is unique in many ways, similar organized displays of national, ethnic, and racial identity are enacted in communities across the United States. The group compositions and labels may vary, but the imperative of publicly claiming and celebrating identities remains the same. New patterns of international migration to the United States, overwhelmingly from sending countries in Latin America and Asia, foreshadow the development of a democratic politics organized around a new racial pluralism. Political theorists have taken up anew the question of how "identity politics" will influence the conduct of contemporary government.[1]

The expectation that a demographic shift toward diversity will have political consequences has multiple origins. Perhaps most compelling is the intuitive appeal of the notion that people with shared ethnic and/or racial backgrounds will naturally join together. Public celebrations of ethnic identity and the successful collective action strategies of African Americans during the civil rights movement are but two examples of the palpable link between collective identity and group mobilization. Equally compelling is a normative premise linking citizen participation with political equality; more voice, particularly among those traditionally disadvantaged, will lead to more-favorable political outcomes that enhance equality (Verba 2003; Verba, Schlozman, and Brady 1995). With a critical mass of racial minorities emerging post-1965 comes the possibility that disadvantaged groups might mobilize into ethnic and multiracial forms that increase their input in democratic politics. Foregrounded thus, it seems reasonable to hope and expect that a shared sense of racial and/or ethnic identity will have political consequences and predict, among other things, higher levels of political participation among those who are so identified.

But does it? Research in sociology and political science examining African American political behavior during the 1960s and 1970s offers strong evidence of the significance of black consciousness for political activity (see Verba and Nie 1972, Olsen 1970, Danigelis 1978, Shingles 1981, Miller et al. 1981). In one of the earliest and most influential empirical studies of Black consciousness, Sidney Verba and Norman Nie (1972) found racial identification to be so powerful as to overcome significant deficits in socioeconomic resources; the effects potent enough to unseat formal education, the mightiest of all explanatory variables for political activity. Subsequent studies found the notion of "linked fate" among African Americans to also contribute to political participation (see, e.g., Tate 1993, Dawson 1994, 2001), though others note that the link between group consciousness and increased activity among is not consistently replicated either among African Americans today or members of other racial and/or ethnic groups (Chong and Rogers 2002).

There is only sporadic evidence that Latinos and Asians have racial/ethnic identities with political kick (see, e.g., Beltran 2003; Lien 2001, 1994; Leighley and Vedlitz 1999; Jones-Correa and Leal 1996; Uhlaner, Cain, and Kiewiet 1989). Nevertheless, there are numerous examples of successful mobilizations of group consciousness to achieve political ends. Just because researchers fail to find it—particularly when looking in data from the large sample survey—does not necessarily mean the phenomenon does not exist. In addition to African

Americans, organized groups of women, gays, Latinos, and Asians have all successfully organized around identities. The women's movement, gay pride, and the development of pan-Latino and Asian coalitions united in opposition to California ballot propositions provide compelling testimony for the possibility of collective action mobilized by identity and consciousness.

The mismatch in expectations and empirical findings leaves us in a curious position. Does ethnic and/or racial identity have political consequences? The answer is an equivocal "sometimes." The recent swell of interest in new immigrant populations and their influence on U.S. politics present an unusual opportunity to build on previous scholarship on racial group consciousness and provide a more unequivocal answer about the circumstances under which it has political kick. My purpose in this essay is to carefully scrutinize four of the assumptions, inferential claims, and normative positions inherent in the reasonable expectation that animates much of the current research on immigrant America in political science: a shared sense of identity based on racial and/or ethnic identity will have political consequences and predict higher levels of political participation among those who are so identified. There are at least four analytically distinct arguments embedded in this expectation:

1. race and ethnicity are meaningful and discernible categories
2. group membership and identity are related, and go together with consciousness
3. consciousness leads to participation
4. participation is good for people in groups categorized by race and ethnicity.

Clarifying and scrutinizing these analytical starting points helps to reveal how we might develop strategies to investigate the circumstances under which racial consciousness mobilizes individual political action. I begin by highlighting the complexity of classifying by race and/or ethnicity. While there is a simple and perhaps even primordial appeal to nationality, ethnicity, and race-based classification, the reality of group membership and identity is both complex and subjective. Second, I echo the concerns of other scholars in the field who observe the tenuousness of the connection between social identity, consciousness and political behavior. Rather than assuming a relationship, new research should seek to systematically observe the situations under which social identities become political, how consciousness is forged, and when participation is mobilized. Finally, I argue that understanding the dynamics of moving from ethnic/racial group identity and consciousness to participation requires a relational analytic strategy with an explicit eye to the social structural context. For instance, modes of political participation such as voting or making a campaign contribution are implicitly acts in support of the maintenance of a political system that may not be in the best interests—instrumental or expressive—for people who benefit least from that system.

In this regard, rather than assume the same set of conditions structures the costs and incentives of political activity, interpretations of findings need to provide space for the likelihood that strategic calculations among individuals categorized by race vary systematically as a function of the location of their group in the social and political hierarchy. Suspending the assumption that groups ought to see participation in the political system as desirable provides the opportunity to train the lens away from the failings of racial mobilizing organizations or inactive citizens, and instead, focus scrutiny on the participatory institutions of democracy that may themselves inhibit the achievement of equality.[2]

Immigration and the Significance of Race
for Political Participation

Race and ethnicity have always been important in the study of political participation, particularly the period in which the power of urban political machines and parties were built on coalitions of ethnic voting blocs. Like immigrants today, the early twentieth-century generation of newcomers spoke languages other than English, came from poor or modest economic backgrounds, often lived in urban ethnic enclaves, were younger than the average native-born American, and on average, had larger families. Questions about their ability to assimilate to American politics and culture were carefully examined (e.g., Glazer and Moynihan 1963, Gordon 1964, Epstein 1978). While the earlier immigrants from Germany, Ireland, Italy, and Eastern Europe were slow to naturalize, once citizens, the strategic mobilization of these new voters by ethnic organizations and the urban political machines of their era created lasting political consequences for politics in the United States.[3]

As time passed, later generations moved out of the enclaves, married members of competing ethnic groups, and in the process, retained some culinary and holiday rituals, but lost the language and identities of their grandparents' home country. One-quarter Irish, German, Italian, and English were eventually shortened to become simply white (see Alba 1990, Waters 1990). This combination of social and political assimilation contributed to an altered understanding of the racial category of "white." Slowly and grudgingly, the once-undesirable immigrants—the Irish, Italians, and Jews—were given and adopted the racial identity of whiteness.[4] It remains to be seen whether the racial marking of new Asian and Latino immigrants will have consequences for the reconstruction of whiteness or the creation of a new set of categories.

As these earlier ethnic identities among voters began to fade, research on the significance of race for political participation began to turn more of its attention to the differences in political behavior between whites and African Americans. Most studies showed that while African Americans were less likely to take part in a range of political activities, their rates of participation were actually higher than what would be predicted given their relatively low socioeconomic status.[5] In addition to resources, mobilization through religious organizations and African American candidates for office has been particularly effective in increasing political participation among blacks (see, e.g., Tate 1993, Harris 1994, Bobo and Gilliam 1990). Systematic research on the participatory behavior of Latinos in the United States produced a companion set of findings.[6] While varying substantially by national origin, Latinos tended to participate well below the rate of activity for whites, and the analyses reveal similar patterns of the importance of social and economic resources for political participation (see, e.g., de la Garza 1995; F.C. Garcia 1988, 1997; DeSipio 1996b; de la Garza and DeSipio 1999; Montoya 1996; Verba, Schlozman, Brady, and Nie, 1993; Leighley and Vedlitz 2000; Junn 1999).

There is a growing, though still small, amount of research on Asian political participation, and studies show that there is a great deal of variation in political activity among Asians based on immigrant generation, national origin, and to a lesser extent, socioeconomic status (see Lien 1994, 1997, 2001; Lien, Conway, and Wong 2004; Ramakrishnan 2005; Tam 1995; Lee 2000; Uhlaner, Cain, and Kiewiet 1989). In addition to research on minority political behavior using quantitative survey data, there are also a number of studies using data from in-depth interviews of small populations of activists, as well as historical accounts of participatory action by groups of minority Americans.[7] Some of the most interesting sociological research on racial and ethnic minorities in the United States is on patterns of assimilation, which have clear implications for participatory behavior.[8]

Three conclusions are readily drawn from the body of research on the significance of race for political participation. First, minority Americans are worse off from a participatory standpoint, and are less likely to take part in politics than are whites. To the extent that citizen participation has an impact on government policies that influence the daily fortunes of people, it would be reasonable to deduce that minority Americans get less from government because they do not raise their collective voices as often and as loudly as whites. Second, social and economic resources at the individual level—particularly education and income—play the biggest role in encouraging political activity.

The standard socioeconomic status (SES) model, with some exceptions, is both ubiquitous and useful for explaining minority political behavior. The most frequently cited exception to this rule is the anomalous finding of relatively low levels of participation among Asians despite high educational achievement. Alternatively, the use of racial and/or ethnic consciousness as a resource for political mobilization has been found to limit efficacy in motivating minority Americans to take part in democratic government. Finally, categories of race and/or ethnicity are of greater concern than national origin, with the big four groups of white, African American, Latino, and Asian dominating the designation of analysis categories. Taken together, these three conclusions raise the imperative for mobilization around racial and panethnic identifications, because successful activation of political consciousness could raise engagement levels among minorities, reduce participatory inequality, and consequently, produce more progressive governmental policies favoring disadvantaged groups.

Bananas and Eggs: Ascribed versus Acquired

One of the first considerations in the study of the significance of race for political participation is deciding how to categorize people into groups. As Kenneth Prewitt (this volume) demonstrates, there has been a profound shift over the long history of the decennial census in how people are classified by their race and ethnicity. Beyond the complexification that is under way with the influx of immigrants from Asia and Latin America and the introduction of a new "Mark one or more" multiracial identifier, are disruptions and reconfigurations ongoing within categories that we think we are familiar with. Similar to the complex reconstruction of the category of whiteness in the early twentieth century, the category of "blackness" is undergoing its own shifts as a result of international migration to the United States from the Caribbean, the African continent, and South America. In 1996, more than 15 percent of the foreign-born residents in the United States came from a sending country in the Caribbean or Africa. Most Africans identify themselves as black, but Cubans and Dominicans of African and mixed descent might, for example, feel equally comfortable with the classification of Hispanic (Rogers 2001, Waters 1999, Kasinitz 1992).

The political consequences of this new data collection strategy for an updated classification system reflecting the nation's complex racial heterogeneity are still unclear (Prewitt 2002, Hochschild 2002, Skerry 2002, Glazer 2002). The analytical choices for social scientists of categorization, however, are now in front of us. How should we deal with the rapidly growing group of Americans whose parents come from different racial and ethnic backgrounds? Popular news magazines such as *Newsweek* (September 18, 2000), are asking these questions and showing the faces of native-born Americans with such racial and ethnic backgrounds such as: "Trinidadian-Sicilian; German Jewish-Korean; African American-German-Native American; Polish-African American-Puerto Rican; and Lebanese-Dominican-Haitian-Spanish." The steadily increasing rate of intermarriage (particularly among Latinos and whites and Asians and whites) foreshadows more growth in the set of hyphenated racial and ethnic categories (Edmonston et al. 2002). While currently in the single digits, this population of multiracial, multiethnic people, combined with those who classify themselves as some "other" race will be difficult to place into one of the big four categories. The stakes will only get bigger over time, because the children of the multiracial and other-racial Americans will have perhaps even more complex racial designations.[9]

The intricacies of racial and ethnic classification extend still further and encompass resistance to categorization into wider racial groups when subjective identities are in conflict with more-objective racial categories. For instance, some minority Americans may refuse an ethnic or racial label, preferring a white honorific instead.[10] When a research subject describes herself as a "banana"—yellow on the outside and white on the inside—what is the analyst to do with her classification? Alternatively, the social phenomenon of the "egg" forces one to ponder the power of acquired identification with minority groups to which one's phenotypic features do not match.

While the eggs might be written off as outliers, the degree of variation and heterogeneity should provide fertile ground from which a robust set of politically relevant classifications for race and ethnicity can be developed. What the diversity of categories indicates is the extent to which such groupings are social constructions, created and maintained by individuals alone, as well as together in society.[11] From the perspective of studying the significance of race for political participation, social scientists need to construct categories for analysis that are both relevant to the people themselves and signify the group's location within the political structure. In other words, a racial and ethnic classification that is salient to political action is one that must be contingent upon both acquired identification and the categorical boundaries imposed and maintained by the social order. A. L. Epstein describes the latter as negative identity, and uses the example of the social category of *mischling*,[12] where "elements of negative identity are nearly always present where ethnic groups occupy a position of inferior or marginality within a dominance hierarchy. Abundant evidence is to be found in colonial situations, but it is no less characteristic, though in varying degree, or minority groups in modern states: it has contributed importantly to the identity of American Blacks" (1978, 102).

Categories of racial and ethnic identity are therefore most fruitfully understood as the interplay of both internal (positive identity) and external (negative identity) forces. Using evidence from his fieldwork in the United States and New Guinea, Epstein argues that this framework is explicitly defined in structural terms. ". . . [E]thnicity quickly becomes intimately interwoven with questions of hierarchy, stratification, and the pursuit of political interests. In these circumstances, the categories quickly become 'social facts' in the Durkheimian sense, increasingly taking on a life of their own, from which it may be extremely difficult for the individual to escape. Identity, as I have suggested, always involves a measure of choice, but here it operates within severe constraints, though these may vary in their intensity as between different groups" (1978, 109). Nevertheless, these categories need not be durable to be useful; rather, their definition and composition should accurately reflect the social circumstances of the time of the analysis.

For example, the reason behind the disappearance in contemporary scholarship on the Irish vote is the same reason why Irish identity in the United States today is most often recognized on what has become a celebratory holiday in March. Being Irish no longer signals one's place at the bottom of the social and political hierarchy, nor does the subjective identification carry with it as substantial a political meaning. Thus, classifications of race and ethnicity that are relevant to political participation should be ones that reflect the social structural forces at play. Potent examples of the interplay of this negotiation of internal sources of racial identity and external labels can be found in studies of racial hierarchies in Brazil, and the contemporary struggle over the racialization of categories of identity for "coloureds" in South Africa (Jung 2000, Nobles 2000, Marx 1998).

For better or worse, anyone writing about race and politics after the 2000 Census must now fumble with the confused and somewhat cumbersome term "race and/or ethnicity." The popular use of the and/or term is perhaps indicative of our uncertainty about how to proceed. Complicated as it may be, when analyzing any category and its relationship to some political dependent variable, parsimony calls, and the analyst is faced with the question of which is more important. When can we use the seemingly simple term race, and under what circumstances must categories be qualified by ethnicity or national origin? While it is tempting indeed to use one of the big four and lump nationalities together into a pan-ethnic category, it is quite possible that grouping Cubans, newly arrived Mexican immigrants, along with third-generation Chicanos, for example, will introduce a different set of inferential difficulties. The same can be said for classification decisions for the multiracial. Resolving the issue of how to classify depends to a certain extent on defining the contours of identity, consciousness, and participation. Defining the categories for classification, in turn, requires an admission of the complexity of the task at hand, as well as additional theorizing to account more fully for the importance of subjective meanings of racial and ethnic identifications among individuals.

The Tenuous Relationship between Identity and Participation

An increasingly complex world forged out of interracial unions producing multiracial people, combined with acquired identities of many flavors, makes taking racial categories for granted problematic indeed. At the same time, however, the political and analytical motivations for pan-ethnicity, combined with the normative goal of increasing participation among traditionally disadvantaged minorities, implies a relationship between racial and/or ethnic identity and political engagement. In getting from here to there, there are a number of difficulties, both conceptual and empirical, along the way.

While the study of identity long ago left the province of social and political psychology, many of the assumptions of social identity theory (SIT) and self-categorization remain intact. Current work on identity traces roots back to the work of Henri Tajfel and James Turner in particular, and (to a lesser extent in the study of U.S. politics), Erik Erikson. While powerful, the social psychological framework and its research present a number of problems for those interested in the political consequences of identity. Leonie Huddy argues that while much attention has been paid to how social identities develop and what helps to reinforce them, correspondingly little has done to see what the consequences of those identifications are (2001). Huddy points to three critical problems in identifying when a social identity turns political: the ability to choose identities, the subjectivity of identities, and gradations in strength of identification. In identifying identities relevant to politics, we need to develop data collection strategies and analytic techniques that can help tell us something about how a social identity encouraging parade revelers turns into an identity forging political activists.

Many studies of race and political participation simply assume group membership implies identity and political consciousness. The elusiveness of findings linking consciousness to political participation, then, often still comes as something of a surprise. It shouldn't. Perhaps the most widely cited piece of research in political science demonstrating the relationship between racial consciousness and political engagement is one that sets forth an explicitly structural theory of the effect of consciousness on participation, along with a fairly stringent definition of consciousness.

The 1981 article by Arthur Miller, Patricia Gurin, and colleagues clearly articulated a distinction between social identity and group consciousness. It argued that while social identity signified awareness of group identification, consciousness had the added feature of incorporating the ideology of the group. Consciousness would lead to participation only if the identified individual recognizes that his or her interests are linked to other members of the group, sees his group in a subordinate position, and believes the system is to blame for this positionality (498). It is as satisfying and comprehensive a framework now as it was at the time it was published. The problem with it is not in its theory; rather, it is with the difficulty analysts have found in replicating the findings. The effects of consciousness on participation are either not there to begin with or wash out after including other potent predictors of political activity.

The Miller and Gurin model specifying a group membership with political consequences is useful in many regards. However, a more generalizable theoretical approach to the question of how and why racial and/or ethnic group identities form can be found in general theoretical analyses of the "political economy" of group membership. Unlike many of the social psychological perspectives that posit nonrational motives for joining groups, the perspective from the interest group and rational choice literatures treats group membership decisions as choices made on the basis of calculations of the incentives and costs of joining. In this regard, social and political group identification is not automatic and reflexive (Hansen 1985).

Take the classic statement of the collective action problem by Mancur Olson (1965). Olson argued that group membership provided both collective and selective benefits. Everybody can enjoy collective benefits, member or not, and thus are insufficient inducements to take part in group activity that would produce such collective goods. As a result, selective benefits are necessary, because they provide incentives for cooperation, and only those who cooperate can get selective benefits.

Olson argued further that people who share interests with a large group join less readily than those who share interests with others in a small group, and that those who join large groups act in the collective interest primarily because they are seeking benefits unrelated to the group's political purpose. The collective activity is, instead, an unintended consequence of this noncollective motivation. While Olson thought of these benefits as monetary in nature, James Wilson (1973) and others have suggested that there are also "solidarity benefits—rewards created by the act of associating" and "expressive benefits including rewards that are derived from a sense of satisfaction at having contributed to the attainment of a worthwhile cause" (Wilson 1973, 34). Prominent among the strategic motivations to join organizations—in this case, to identify with and organize on the basis of racial and ethnic groupings—are responses to disturbances in their social environments (see Truman 1971, Hansen 1985). Incorporating elements of a rational perspective to augment the social psychological approach to understanding the dynamics of group membership will aid in discerning when that membership has political consequences.

Race as Agency versus Social Structural Constraint

New data on minority and immigrant Americans should help us to describe and map racial and ethnic identities with political kick. They should also provide insight into the permanence or malleability of these identities and enumerate the circumstances under which identities come under pressure and change. At the same time, these data need to be accompanied by better analytic strategies to tease out the inferential relationships in question. In this section, I argue that one particularly durable theoretical perspective impedes our ability to make sense of the empirical findings about the significance of race for political participation.

Scholarship in political science and complimentary disciplines provides ample evidence of the racial biases in American political institutions, jurisprudence, and public policies. While scholars disagree as to the scope of the bias and the intention of the policymakers who created the policies and institutions that continue to structure government in American today, there is nevertheless wide acceptance of the notion that race, broadly speaking, has played a major role in American political development and that minority citizens have usually been on the short end of the stick. While much research on citizen participation in the political behavior tradition is mindful of this legacy, the emphasis on individual-level survey data and the practice of estimating inferential statistical models predicting political participation often leads analysts to see individuals in greater social isolation than is warranted. The complaint here is less one of model specification — that is, for including some independent variables that help to reflect the structural context of individual citizens — and directed more at the interpretation of these findings.

Even if we are successful in developing politically relevant categories of race and then specifying important aspects of the structural context, the logic of the "socioeconomic status" (SES) model still remains. Measures of SES account for the lion's share of variance in models predicting participatory behavior. In this regard, even models including measures of identity-based mobilization or structures of local government must contend with the dominance of these individual-level factors for behavioral outcomes. The fact that measures of SES are nearly always important predictors is noncontroversial; rather, what is at issue is the interpretation of the relevance of their significance. The consistency of the findings about the significance of SES has contributed to a more reflexive rather than purposive response, and in the process, has helped turn what should be an explicit assumption about individual agency into more of an implicit one. The interpretation that has most often prevailed is an assumption about the equality of individual agency that is best exemplified in model specifications, including separate controls for race and class. A companion assumption is one about representation—that more participatory input from citizens means that there will be more responsiveness from political representatives. Both are reasonable assumptions, but they are just assumptions about which individual-level data on political behavior data provide little certainty. The more significant problem, however, arises when these two assumptions are bundled with a popular normative perspective about democracy that advocates more political activity. This combination encourages conclusions from the findings about the significance of race for political participation that may be contradictory to the interests of minority populations.

The equality of individual agency assumption is appealing, because it is something we want to believe: one more year of education will garner the same increase in political engagement for whites as for blacks. But if there is evidence that there is an interaction between antecedents to political activity—a set of structural constraints that present unequal contexts for opportunity among individuals classified by race—then the assumption becomes much more problematic. The same is true for the representation assumption. If it is the case, both objectively and subjectively, that a black man's letter to his congressman receives the same attention and action as the white man's, then this assumption is justifiable. But if there is something systematic in the political process that makes the campaign contribution from the Asian American worth less than the same dollar amount from a white American, we can be less sure about this assumption, and we need to find ways to account for the interaction between race and representative responsiveness.

Finally, it is worth reconsidering, within the context of what we know about the significance of race for political participation, one of the more enduring normative positions that more participation is good. More political activity—in this case, expanded expression of voice among individuals—has been advocated as a procedural and substantive solution for distributional inequities in social and political goods. Increasing political activity among those traditionally disadvantaged and politically underrepresented can help create public policies that take their interests into account as well as empower those previously disenfranchised to take political stands in order to develop and forward their interests. Because minorities tend to participate in politics at comparatively lower rates, people in these groups have become the target for calls for political activity through naturalization and voter registration drives.

Such well-intentioned campaigns seek greater equality in political outcomes by making the electorate more descriptively representative of the population at large. The inference is that policies beneficial to those previously disenfranchised are most likely to be adopted when the face of the electorate mirrors the face of the polity. Conversely, undesirable political outcomes are reasoned to be the result of the lack of political activity among those whose interests are at stake. Under circumstances of relatively modest rates of political activity among minorities, what falls under scrutiny for change are the individuals who supposedly influence the institutions and process of democratic government, rather than the institutions and practices themselves.

In this regard, the analytic emphasis on the individual-level subject has trained the focus for change on the nonparticipant citizen at the expense of a more critical examination of the institutions of democracy in which agency is acted out. But if we relax the assumption that the political process—the democratic culture, practice, and institutions of democracy—provides equality of agency for all regardless of race or some other politically relevant category, then the comparatively low rates of participatory activity among minority Americans can be interpreted in another way, as an indicator of the structural inequalities present.

Thinking of racial and ethnic group identification as a constraint as well as an incentive is instructive. There are a number of illustrations of how racial group membership continues to restrict the opportunities to participate, leaving suspect the claim that structural barriers based on race no longer exist in the U.S. political system. The 2000 presidential election revealed not only widespread incompetence in voting administration in the states, but more deliberate—even if by omission only—structural obstacles for blacks, particularly in poor districts and southern states. Statutes disqualifying convicted felons legally disenfranchise 4.7 million adult citizens, 1.8 million of whom are African Americans. Statistical estimates of how immigrants are affected by disenfranchisement laws are not currently available, but a recent study by the Mexican American Legal Defense and Educational Fund shows that Latinos too are disproportionately affected by such exceptions to the right to vote (Uggen and Manza 2002, Demeo and Ochoa 2003). Race acts as an agent of resources as well as serving as a marker for positionality. But for racial minorities, it is more often a structural constraint (see, e.g., Sidanius and Pratto 1999, Hochschild 2003b).

Conclusion

Under what circumstances does a racial and/or ethnic group consciousness have political consequences? To satisfactorily address the question, I have argued that we need to more carefully examine the assumptions implicit in the expectation that a shared sense of identity will foster more participation in politics among minority Americans. Classifying by race is complex and contested because of the heterogeneity and subjectivity of racial and ethnic identities. It is also complex and contested because of the uneven incorporation of new immigrant groups to a preexisting classification system—a process defined by the dual pressures of immigrants to adapt to existing categories of race and ethnicity and, reciprocally, for government agencies to adapt their classification systems to the new immigrant realities of national origin, racial and ethnic diversity, and the political mobilization of interests. Further, the jump from racial and/or ethnic identity to political activity is not universal; rather, the development of a political consciousness based on race is contingent on the relationship between the individual's group and the governing forces that allocate benefits. Most clearly explicated by Miller and Gurin and colleagues (1981), a consciousness with political kick is characterized by deprivation, blame attribution, and collective action.

Combining social psychological theories of social identity along with political economy perspectives highlighting the importance of rational strategic calculations will provide a more robust set of theoretical perspectives from which we can discern the significance of racial consciousness for participation. With the aid of methodological strategies designed to observe differences in identity and strategic behavior as a result of a systematically altered context, we can move away from assuming or hoping for a relationship, and toward identifying the circumstances under which social identities organized around race and ethnicity become political.

Racial group consciousness is significant for politics, because it has bearing on political participation. But racial group consciousness is more than an independent variable in the conventional sense. Rather, the extent to which racial consciousness makes a difference for individual behavior also tells us something about the structural conditions in U.S. democracy that produce social constraint and individual agency.

Notes

1. See, e.g., Gutmann(2003), Benhabib (2002), and Hochschild's recent work (2002, 2003a, 2003b). To the extent that minority group status and social class are correlated, the demographic shift also hints at the possibility of a renewal of class-based politics.

2. This perspective is taken from Charles Tilly's *Durable Inequality* (1998). Tilly argues that inequalities have their roots in exploitation and opportunity hoarding embedded in the structure of social, economic, and political institutions. Two additional properties of emulation and adaptation serve to maintain this structure and further exacerbate inequality.

3. Kristi Andersen's analysis (1979) of presidential voting between 1928 and 1936 identifies the political activation of immigrants as one of the chief reasons behind the New Deal realignment.

4. Jacobson (1998) provides an interesting account of these three groups. See also Ignatiev (1995) on the Irish Americans' quest for inclusion among whites and Anderson (1988) on the evolution of the race question in the Census.

5. Verba and Nie (1972) were the first to demonstrate this finding with survey data from the U.S. population. See also Verba, Schlozman, Brady, and Nie 1993; Danigelis 1978, 1982; Dawson 1995; Dawson, Brown, and Allen 1990; Ellison and Gay 1989; Guterbock and London 1983; Leighley and Vedlitz 2000; and Shingles 1981.

6. The Latino National Political Survey (LNPS) was conducted by Rodolfo de la Garza, Louis DeSipio, F. Chris Garcia, John Garcia, and Angelo Falcon, and the study is detailed in their 1992 book, *Latino Voices*.

7. Michael Jones-Correa's study of New York (1998) and Carol Hardy-Fanta's work in Boston are two examples of work on Latinos. On Asian Americans, see Espiritu (1992) and Wei (1993).

8. See Portes 1996, Portes and Rumbaut 1996, Waters 1999, Gans 1992, and the June/July 1999 issue of the *American Behavioral Scientist*.

9. Interestingly, however, Harrison (2002) reports that only half of children of interracial couples report being more than one race.

10. Andrew Hacker uses this memorable phrase to describe the location of Asian Americans in the American educational system in *Two Nations* (1992).

11. Omi and Winant (1994), provide a useful discussion of how racial groups were created and changed in the United States.

12. Epstein defines *mischling* as "the offspring of marriages between Jew and Gentile who have usually been brought up on neither a Jewish nor a Christian tradition, and where the home environment has laid little emphasis on ethnic origins" (1978, 102).

Part 2

Citizenship
Here and Abroad

Rethinking Citizenship
Noncitizen Voting and Immigrant Political Engagement in the United States

Lisa García Bedolla

In June 2003, the Office of the Inspector General in the Justice Department released a report documenting the treatment of post-9/11 detainees held in New York and New Jersey. The report found that both the Immigration and Naturalization Service (INS) and Federal Bureau of Investigation (FBI) made little distinction between detainees who were being held under suspicion of terrorist ties and those who happened to be captured as a result of FBI sweeps, and that detainees' conditions were "excessively restrictive and unduly harsh." The Inspector General's December 2003 supplemental report focusing on allegations of prisoner abuse found that detainees were filmed during strip searches, verbally threatened, slammed against walls, hung by their restraints, and kept restrained for extended periods of time (Office of the Inspector General 2003). Not excusing the behavior, the report makes reference to the heightened emotional atmosphere in the facility's Brooklyn, New York, location and the fact that many of the guards had lost relatives in the 9/11 attacks. These behaviors point to a significant change in attitudes toward immigrants and immigrant rights that has occurred in the United States after 9/11.

Thus, the movement in the United States has been toward restricting, rather than enhancing, immigrant political incorporation and rights. Yet, despite the growth in anti-immigrant rhetoric and limitations on immigrant rights, levels of legal immigration have not changed significantly since September 11, 2001. It is reasonable, therefore, to assume that the United States will remain home to a foreign-born population in significant numbers for the foreseeable future. Currently one in five Americans is either foreign born or the child of foreign-born parents. Given the relative size of the population, it is important that we consider how these immigrants are being incorporated into the U.S. polity. In particular, this essay considers the question of noncitizen political incorporation. It begins with a historical look at noncitizen voting and an analysis of its legality. It then takes a theoretical look at the Lockean ideals underlying current attitudes toward immigrants and immigration. I argue that not only is the incorporation of legal permanent residents into the political system through voting and other forms of local participation constitutionally legal, but, given the large numbers of noncitizens currently living, working, and paying taxes in the United States, it also is necessary for the continued legitimacy of our democratic institutions.

Noncitizen Voting in Historical Context

Currently, noncitizen voting is the exception rather than the rule in the United States. However, for the bulk of American history, noncitizen voting was common at the local, state, and federal levels.[1] During the nineteenth century, at least twenty-two states and territories had alien voting rights. During the colonial era, noncitizens voted and held public office throughout the colonies—a practice that was in opposition to established British policy.[2] These policies were maintained after independence. As Gerald Rosberg points out, there was, in fact, "little effort in the latter part of the eighteenth century to declare specifically that only citizens could vote (Rosberg 1977, 1097). As such, "the line between national and state citizenship during the eighteenth and early nineteenth centuries was not clearly demarcated, so those states that permitted noncitizen voting allowed it at all levels, local to national" (Harper-Ho 2000, 274).

Thus, during the first few decades of U.S. history, race, property, and residence were the key criteria for voting rights, rather than citizenship. Most state constitutions referred to members of the political community as "inhabitants" rather than "citizens" (Rosberg 1977, 1097). This state of affairs changed during the early nineteenth century. States admitted into the union, such as Louisiana (1812), Indiana (1816), Mississippi (1817), Alabama (1819), Maine (1820), and Missouri (1821), all had constitutions that referred to citizens as voters (Rosberg 1977, 1097). Other states that had previously allowed noncitizen voting also moved to define voters as "citizens" rather than "inhabitants" in their new Constitutions.[3] Some argue that these changes were the result of a growing national consciousness that came out of the war of 1812. Others suggest that it was a reaction both to the growth of non-English immigration during this period and to concerns about the "assimilability" of new immigrants (see Rosberg

1977, Harper-Ho 2000, Hayduk 2002). With westward expansion, the trend changed again. Many of the newly admitted states allowed noncitizen suffrage in order to encourage immigrants to settle in their areas. Congress approved noncitizen voting in Illinois, Indiana, Kansas, Kentucky, Michigan, Minnesota, Missouri, Nebraska, Nevada, North Dakota, Ohio, Oklahoma, Oregon, South Dakota, Washington, Wisconsin, and Wyoming.[4]

What mattered most for suffrage during this period was a person's race and gender, rather than their citizenship status. For example, in 1850 Maryland gave all white male residents the right to vote regardless of their citizenship status. In fact, states "shied away from making citizenship the key criterion for suffrage rights, in part because many feared it would also justify the enfranchisement of women and blacks" (Harper-Ho 2000, 279). States saw providing noncitizens voting rights as a way to teach civic ideals and to encourage immigrants to settle in their state. During the Civil War, alien suffrage was used as one justification for requiring noncitizens to serve in the military. After the war, some states in the South adopted alien suffrage to attract settlers.[5] But race remained an issue—Jim Crow laws were in force in all these states, and South Carolina only enfranchised European declarant immigrants. The year 1875 marked the height of noncitizen suffrage in the United States, with twenty-two states and territories granting immigrants the right to vote.[6]

Around the end of the nineteenth century, the pendulum swung again, as concerns arose regarding the power and influence exercised by immigrant groups. As anti-immigrant sentiment grew, states began to retract their support of noncitizen suffrage. Many states passed constitutional amendments limiting the franchise to U.S. citizens. As Leon Aylsworth points out, 1928 was the first national election in over 100 years "in which no alien in any state had the right to cast a vote for a candidate for any office—national, state or local" (1931). The demise of noncitizen voting coincided with moves to limit immigration generally, exemplified by the passage of the National Origins Act in 1924. Thus, for much of our nation's history, citizenship and voting have not been directly connected. We will see below that the reasons underlying current limitations to immigrant suffrage are largely political, rather than legal.[7]

Most legal analysts agree that the courts have found that, while states are not *required* to allow noncitizens to vote, there are no legal impediments to their doing so if they choose. Harper-Ho finds that "neither the Constitution, nor Amendments relating to the franchise, bar states from giving noncitizens the right to vote. Similarly, the Voting Rights Act contains no provisions that would prevent the enfranchisement of noncitizens" (2000, 285). Likewise, Tiao argues "the [Supreme] Court has not provided a convincing explanation for excluding noncitizens [from voting]. Each state can define its political community as it wishes" (1993, 179–80). Tiao goes on to argue that the assumptions regarding unequal access and the franchise as a fundamental right that underlie the Voting Rights Act provide strong support for enfranchising noncitizens.

The Supreme Court has determined that Article I, Section 2 of the Constitution gives the states, not the federal government, the responsibility to regulate voter qualifications (Harper-Ho 2000, 288). The Court has found that "beyond the provisions of the Constitution which define the 'core electorate,' that is, the Fifteenth Amendment (prohibiting race restrictions), and Nineteenth (prohibiting gender restrictions), the Twenty-Fourth (prohibiting the poll tax), and the Twenty-Sixth (granting 18-year-olds the vote) the states' right to determine voter qualifications cannot be limited" (Harper-Ho 2000, 288). In addition, the Court has found that giving noncitizens the right to vote is not the equivalent of naturalization, an exclusively federal power.[8]

Thus, what makes state noncitizen voting possible is the Supreme Court's recognition that individuals can be citizens of a particular state *and* of the nation (Raskin 1993, Harper-Ho 2000, Hayduk 2002). In other words, legally, state citizenship does not equal national citizenship and vice versa. Articles I and II of the U.S. Constitution give states the right to define the electorate and to regulate voter qualifications, including granting voting rights to noncitizens. Conversely, the Court has ruled that states can deny voting rights to certain citizens if they can prove a compelling state interest.[9]

Given that noncitizen voting was common in U.S. history and is perfectly legal according to U.S. courts, the impediments to it are largely political. As such, it is important to consider how denying suffrage to a large and growing portion of our population may affect the legitimacy of our democratic institutions.

A Crisis of Democracy: Immigrant Voice, Representation and Consent

Although the foreign born make up only 10.4 percent of the overall U.S. population, it is the fact that they are concentrated in particular geographic areas, which raises problems for issues of democracy and of representation.[10] For example, the state of California has twelve municipalities where noncitizens make up more than 50 percent of the adult population.[11] Eighty-five California cities have over one fourth of the adult population that is noncitizen (Avila 2003). Around the nation, the foreign-born population tends to be concentrated in metropolitan areas. As of 2000, the New York, Los Angeles, San Francisco, Chicago, and Miami metropolitan areas all were home to more than one million foreign-born residents (Schmidley 2001). As a result, in these areas "a substantial number of persons, who contribute to our economy and our government's revenues, are being denied political representation" (Avila 2003, 1).

Immigrant rights advocates argue that since noncitizens are subject to the same obligations of citizens, including paying taxes, following the law, and so forth, they should enjoy some of the same privileges. It is important to consider what this exclusion means for the U.S. polity in terms of our democratic ideals, as well as for the future of our democratic governance. Such consideration requires that we examine how Lockean understandings of membership and consent affect how we conceptualize democracy, immigration, and immigrant rights in the United States.

In his arguments in favor of promoting democracy internationally, President George W. Bush often equates democratic decision making with "freedom" and "liberty." The argument is that democratic governance is superior to other forms of government because it gives voice to "the people." Thus, having and exercising "voice," which most often is equated with the right to vote, is often described as fundamental to democratic government. Yet, if we look at the writing of John Locke, arguably one of the foundational theorists in favor of liberal democratic government, we see that Locke did not believe that the "consent" principle required voting rights for all citizens. On the contrary—the exclusion of women and the "lower orders" was entirely consistent with his argument (1988, 29–30). The persistence of this Lockean understanding of rights could help explain much of how immigrants, and immigrant voting, are discussed currently in the United States.

Locke saw the formation of government as a two-stage process. All individuals began in the state of nature. The first stage entailed the individual choosing to leave the state of nature, and therefore give up their power within it, to form a civil society. Here is where individual consent was crucial to Locke—since all were political equals within the state of nature, only the individual could choose to give up the power he or she held there (1988, 26). The second stage is where the community chooses its form of government. In this instance, the choice did not have to be democracy; oligarchy and monarchy were also possible. In addition, for Locke, the decision regarding the form of government did not have to be unanimous. By consenting to the original compact to form a civil society, individuals tacitly agreed to cede to the will of the majority, even if that tacit agreement resulted in their disenfranchisement within the new government (1988, 30–31).

With regard to the status of "aliens," in particular, Locke argues that the state has the power to enforce laws on "aliens." In other words, noncitizens within a state's borders, regardless of consent, would still be subject to its laws (Schuck and Smith 1985). This Lockean framework, that individual consent does not require suffrage rights and aliens being subject to governmental laws regardless of consent, underlies much of the current discussion regarding undocumented migration in the United States.[12] For example, in *Citizenship without Consent* Peter Schuck and Rogers Smith argue that undocumented migration has reached "critical proportions" in the United States and threatens to destabilize our democracy (1985). They contend that the crisis is one of consent, namely, that undocumented migrants are present without the consent of the larger polity, or, in Locke's terms, against the will of the majority. Their presence, therefore, undermines our democratic institutions. While these arguments may appear largely theoretical, concerns about consent formed a large part of recent congressional hearings on abolishing birthright citizenship in the United States (Schuck and Smith 1985, 10–12).

The immigration debate in the United States currently centers on the question of the extent to which the political community has the right to decide who is in, and who is outside, its borders. But, because these arguments are based on a Lockean framework, they tend to ignore an equally important concern: What rights and privileges do political communities have to grant those who reside under its jurisdiction?

Locke was concerned with individuals' rights and power vis-à-vis the state, and was trying to develop a justification for expatriation. Under English common law at that time, a person was born under the protection of a monarch and thus owed their loyalty and allegiance to that monarch for life.[13] One of Locke's main concerns was justifying an individual's right to rebel against an unjust state, even if it was a monarchy.[14] As such, he was less concerned with the responsibilities of the state vis-à-vis the individual, particularly if that individual was in the minority.[15] This tendency to focus on individual action, rather than that of the state, remains true within American immigration debates. Yet, by focusing solely on the actions and responsibilities of individual immigrants, they ignore the role of the state, and state-sanctioned economic actors, in facilitating, subsidizing, and making possible documented and undocumented migration.

To begin, the documented/undocumented dichotomy is a false one, most obviously because it assumes that these kinds of migration are mutually exclusive. The popular conception that undocumented migrants gave up their rights when they violated U.S. law assumes a number of things. First, it assumes that migrants who are currently undocumented always have been, and that the same applies for legal migrants. This is often not the case. Many immigrants come to the United States legally under particular visa programs, only to have the visa rules change after they arrive, or their visas expire. While they are theoretically "breaking the law" if they remain after their visas expire, many are often in the process of trying to regularize their status when this happens, making their legal status at the very least "fuzzy." Both documented and undocumented migrants can have periods when their migration status is unclear, blurring the line between the two categories.

Second, and relatedly, who is in the country legally or not is determined by the state. The U.S. state, in particular, historically has had a strong interest in allowing the presence of undocumented migrants within its borders. One need only look at the long history in the United States of supporting guest worker programs to see examples of this.[16] The state also periodically changes immigration law in response to foreign policy needs or other political goals. For example, during the 1980s, the United States was very slow to support the political asylum petitions of Central American migrants from countries led by military regimes that we supported. Since the passage of the Nicaraguan Adjustment and Central American Relief Act (NACARA) in 1997, we treat asylum seekers from Nicaragua and Cuba completely differently from those from El Salvador and Guatemala simply because they were fleeing communist regimes rather than right-wing military dictatorships. As a result, many long-term residents from El Salvador and Guatemala are now being brought into deportation proceedings and expected to return home. Most of these immigrants have been in the United States legally for more than twenty years, have native-born

children, and own homes and businesses. These are just a few examples of how U.S. immigration policy can change significantly over
time, making the illegal/legal dichotomy a false one.

In addition, as we see in Schuck and Smith's work, the liberal framework tends to characterize migration as a choice made by an individual migrant, rather than situating migration flows within the larger
structural requirements of global capitalism. Gilbert González and
Raúl Fernández argue that Mexican migration patterns cannot be understood outside of the United States' economic intervention in, and
dominance over, Mexico (2002, 2003). Thus, migration patterns are
not simply the result of individual choices but are also greatly influenced by this larger global context. As such, the role of the state in encouraging both legal and undocumented migration, and in rewarding
companies who facilitate the employment of migrants upon arrival,
weakens the liberal argument that undocumented migrants enter the
United States "without consent."

In fact, these migrants have the tacit consent of important economic
and governmental constituencies. In addition, the labor of these migrants is integral to the economic production of the receiving areas—
they take care of the children, clean the houses, cut the grass and wash
the dishes—freeing other residents to spend their time on other kinds
of work. To say that the society has no moral obligation to migrants
because they come here "on their own" is to ignore the web of economic interdependence that connects all of us and the degree to which
migration is the result of structural, rather than individual, processes.

This focus on the role of the state and society in facilitating and
maintaining migration patterns shows the degree to which any discussion of the liberal ideals of consent and reciprocity must be located
within the "real world," including real-world international power relations. Locke believed that consent implied reciprocity—members
of a political community give their consent to the community and in
return receive the protections of civil society. For immigrants, that
means that while they are denied rights in their new political community, this is not a moral problem, because they remain subject to the
protection of their home country. While this works well in theory, in
practice this formulation becomes problematic when the home country is politically much weaker internationally than the host country. In
that situation, it becomes difficult for the home country to ensure the
protection of its citizens abroad.

One example is the continual attempts on the part of the Mexican government to keep its nationals from being subject to the death penalty in the United States.[17] Three Mexican nationals have been executed in Texas over the past ten years, and seventeen are currently on death row. It is understood that the United States' actions in these cases violate international law, yet the Mexican government, and these Mexican nationals, have had little recourse. Thus, the practical experience of immigrants in this situation is that they are left "stateless," without adequate protections from either the host state or the home country.

The Bush administration's recent immigration proposals highlight the degree to which these Lockean formulations remain constitutive of U.S. immigration policy. In 2003 President Bush proposed his administration's first major immigration initiative—a guest worker program. This program would create an employment database where employers could post job openings. If employers could not find U.S. citizens to fill those jobs, they would be allowed to bring in foreign guest workers. The guest workers would get a three-year visa to work in the United States legally, with no guarantee of renewal. At the end of three years, the expectation would be that the immigrant returns to the home country, and some monetary benefit is proposed to ensure that happens. The stated goal is to decrease the number of undocumented immigrants working the United States, in the interest of homeland security.

Clearly, this policy reflects liberal, individual understandings of migration patterns. It assumes immigrants act as individuals and will come for three years, unencumbered by family, and leave when asked, similarly untied to the United States. This formulation flies in the face of historical experience. These workers are likely to get married and have children during their time here. Those family members are likely to be U.S. citizens. Are they supposed to simply leave as well? In addition, the Bush administration expects undocumented immigrants here currently to "regularize" their status by signing up for these three-year visas. But, if someone has been in the United States for ten years, what incentive do they have to bring themselves to the attention of the U.S. government in order to be "legal" for three? The main problem with this, and most, approaches to immigration and immigrants in the United States is that they fail to see immigrants as important, and permanent, parts of our political community. With this proposal, the Bush administration is trying to use immigrant labor without granting immigrants any rights or privileges in the United States. They are seen as temporary workers we can use for their labor and then send home, not as human beings that contribute to our society and to whom we owe reciprocal responsibility.

Regardless of current U.S. policy, given that states are intimately involved in facilitating migration, that much of migration is driven by structural processes outside the control of individual migrants, and that modern migration often results in immigrants being left without the protection of any state, it becomes important to consider more deeply the responsibilities states have toward their migrant populations. In his criticism of some of the assumptions of liberal theory, Michael Sandel critiques the idea of the "unencumbered self" (1984). Building on Sandel's concept of the "unencumbered self," I would argue that currently the United States sees itself as an "unencumbered state" that only has reciprocal responsibilities toward its actual citizens rather than to all people living and contributing within its borders. Instead, the United States could choose to see persons located within its borders as forming an organic community. As such, noncitizens within a state's territory would hold a "moral claim to citizenship in its governing policy—a claim that strengthens as the individual's presence lengthens" (Schuck and Smith 1985, 40). Liberal theorists could respond that a territorially based claim abrogates the political community's right to self-determination. Yet, given the tacit state consent implicit in the presence of migrants within its borders, self-determination alone is not a sufficient justification for the state ignoring its moral obligations to those noncitizens whose presence is integral to the functioning of its economy and society.

Given the structural factors involved in migration, the liberal Lockean focus on the individual cannot fully address the questions surrounding immigrant political rights and responsibilities. A more structural, communitarian understanding of the immigration experience, then, could serve as a foundation for a view of state responsibility that entails a more substantive understanding of mutual reciprocity between immigrants and their receiving country.

Immigrant Political Incorporation: Local-level Noncitizen Participation

Such a new formulation could lead to important changes in how the United States frames immigrant political incorporation. Currently there are twenty-two million noncitizens in the United States, who make up approximately 8 percent of the nation's total population

(U.S. Bureau of Census 2002). As I mention above, there are numerous municipalities in the United States where noncitizens make up the majority of the adult population. Their exclusion results in strange situations, like that of the first city council district in Los Angeles, where two-thirds of the adults are noncitizens that cannot vote (Rohrlich 1998, 1). As a result, even though whites only make up 10 percent of the district's population, they constitute a majority of the voters. Given that significant differences have been found among racial groups in terms of policy preferences, this situation ensures that the preferences of one racial group is overrepresented, while those of another are underrepresented.[18]

Such a state of affairs limits the ability of democratic institutions to be characterized as substantively "representative." Since immigrants already present in the United States are most likely to remain, a framework that focuses on state responsibility and democratic legitimacy would lead us to consider ways to encourage the political engagement of all those present in the United States, citizen and noncitizen. To this end, I suggest two avenues for increasing immigrant political engagement: noncitizen voting at the local level and expanding opportunities for participation within community decision-making structures.

Ian Shapiro provides a useful framework for conceptualizing immigrant voting rights (1999). In *Democratic Justice,* Shapiro tries to bring together theories of democracy and distributive justice to develop a theory that "offers the most attractive political basis for ordering social relations justly" (5). Shapiro argues that while democracy is not sufficient for social justice, it is often necessary. Like Locke, he begins with the presumption that the people are sovereign, therefore, "everyone affected by the operation of a particular domain of civil society should be presumed to have a say in its governance. This follows from the root democratic idea that the people appropriately rule over themselves" (37). In terms of political participation, specifically, Shapiro argues that "those whose basic interests are most vitally affected by a particular decision have the strongest claim to a say in its making" (37). For him, the right to participate "comes from one's having an interest that can be expected to be affected by the particular collective action in question" (38). As such, "the structure of decision rules should follow the contours of power relations, not those of memberships" (38).

This argument seems especially applicable in the case of noncitizen parental voting at the local level, particularly in school board elections. Noncitizen parents have a stakeholder interest in the work of their children's school board. Those boards decide on curriculum, school programs, budgetary priorities, teacher hiring, and professional development. All these decisions will have an immediate and important impact on the educational experiences of their children. In school districts with large numbers of immigrant children, like Los Angeles and New York, noncitizen parents can make up over a third of the parents of school-age children. At least in Los Angeles, these parents have no say in who sits on the board and what kinds of policies that board pursues. This state of affairs does not satisfy Shapiro's requirements for either democracy or justice. Clearly, the decision rules here follow the contours of membership rather than power relations. Given the importance of education to children's life chances and the future of society as a whole, it seems that it would be in democracy's interest to have those children's parents more involved in school decision-making structures, rather than less.

Currently, a number of municipalities allow noncitizen voting.[19] One of the most liberal statutes exists in Takoma Park, Maryland, where since 1992 noncitizens have been allowed to vote in local elections and hold municipal office regardless of migration status (Kaiman and Varner 1992, Arnold 1993). A number of other municipalities, including New York, Washington, D.C., and Los Angeles, have recently proposed expanding immigrant voting rights (Worth 2002, 2004). In Massachusetts, the Amherst and Cambridge city councils have approved noncitizen voting, but state law requires state legislative approval of such changes, and the Massachusetts state legislature has failed to do so (Harper-Ho 2000, Worth 2004). The need for state legislative approval of local immigrant voting initiatives, which is the case currently in all states with large immigrant populations, makes it far less likely for immigrants to obtain the right to vote. But again, these obstacles are political, not legal, and relate to two main arguments against noncitizen voting: that it undermines the value of U.S. citizenship and that immigrants should simply naturalize if they want to vote. I will address each in turn.

Those concerned about undermining the value of U.S. citizenship argue that granting individuals the right to vote without citizenship gives them, ahead of time, one of the main benefits of citizenship, namely voting (Nelson 1991). Yet, the conflation of citizenship with voting rights is a fairly recent phenomenon. As Rogers Smith, Bonnie Honig, and James Kettner point out, for most of U.S. history, U.S. citizens have not necessarily had voting rights (Smith 1997, Honig 2001, Kettner 1978). In many states, noncitizens had voting rights so long as they met the race, property, and gender qualifications set out by the state. To say that noncitizens should not be able to vote now because voting is such an important aspect of U.S. citizenship is an artificial construction that flies in the face of the bulk of U.S. history.

The second most common argument against noncitizen voting is that noncitizens can have a formal say in the system once they naturalize. Thus, the length of the voting restriction is up to them. Because the transition from noncitizen to citizen is up to the individual, society is not placing an unreasonable limitation on their democratic rights by denying them the vote before they naturalize. Again, the focus is on the individual agency of immigrants, rather than the structural constraints they face, such as how long it usually takes people to become citizens, even if they begin the process as soon as they become eligible. Although naturalization is supposed to take only five years, in practice it takes much longer, with an average of over a decade.

In addition, some national-origin groups have been found to have their citizenship applications rejected on administrative grounds at higher rates than others, indicating that the naturalization process is structurally constrained and not completely under the immigrant's control (DeSipio and Pachon 1992).[20] This also makes it reasonable for immigrants to choose to remain legal permanent residents to avoid the possibility of having their citizenship application rejected. At the most basic level, legal permanent residents can be in this country for more than a decade before they have the opportunity to become naturalized citizens. During that time, they obey U.S. law, pay taxes, have children who are U.S. citizens, and are directly affected by government decisions. From the standpoint of Shapiro's principles of democratic justice, it is difficult to justify denying them a formal say in host-country politics during that entire time, simply because they have not undergone a formal administrative process.

That is why, in terms of a specific policy proposal, the most straightforward argument to be made is that permanent residents should receive the right to vote. Their having applied for residency suggests a long-term commitment to this country, the current equivalent of the nineteenth-century requirement that immigrant voters be "declarant aliens." In terms of residency requirements for the particular locality, Paul Tiao argues that, since the courts have outlawed extensive residency requirements for citizens, the Fourteenth Amendment precludes extensive residency requirements for noncitizens (DeSipio and Pachon 1992). Politically, it would be easier to make the argument for inclusion if an individual had to be living in, and therefore contributing to, their particular community for six months or more. But, from a normative standpoint, legal residency alone should be sufficient to justify political inclusion, and it would be difficult from a legal standpoint to justify unequal treatment in terms of residency once the right to vote has been granted. That said, a great deal of political opposition is likely to remain regardless of the particular requirements laid out for noncitizen voters.

Yet, even if we were able to overcome the significant political obstacles to granting immigrant voting rights, given overall participation patterns in the United States, it is unlikely that overwhelming numbers of noncitizens will take the opportunity to vote.[21] That is why a program of immigrant political incorporation should also entail institutional changes designed to enhance the political engagement of both citizens and noncitizens at the local level. Currently, both scholars and political pundits are concerned about the state of democracy and civil society in the United States and the rest of the world (e.g., Putnam 1993, 2000). In the United States, participation rates are at record lows, and general feelings of efficacy and trust in government are also in decline (Diamond 2001). Many argue that this disaffection reflects a deeper crisis of legitimacy for democracy itself. Citizens of democratic states increasingly see their governments as distant, inaccessible and, in some cases, corrupt. According scholars like Robert Putnam and Larry Diamond, the development of social capital and civil society is key to resolving this crisis of democracy.

But, the question becomes how to best develop that social capital. Recently, political theorists have begun to emphasize deliberation as a way to improve decision making, build social capital, and increase democratic legitimacy.[22] Deliberative democracy has been suggested as a way to deepen democracy and improve the quality of democratic decision making (see, e.g., Fung and Olin Wright 2003, Habermas 1998, Gutmann and Thompson 1996, Young 2000, Rawls 1993, Dryzek 2000). They argue that democratic decisions are most legitimate, compelling, and defensible when they are developed through public, reasoned arguments oriented toward developing mutual understanding.[23] Many localities are already using deliberative models to develop their long-range and regional master plans. These deliberative groups meet for long periods—often for nearly a year—and arrive at policy recommendations that they present to the appropriate decision-making bodies. Municipal and regional governments like these deliberative exercises because it gives the key stakeholders a high degree of "buy in" and addresses points of contention before the debate reaches the governmental body. They also believe that the openness of these "visioning" exercises gives the policy recommendations automatic democratic legitimacy.

The expansion of these kinds of deliberative decision making processes on the local level to address local policymaking issues would serve a number of purposes. First, it would deepen the avenues of political participation and engagement available to all on the local level, especially for noncitizens. This could serve as an important venue for noncitizens to become more knowledgeable about and engaged in the U.S. political system. Given that they, and their children, are likely to stay in the United States, these opportunities for substantive political engagement at the local level could have long-term beneficial effects on participants' political participation rates. Second, it would make local residents feel they have more of a say in how their government works and how it makes decisions. The development of deliberative decision-making structures at the local level could help make participants feel closer to their representatives and their local government, again enhancing feelings of efficacy and perceptions of governmental legitimacy. These potential outcomes—greater noncitizen and citizen political engagement, feelings of efficacy, and trust in governmental decision making—all would be beneficial for American democracy overall.

Yet, there are many practical obstacles to this plan. The first is simply time and logistics. Immigrants tend to live in lower-class communities and have limited time available. This kind of participation would take up a great deal of time and energy, and it is unlikely that citizens or noncitizens in lower-class communities will engage in this way. Potentially, an Alinsky-style model of political organizing could be useful in this regard.[24] Saul Alinsky argued that it was best to mobilize people about what was happening close to them, in their workplaces, neighborhoods, and so forth. Municipal government is very close and deals with issues that affect people's everyday lives. If individuals are led to believe that they can actually substantively influence those decisions, it is likely they would participate at higher rates than they do now.

The second is that, while deliberation has been promoted as a way to break down hierarchy, some fear that these kinds of structures will simply reinscribe the same hierarchy on a different set of institutions. In other words, it is likely that the most educated are likely to be the most articulate, and that immigrants' lack of facility in English could negatively affect their ability to participate in a forum that depends on public discussion and communication. But, the fact of the matter is that the United States is highly segregated. On the local level, it is unlikely that community groups will contain extreme class or racial diversity. While this segregation should not be seen as positive, recent work on the development of social capital in marginal communities strongly suggests that social capital is easier to develop within racially homogenous communities (Hero 2003, Portney and Berry 1997). This tendency should serve to make immigrant deliberative groups work fairly well together and make these deliberative environments somewhat more egalitarian than would be the case if they were representative of society as a whole.[25]

Despite these obstacles, the potential benefits of greater noncitizen political engagement for American democracy are too great to ignore. One in five Americans is currently foreign born or the child of foreign-born parents. It is important that this large segment of the U.S. population be formally incorporated into U.S. politics. The political party machines that did this work at the turn of the twentieth century are not doing that work now. If we socialize new immigrants into a more participatory and engaged politics, at least on the local level, this may translate into a deepening of U.S. civil society in the long term. Relatedly, the current U.S. approach to civic engagement is clearly not working. As Robert Putnam bemoans in *Bowling Alone,* participation rates in all kinds of collective organizations are on the decline. The development of institutional mechanisms that increase the engagement of citizens and noncitizens can only be beneficial to U.S. democracy as a whole. Finally, local governments and school boards have direct and often significant effects on people's lives. The creation of opportunities for greater public discussion and debate about local issues will help decision makers make better and more representative decisions. That will increase democratic legitimacy and, ideally, improve the quality of life for all residents of a particular locality, whether they are citizens or not.

Conclusion

Political scientists have expressed concern about the differential levels of participation among groups in the United States, because the result is that "policy makers are hearing less from groups with distinctive needs and concerns arising from their social class and group status" (Verba et al. 1993, 495). In addition, in countries like the United

States, with large immigrant populations and increasing political disinterest among citizens, it is the interest of all to develop a deeper sense of citizenship and political engagement among community members. Bonnie Honig argues the goal is to create a citizenship that "is not just a juridical status distributed (or not) by states, but a *practice* in which denizens, migrants, residents, and their allies hold states accountable for their definitions and distributions of goods, powers, rights, freedoms, privileges and justice" (2001, 104).

At least with regard to voting, policymakers do not hear at all from the millions of noncitizens who live and work in the United States. But, we cannot simply assume that more participation on the part of marginalized groups will automatically result in more egalitarian decision making. When considering the participation of subordinate groups in U.S. society, it is important to keep in mind Jane Junn's caution in this volume, that increased participation on the part of minorities can change the structures of inequality in society only if those institutions of democracy are indeed neutral, and if the common understanding of agency and citizenship is fluid. If these assumptions are not met, more participation will only, on the one hand, reinforce and legitimate existing structures of domination, and, on the other hand, force groups that are different from the norm to either assimilate or exit the system. That is why it is important that we reconsider how we think of immigrants, and citizenship, as part of the process of expanding noncitizen political rights.

As a result, increased participation of noncitizens must be encouraged in ways that will facilitate the political integration of immigrants and deepen democracy, in the spirit of the work of Junn, Will Kymlicka, and Honig (Junn this volume, Kymlicka 2001, Kymlicka and Norman 2000, Shapiro and Kymlicka 1997, Honig 2001). In *Politics in the Vernacular,* Kymlicka argues that in multicultural societies, the principle of fairness "requires an ongoing, systematic exploration of our common institutions to see whether their rules, structures and symbols disadvantage immigrants" (2001, 162). For him, justice also requires that everyone have the opportunity to become active in the polity, which means eliminating economic and/or social barriers to participation (297). Similarly, Bonnie Honig argues for the development of what she calls "democratic cosmopolitanism," which is a democracy that includes a "commitment to local, popular empowerment, effective representation and the generation of actions in concert across lines of difference" (2001, 103). Such a democracy would require the incorporation of all residents under the jurisdiction of a particular government.

For such a democracy to occur in the United States, we would need to reconceptualize not only the responsibilities of the state toward its people, but also what it means to be a "citizen." Joseph Carens's formulation is helpful in this regard. In *Culture, Citizenship and Community* (2000), he lays out three dimensions of citizenship: legal, psychological, and political. The legal definition applies to members' formal rights and duties, the psychological to the individual's identification with the political community, and the political to the sense of political legitimacy the individual attaches to those who act in the name of that political community. This multidimensional framework is useful, because it moves us away from a one-dimensional understanding of citizenship as simply a legalistic question of rights, rather than a deeper commitment to a particular political community. If we were to see citizenship as fundamentally a question of commitment, then it would be in society's interest to do whatever necessary to foster that commitment. Under such a conceptualization, encouraging immigrant political engagement becomes fundamental to the development of the "citizen" and of democracy. Such a reconceptualization of our understanding of citizenship, and of the state's responsibilities toward those living within its borders, could result in a more inclusive, vibrant, and healthy American democracy.

Notes

I would like to thank Becki Scola for her research assistance.

1. This section is based on information found in Raskin (1993), Harper-Ho (2000), and Hayduk (2002).

2. Aliens could vote under the early constitutions of Maryland, Massachusetts, New Hampshire, New Jersey, New York, North Carolina, Ohio, Rhode Island, Vermont, and Virginia. They could hold office in Maryland as early as 1692, South Carolina in 1704, Pennsylvania in 1747, and in the Northwest Territories after the Ordinance of 1787.

3. For example, Maryland (1810), Connecticut (1818), New York (1821), Massachusetts (1821), Vermont (1828), and Virginia (1830).

4. Most of these states only required that aliens be white, male, and that they declare their intent to naturalize. In Ohio, Illinois, Michigan, and Indiana, noncitizens not only were granted the right to vote in their states' constitutions, but they also were allowed to participate in the state constitutional conventions. See Rosberg (1977, 1098) and Harper Ho (2000, 278).

5. This included Alabama, Florida, Georgia, Louisiana, South Carolina, and Texas.

6. States and territories allowing voting by declarant aliens in 1875 included: Alabama, Arkansas, Colorado, Illinois, Indiana, Kansas, Kentucky, Michigan, Minnesota, Missouri, Nebraska, Nevada, North Dakota, Ohio, Oklahoma, Oregon, South Carolina, South Dakota, Texas, Washington, Wisconsin, and Wyoming.

7. While law is, of course, subject to politics, the fact that the legality of noncitizen voting is well established suggests that the denial of alien voting rights is more the result of political/social concerns about the rights of immigrants rather than concerns about its legality under the U.S. Constitution. See Tiao (1993), Harper-Ho (2000), Rosberg (1977), and Raskin (1993).

8. The status of voting and state citizenship as distinct from national citizenship is well established under U.S. law. See Harper-Ho (2000) and Raskin (1993).

9. This is why it is legal, for example, for states to deny convicted felons the right to vote.

10. I am defining consent as the ability of an individual to have a formal voice/say in the political decision-making process. The most obvious method is through voting.

11. They are the cities of: San Joaquín, 63.5 percent; Maywood, 59.5 percent; Cudahy, 58.9 percent; Bell Gardens, 56.5 percent; Huron City, 55.9 percent; Huntington Park, 55.9 percent; Bell, 53.9 percent; Arvin, 53.8 percent; Mendota, 53.5 percent; King City, 52.3 percent; Santa Ana, 51.9 percent; Orange Cove, 51.6 percent (Avila, 2003).

12. For a more in-depth discussion of "consensual citizenship" see Jacobson (2003).

13. For an overview of British common law and its relationship to American citizenship law, see Kettner (1978) and Smith (1997).

14. The justifications for rebellion were the main topic of Locke's second treatise, which has received much less attention than the first. See Locke (1988, 58–82).

15. In the second treatise, Locke delineates the grounds for justifiable rebellion against the state, which included the government failing to enforce the law of nature, failing to further the common good, or acting within the bounds of positive law. Especially key was the loss of government trust, but again, if the majority still trusted the government, the minority had no right to rebel, regardless of their loss of trust (1988, 60–71).

16. The best example of this is the Bracero program, which is credited with increasing both undocumented and documented migration from Mexico while it was in existence.

17. For a summary of this problem within the context of international law, see the Web site of the Justice Project: http://www.internationaljusticeproject.org/nationalsJMedinaMexNationals.cfm.

18. Given the significant racial and socioeconomic differences that exist between the California electorate and its voters, this problem is also present statewide. See García Bedolla (2005). For a discussion of racial differences in public opinion, see Dawson (2000).

19. These include five cities in Maryland: Takoma Park, Barnesville, Martin's Additions, Somerset, and Chevy Chase. Noncitizens can vote in school board elections in the city of Chicago. Noncitizen parents can vote for and serve on community and school boards under New York state education law so long as they have not been convicted of a felony or voting fraud. As of 1992, there were 56,000 noncitizens registered as parent voters in New York. See Harper-Ho (2000) and Hayduk (2002).

20. They find that Latino applicants are more likely to be denied citizenship on administrative grounds than those from other parts of the world.

21. This is largely because socioeconomic status has been found to be the strongest predictor of political participation, and most immigrants possess low socioeconomic status (see Verba, Schlozman, and Brady, 1995). In a study comparing native born and foreign born voting in New York state, Minnite, Holdaway and Hayduk (2001) find that nativity has a significant negative impact on participation rates across a number of modes of participation.

22. My thanks to Shawn Rosenberg and Molly Patterson for helping me to develop many of the ideas in this section.

23. For an overview of these perspectives, see Benhabib (1996), Cohen (1997), and Gutmann and Thompson (1996).

24. For an overview of the Alinsky approach to organizing within the Industrial Areas Foundation (IAF), see Marquez (2000).

25. This picture does have one very important caveat—given findings in my previous work and that of others that shows native-born hostility toward immigrants in the Latino community, it is important that those power relations not be reproduced within these deliberative contexts. See García Bedolla (2003) and Gutiérrez (1995).

Jus Meritum
Citizenship for Service

Cara Wong and Grace Cho

According to scholars of citizenship, there are two main principles
that have been used by nations to decide citizenship (and nationality): lineage and land (Aleinikoff and Klusmeyer 2001, Faulks 2000,
Heater 1999, Kondo 2001, Shafir 1998). *Jus sanguinis,* or "right of
blood," refers to a law of descent, whereby citizenship is accrued from
one's parents.[1] *Jus soli,* or "right of the soil," refers to the method of
granting citizenship to an individual born in the territory of the state.
These two principles are often placed in sharp contrast, with Germany
as an exemplar of a nation of descent based on *jus sanguinis*—stressing ethnic origins—and France as a case of a nation based on *jus soli,*
or birthright citizenship—representing a more "progressive" attitude
toward assimilation (see Brubaker 1992 for an excellent discussion).[2]

Nevertheless, the comparison is exaggerated, as most authors would
explain (Brubaker 1998, Faulks 2000); many nations use a combination of both *jus soli* and *jus sanguinis* in determining citizenship. For
example, in his comparison of twenty-five nationality laws, Patrick
Weil (2001) reported that Australia, Belgium, Canada, France, Germany, Ireland, Lithuania, Mexico, the Netherlands, Portugal, Russia,
South Africa, and the United Kingdom all use a combination of the
two principles, with a variety of conditions. The other countries all
rely on some variation of *jus sanguinis* or *jus soli.*[3] In other words, one
or both principles form the bases of citizenship and nationality laws
in all nations studied.

Citizenship in the United States is also described—by Weil, Atsushi
Kondo, and others—as membership based on the principles of both
jus soli and *jus sanguinis.* Individuals born in the United States and
those with an American parent are legally Americans. Birthright citizenship was established in the Fourteenth Amendment to the Consti-

tution, and *jus soli* is also part of our colonial heritage inherited from Britain. *Jus sanguinis* was first recognized by Congress when it decided in 1790 that a child born to an American father would automatically acquire U.S. citizenship. Together, they form the bases of who is generally recognized as an American.

However, these two principles only address the question of who is *born* an American, not of how adult foreigners are transformed into adult Americans.[4] Naturalization is an important part of the story of a "nation of immigrants," a nation that "glows world-wide welcome" according to the Lazarus poem on the Statue of Liberty. Therefore, in addition to citizenship by birthplace or lineage, U.S. citizenship is given to immigrants who have lived in the country for a prescribed amount of time and have displayed knowledge of the English language and American history.[5] Applicants for U.S. citizenship must also swear an oath of allegiance, but there is no accompanying test of that loyalty. Although the government does selectively open its doors to certain immigrants, the ideology enshrined in American laws concerning naturalization is that once immigrants reside within the nation's borders, no single applicant is worthier than another of *becoming* an American.[6] The tenure requirement, language proficiency, and civics knowledge are all intended to ensure that immigrants have been socialized and are ready to become informed, able citizens, as "American" as those born of the land or blood (Pickus 1998).

These descriptions of American citizenship have largely ignored one major historical fact: immigrants also become Americans through service, both involuntary and voluntary. In other words, in addition to principles of *jus sanguinis* and *jus soli,* American citizenship is also based on a principle of service (what perhaps could be called *"jus meritum"*). While other nations may also grant citizenship for service, this essay focuses on the United States as a case study of where membership in a nation is granted as a direct result of service by an alien, sometimes with no waiting period needed.[7] The history of noncitizen soldiers in the United States provides clear evidence that, in addition to relying on principles of blood and soil, citizenship is also granted on the basis of service.[8]

This missing part of the story is not only important in adding another category to the study of citizenship. It fundamentally changes how one thinks about the relationship between citizens and their state. Scholars in recent years have worried about the overemphasis in the literature on citizen rights to the exclusion of discussions of citizen responsibilities (Dionne and Drogosz 2003, Etzioni 1993, Janoski 1998,

Janowitz 1983, Nussbaum 1996). The relationship between citizenship and obligations appears anemic, given that military service, voting, and jury duty—three common duties—are, in large part, voluntary or infrequent in the United States. However, if service is also recognized as a guiding principle upon which citizenship is based, we are forced to acknowledge the explicit relationship between acts on behalf of the state and citizenship. In other words, if membership in a political community is not simply automatic and beyond the control of a newborn citizen—depending on where one is born or who one's parents are—but also the reward for service, then the study of citizenship must incorporate a discussion of obligations. The emphasis of the literature on identity and rights is not therefore simply reflecting a fashionable or normative trend about citizenship; it is misguided, ignoring an empirical reality that comprises a third principle guiding American citizenship.

History of Aliens in the U.S. Military: Wartime Service

Because of a demand for labor, noncitizens have been engaged in battles throughout American history as both volunteers and conscripts. At the founding of this country, military service in some states could be substituted by white males for the property requirement to gain one of the rights of citizenship, the eligibility for the vote. Congress also offered bounties of cash and land, above and beyond regular pay, to attract soldiers. Therefore, the Continental Army was initially composed of those less well-off, including workers—semiskilled, unskilled, and unemployed—and those men with few rights—captured Hessians and British soldiers, indentured servants, and former slaves. However, as the Revolutionary War dragged on, the calls to arms that were based on patriotism and money or land failed to gather enough recruits. As a result, some states' militias were expanded to include noncitizens, often using state citizenship as an inducement for military service (Chambers 1987, 22, 231). Both the British and the Continental Armies also promised freedom to slaves if they deserted their masters and fought for the king or Colonies, respectively.[9]

The service of propertyless whites, free blacks, slaves, aliens, and convicts in local self-defense led to greater (or restored) political rights and the right to vote at the local level. As Meyer Kestnbaum (2000) explains, "in doing so, [Congress and the separate states] inverted the historical relationship between military service and citizenship that had been affirmed at the outbreak of hostilities. Now, citizenship flowed from military service, rather than service forming the expression of citizenship" (21).

It had always been assumed that services were owed in exchange for the protection and benefits of the state; the converse, however, was true as well. Along similar lines, the states and Congress eased the American property requirement to vote in electoral assemblies for soldiers who fought in the Continental Army.[10]

After the Revolutionary War, noncitizens were still recruited for military service during peacetime (Jacobs and Hayes 1981). During the War of 1812 and the Mexican War, the service of noncitizens gave the country a volunteer force of sufficient size to avoid drafting soldiers. The idea of conscription arose in the War of 1812 and in the war against Mexico, but the national government did not want to have to enforce such an unpopular policy. The issue was avoided, because enough volunteers—citizen and alien—were attracted by cash bounties.

However, the inclusion of noncitizens in the military was largely determined by expediency and need for soldiers, particularly during wartime labor shortages. In the 1820s, for example, there were many Irish and German soldiers in the peacetime army, but as a result of a nativist backlash, these immigrants were later excluded from state militias and national guards. The desire was to create a "pure" American militia, not one that was Catholic or "ethnic" in any way (Chambers 1987, 38). There was no shortage of soldiers at that time, so political leaders had the luxury of picking and choosing whom they considered "ideal" Americans to fill the ranks.

During the Civil War, though, the military once again faced a labor shortage, and immigrants—naturalized or not—were again recruited for the Union Army. When the first national draft was adopted in 1863, all immigrant males who had legally declared their intention to naturalize ("declarant aliens") were included. The following year, an amendment to the draft law stated that declarant aliens who refused to be conscripted could be deprived of their political rights and deported. As one congressman explained, every man should "fight, pay, or emigrate" (Chambers 1987, 59); the sentiment was that aliens should not receive the benefits of living in America without bearing part of the burden as well. Tens of thousands of resident aliens were affected by this change, because it applied not only to declarant aliens, but also to any foreign-born males who had voted; by voting, these individuals were assumed by Congress to have implicitly declared their intention to naturalize (Walzer 1970, 107–8). Experiencing any of the benefits of citizenship became tied to obligations of that citizenship.

Chambers documents that about a quarter of the Union Army was staffed by foreign-born soldiers (1987, 49).

The first time military service affected naturalization at the *national* level was during the Civil War. The Act of 17 July 1862 allowed alien veterans to skip the "first papers" that declared their intent to apply for citizenship in the two-step naturalization process; they also would not have to wait the normal five year residency period ordinarily required (Kettner 1978).[11] The right to naturalize, in other words, served as both reward and incentive to serve in the military. These "one-paper naturalizations" served as an important inducement to recruit aliens to serve in the Union Army. Aliens who served the U.S. Army, received an honorable discharge, and had one year's residence were to be granted citizenship upon their petition. In 1894 the legislation was extended to veterans of the Navy and Marines.

By 1894, though, the United States was between wars and the demand for soldiers was low. That year, Congress again passed legislation excluding aliens that stated: "In time of peace no person . . . who is not a citizen of the United States, or who has not made legal declaration of his intention to become a citizen of the United States . . . shall be enlisted for the first enlistment in the Army" (Act of 1 August 1894). However, while low demand for noncitizen military labor complemented beliefs in excluding aliens, there were growing views about the need for the Americanization and assimilation of immigrants. For example, Israel Zangwill's play, *The Melting Pot,* opened in 1908 and was a resounding success among audiences and politicians. Therefore, at the turn of the century, there again was strong support for immigrants to serve in the military. During the 1910s (and continuing in the 1920s), some political leaders viewed military training as one method for "Americanizing" immigrants, with the armed forces serving as the crucible for the melting pot. According to this view, military training would homogenize the different ethnic groups, and it would integrate them into the fabric of American society.

During World War I, the draft was reinstated to meet the demand for soldiers. Those immigrants who had not yet naturalized were considered exempt from the draft because of their noncitizen status; nondeclarant aliens who had not yet filed the paperwork stating their intention to naturalize still had to register, but they would not be called to serve. As a result, immigrants who were not volunteering or being recruited by the draft were the targets of resentment. Besides the symbolic problem of Americans dying for "parasitic" foreigners in the United States, a logistical issue also was at stake: over 15 percent of registrants for the selective service were exempt because of the vast numbers of nondeclarant aliens in the country at that time. Since the number of men drafted in a local area was based on *total* population and not eligible registrants, there was the sense that these "loafers" were also increasing the draft burden for American citizens and declarant aliens living in their communities (Chambers 1987).

As newspaper editorials explained, "Those who are most patriotic and most intelligently loyal are necessarily sacrificed in the defense of the least patriotic and least loyal . . . " (Chambers 1987, 162) and "The country that is good enough to live in is good enough to fight for" (Chambers 1987, 228). In other words, "good Americans" were dying for free-riding "slackers" and "loafers" (Chambers 1987, 163). One civic leader from Wisconsin combined the idea of fulfilling obligations with the notion of Americanization: "We have in this country over two million Jews of military age and many more millions of pacifics [sic] and pacifics [sic] sons of like age, none of whom will volunteer. Compulsory service will make good American citizens of these classes. My ancestors fought in the revolution and rebellion and I can assure you this is the feeling of the intelligent men of this section" (Chambers 1987, 163).

Furthermore, the additional idea existed that American citizens should not be fighting while resident aliens remained behind in safety *and* enjoyed all the benefits of their adopted home. In 1918 Congressman John Rainey of Illinois was particularly passionate about what he saw as an unjust imbalance of service:

> . . . great many aliens have taken citizenship papers not because of their desire of becoming Americans, not because they knew of this Government's ideals, not because they appreciated the air of freedom afforded by this land, not because of any particular knowledge of this country's past and destiny, but in many cases because of qualifying for a position of pecuniary advantage they could not otherwise obtain or to avoid certain obligations to their foreign country.
>
> . . . Our boys left their positions, sacrificed their future, tore themselves away from their mothers and fathers or wives; they placed on the altar of patriotism their all, and offered all for the greater glory and the safety of the Stars and Stripes. But the alien stayed behind . . . stepping into our boys' position, reaping the harvest while the sower is away. Waxing fat with the riches of this land while our boys, those preeminently entitled to such riches, are spilling their blood on foreign soil. Is there any justice in such condition of affairs?
>
> . . . any inhabitant of this country enjoying the benefits of the land

who would act or speak in such a way as would make one infer that he thinks that this war is not his war, that he has no obligation of patriotism and loyalty to the land he has adopted, in not worthy of our companionship as fellow men, is not worthy to tread upon the soil made sacred by the blood of the first foreigners and aliens who came here years ago, has no place beneath the American sky, and should be sent back to the land he came from . . . [12]

Political leaders like Rainey believed that people who enjoyed the rights or benefits of a country's citizenship—regardless of motivation—should also bear the burdens of citizenship, specifically the duty to defend that country.

The debates over selective service in World War I also focused on how to balance questions of noncitizens' loyalty with the need for them to share the obligations of Americans.[13] While there was also disagreement about whether citizenship was a worthy or appropriate reward for military service, in the end, a majority decided that aliens who fought for the U.S. had indeed proven their loyalty and deserved to become citizens. They agreed with the sentiments expressed by Congressman John Rogers during the debate about naturalizing World War I noncitizen soldiers; he argued the following: "[They are] men who have shown they have patriotism by volunteering or by declining to claim exemption, as they had a right to do under the draft; men who, in other words, are as worthy of American citizenship as any men in the entire United States."[14]

In the end, roughly 20 percent of wartime draftees during World War I were foreign born, and approximately 9 percent were not citizens. The practice begun in the Revolutionary War of granting (state) citizenship for military service in wartime was also continued after World War I.[15] Over a hundred thousand aliens were granted American citizenship as a result of their service. The Act of 9 May 1918 consolidated the two Civil War bills to cover both military and naval service.[16]

The practice of expediting citizenship for alien veterans of wars continued in subsequent wars and military engagements. According to the Immigration and Naturalization Service (now the U.S. Citizenship and Immigration Services under the Department of Homeland Security), from 1911 to 1920, 244,300 soldiers were naturalized ("Naturalizations" 1977–78). Between World Wars I and II, there were 80,000 such military naturalizations, and between 1942 and 1947, 121,342 more alien soldiers were naturalized. The practice was repeated during World War II, the Korean War, the Vietnam War, the Persian Gulf Conflict, and the more recent wars in Iraq and Afghanistan (which we will discuss more in this essay's conclusion). In all of these instances, naturalization did not depend on time that was spent in active duty during the war, and it was granted regardless of where the service took place.[17]

Maintaining the Peace

As mentioned earlier, noncitizens did not *only* serve in the military in times of war; they also joined, when allowed, in peacetime. In addition to their pay, these alien soldiers were also rewarded for their service with easy access to U.S. citizenship. As part of section 328 of the Immigration and Nationality Act (passed in 1952 and amended in 1965 and 1990), noncitizens who served for three years in the military during peacetime and were honorably discharged could also be naturalized without the usual five-year tenure requirement. No actual residence or physical presence in the United States is required. As a result, many soldiers who served in peacetime were also able to gain citizenship.

In addition to enlistment by alien residents, during the cold war, some noncitizens were explicitly recruited to work for the country—from the United States as well as from abroad—as a result of the 1950 Lodge Act, which provided for the enlistment of aliens for their knowledge of foreign technology, weaponry, languages, and geography. While the actual numbers of noncitizens affected were small and these debates echoed earlier arguments about granting citizenship for service, the concerns about trust and exchanging citizenship for service were often made more explicit.

Numerous questions of loyalty and patriotism were first raised by both sides of the 1950 legislative debate. For example, Congressman Leo Allen expressed concern about Nazi and Communist spies: "In times like these when we hear about all our other departments of the Government having reds and Communists and subversives in them, above all, I want to see that the United States Army is 100 percent American."[18] In remarks reminiscent of concerns expressed in the 1820s—and expounded by the Know-Nothings—Congressman Robert Rich elaborated on what it meant to be "100 percent American": "I want the Chief of Staff of the American Army to see that we educate our own American boys to be in our Army . . . men whom you can trust, men who are good American citizens, born in America or naturalized American citizens, men that we are going to pay with American dollars, men that are Americans from the top of their head to the soles of their feet . . . I do not want any foreigners."[19]

Note the distinction being made between *naturalized* citizens and the Lodge Act's beneficiaries, who would be *potential* citizens; the immigrants who had already become citizens did not necessarily act in any patriotic way, other than swear an oath of loyalty at the time of naturalization, but they were considered Americans.[20] In other words, legal citizenship status was seen to have a transformative power, such that immigrants who had naturalized had crossed the boundary to become part of the community; they were Americans from head to toe. Military service, in contrast, would not make someone a good citizen in the mind of this one representative. However, this was ultimately a minority position.

Congressman Thomas Abernethy also argued in opposition to the Lodge Act that "American citizenship is something which is coveted around the world. Does not [the bill's supporter] think that we are lowering it to a very ordinary category when we use it as a lure to get spies into the Army of the United States?"[21]

Proponents of the Lodge Act acknowledged those concerns and used prominent historical examples as heuristics to mitigate those fears. Congressman Dewey Jackson Short from Missouri explained that he, too, had been taken aback by the legislation at first: "Naturally, one would think of foreign legions, of hired Hessians, and wonder if we have reached such a low level in this country that red-blooded Americans are not any longer willing to face danger and, if necessary, die for their country but would have to depend on foreign mercenaries."[22] However, he concludes his speech with the following history lesson: "George Washington, a British subject, led our American Revolution and Lafayette, a citizen of France, helped him win our independence. We do not have to question the patriotism of any of these foreigners or aliens who are willing to join us because of their comparable political background, because of their love of freedom, because of their devotion to liberty, because of their similar philosophy of life."[23]

In essence, Short implied that if someone is willing to risk his or her life for a country, there is an obligation to reward that sacrifice.[24] This exchange of citizenship for service was obvious to some legislators and problematic to others. Senator Henry Cabot Lodge Jr., in defense of his bill, argued that "this proposal is truly one for the benefit of the United States. It is not a 'hand-out.' It is no cold-blooded hiring of

mercenaries. It is an honorable exchange whereby both parties benefit—and therein, I think, lies its special strength."[25] The Lodge Act
passed, but partially because an upper limit of 2,500 such recruits was
established, so as to mollify fears of a large-scale Communist infiltra-
tion of American military forces.

Overall, through voluntary service and drafts, a large number of
noncitizens have become Americans as a result of their service in state
militias and the different branches of the U.S. armed forces. The annual *Statistical Yearbook* of the Immigration and Naturalization Service reports that from 1945 to 1990 there have been over 260,000
noncitizens whose naturalization was expedited because of military
service during times of war and peace. Figure 1 shows the rise and fall
of the numbers of naturalizations that resulted from these military provisions, with peaks unsurprisingly occurring after wars and conflicts.[26]

While the proportion of soldiers obtaining citizenship through service may be a small proportion of the total number of naturalizations
in any given year, the practice has served the interests of the U.S. military. Immigrants made the difference in recruiting in the late 1990s,
as the Army missed its recruiting goals by tens of thousands of soldiers; it would have missed by even more without noncitizens. David
Chen and Somini Sengupta (2001) note that immigrants, at least in
some major metropolitan areas in recent years, seem to be more likely
to enlist than their native-born peers are. For example, in New York
City, 40 percent of Navy recruits, 36 percent of recruits for the Marines, and 27 percent of Army recruits were green card holders—levels far higher than the proportion of green card holders among young
adults living in the city. Figures on enrollment at the national level indicate that noncitizens accounted for 5 percent of recruits for all services during the late 1990s and increased from 3 percent at the start
of the decade. Put another way, from 1988 to 2001 over 90,000 noncitizens served in the Army, Navy, Marine Corps, and Air Force.[27]

How should one think of these percentages? On the one hand, these
numbers could be considered relative to the proportion of noncitizens
residing in the United States. (less than 7 percent of the population,
calculated as the percentage of the foreign-born population who are
not naturalized citizens, according to the 2000 Census). In similar
ways, the percentage of African Americans in the population (less
than 15 percent according to the 2000 Census) could be compared
with their percentage in the Army (29 percent in 2001). However, the
presence of aliens does not simply raise an issue of under- or overrepresentation of a group in the nation's armed forces. Instead, it

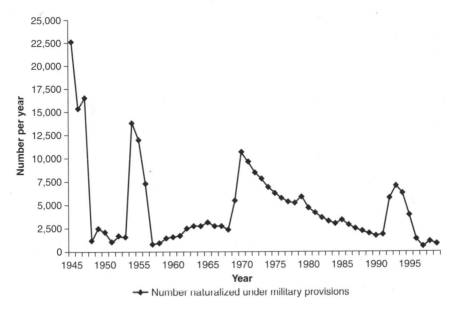

Figure 1 Number of naturalizations under military provisions per year, 1945–1999

should also be clear that aliens have been serving on behalf of the United States for over two centuries, and they were granted citizenship as a result of that service to the nation. Also, given that resident aliens are required to register with the selective service, the role of noncitizens in the military would certainly increase with any wartime draft. With changing demographics and shifts in the structure and composition of the military, it is impossible to predict whether the proportion of noncitizens will increase over time. However, evidence from the recent past indicates that the share of alien soldiers grew steadily during the 1990s and remained stable at the turn of the twenty-first century.

Conclusion

On July 4, 2002, President George W. Bush announced that all non-citizens serving in the U.S. Armed Forces would be eligible for citizenship immediately. His executive order allowed about 15,000 active-duty members of the military to apply for expedited citizenship as a reward for their efforts:

> Thousands of our men and women in uniform were born in other countries, and now spend each day in honorable service to their adopted land. Many of them are still waiting for the chance to become American

citizens because of the waiting period for citizenship. These men and women love our country. They show it in their daily devotion to duty. Out of respect for their brave service in this time of war, I have signed an executive order allowing them an immediate opportunity to petition for citizenship in the United States of America.[28]

On the one hand, this announcement in his Independence Day speech was unremarkable because Bush's executive order was simply a repetition of what other presidents before him had done. On the other hand, in a time when immigration is a controversial issue—with its defenders and detractors battling about amnesty for undocumented immigrants, antiterror provisions, H1B visas, and ethnic and religious profiling, among other issues—it is surprising that the fanfare and media's attention were not focused on the president granting citizenship to thousands of aliens. Instead, the focus of stories about the speech was on Bush's opinion of the Pledge of Allegiance and whether the phrase "under God" belonged in it.[29] There was very little emphasis (and no debate) by reporters or pundits on the idea of citizenship in exchange for service, and very little public reaction to the announcement.

Less than nine months later, the story changed. The media began reporting numerous stories about how citizenship was being granted to the "green card troops" for their heroic efforts (Navarrette 2003). Political leaders also began to call for legislation to simplify the naturalization process and grant greater benefits to these noncitizen soldiers and their families (Bustos 2003, Wilkie 2003).[30] One reason for the sudden news interest and focus was that noncitizen U.S. soldiers were some of the first casualties in Operation Iraqi Freedom. For example, Lance Corporal Jose Gutierrez, who arrived in the United States as an illegal immigrant, was the second U.S. serviceman to die in combat, and in the first month of the war, at least seven of the casualties were noncitizens (Sanchez 2003, Weiner 2003). There appeared to be a consensus, at least evident in the news stories, that the service of these immigrant soldiers was praiseworthy and should be rewarded, and that "there are none worthier of U.S. citizenship" ("Defenders" 2003, Ibarguen 2003).

What was not being discussed much was the policy of allowing noncitizens to serve in the military and expediting their application for citizenship. Some liberals noted the casualty list and disapproved the idea of using members of a disadvantaged group as cannon fodder, but this criticism essentially echoed concerns about the overrepresentation of racial minorities in the military. These critics argued that the government was using poor immigrants' desires for citizenship to exploit them; for example, Constance Rice, a civil rights attorney, argued that, "Especially at a time when the doors for citizenship are closing, this may be one of few routes left. It's a tough but well-worn path. Is it fair? No" (Connell and Zamichow 2003).

In the end, few critics asked *why* we have noncitizens in our military in the first place (see, for a rare example, Krikorian 2003). In this essay, we argue that granting citizenship for military service has been an integral part of American military policy from its founding to the present day. While only about 5 percent of current recruits are noncitizens and about 30,000 resident aliens are now serving in the U.S. military, this expedited process of granting citizenship has affected a large number of Americans in total.[31] The case of aliens in the U.S. military provides compelling support for the argument that *jus meritum* is a third guiding principle—in addition to *jus sanguinis* and *jus soli*—upon which American citizenship is based.

The case of alien soldiers also highlights the fundamental relationship between membership in a political community and the responsibilities of citizens. While it is often assumed that rights and responsibilities follow from citizenship, the converse can also be true: the fulfillment of one responsibility—military service—can lead to citizenship.[32] This policy emphasizes the very real link between citizenship and duties; the relationship is not simply a theoretical or normative one, it is empirical fact.

While scholars bemoan the dominant presence of rights in the citizenship literature, political leaders and pundits note that citizens' sense of duty to their nation is disappearing. Even given the patriotic reaction to the 9/11 events, the idea of a draft is politically infeasible (Holmes 2003, Rangel 2002); voter turnout is consistently low, relative to both other countries and American elections in the past (Blais 2000); and proposals to raise the monetary compensation for jury duty are being debated, in the hope of countering citizens' reluctance to serve (see, for an example, Craig 2004). The fact that aliens who fight on behalf of the United States are immediately eligible for citizenship highlights that, regardless of the literature's focus and concerns that the solitary, unengaged American may see citizenship as a one-way relationship, citizenship and service are inextricably tied together in very tangible ways. These ties have continued for more than two centuries, and they ought to be as much a part of the theoretical discussions as *jus soli* and *jus sanguinis*.

Finally, the notion of citizenship for military service raises questions about whether other types of activities also should qualify. As noted by Karthick Ramakrishnan in this volume, a sizable proportion of noncitizens are engaged in civic volunteerism. Some may argue that acts of service to one's local community should be included in considerations of citizenship. For example, Rodolfo de la Garza and Louis DeSipio propose that permanent residents be allowed to vote; after exercising this right/responsibility for five years—essentially behaving as citizens—they should be allowed to naturalize without meeting some of the current requirements of naturalization (de la Garza and DeSipio 1993, cited in Pickus 1998). Other scholars argue that there is something unique about military service—both from the point of view of political leaders expediting naturalization and from the point of view of public opinion in America—that makes it incomparable to other forms of service or participation (Feaver and Kohn 2001, Hess 2003).

Regardless of whether *jus meritum* is extended to include other forms of public service in the future, recognizing the presence of noncitizen soldiers in the United States should change how we think about the face of the American citizenry. Models of citizenship need to change to acknowledge this third principle of service, especially since it helps balance discussions of rights and responsibilities of citizens. And, as both academics and political leaders debate the merits of public service (see, for example, the chapters in Dionne et al. 2003), they should consider the value of service to individuals. It is not simply a normative ideal to raise the (aggregate) levels of civic engagement, with the goal of ensuring the health of American democracy. For many immigrants, service—via fighting and risking one's life—is worth citizenship.

Notes

For their helpful comments and suggestions, we would like to thank Jake Bowers, Anthony Chen, Don Herzog, Anna Kirkland, Anna Law, Frank Wu, and the participants in the conference "A Nation of Immigrants: Ethnic Identity and Political Incorporation," sponsored by the UC Berkeley Institute of Governmental Studies.

1. While in the past, some nations followed *patrilinial jus sanguinis* (like Japan), many now have systems of *jus sanguinis a patre et a matre,* allowing children born of *either* a citizen father or mother to be citizens of a nation (Kondo 2001).

2. "Progressive" is a rather ironic description of the latter, given that feudalism is the origin of *jus soli*. In rebelling against the ideas of the aristocracy, the French Revolutionaries repudiated the idea of individuals being born to the land, automatically beholden to the landowning lords. At the end of the nineteenth century, *jus soli* returned as a principle in France, in addition to *jus sanguinis*.

3. This list includes Austria, Denmark, Estonia, Finland, Greece, Israel, Italy, Latvia, Luxembourg, Spain, and Sweden.

4. Weil also argues that two other factors besides birthplace and bloodline are often ignored in studies of nationality laws: marital status and residence in a country (2001, 17). However, he does not make the categorical distinction that the latter two apply to the naturalization of immigrants, while *jus soli* and *jus sanguinis* apply to citizenship at birth. Both factors usually also require a certain period of time to pass—either as a newlywed or new resident—before an application for citizenship is permitted.

5. Since 1795, the period of required residence for naturalization has been at least five years.

6. The exceptions to this rule fall along the lines of *jus sanguinis*, stressing lineage and family ties, although not always *blood* ties. The waiting period for naturalization is shorter for an individual married to an American citizen, and a foreign-born child adopted by American parents automatically becomes a citizen. However, while the foreign-born child of an unmarried American woman is automatically an American, the foreign-born child of an unmarried American man is only eligible for citizenship if the father declares paternity before the child reaches the age of majority (see *Tuan Anh Nguyen v. INS*, 533 U.S. 53 [2001]).

7. We use the term "alien" in this essay for two reasons: (1) it allows us to make a distinction between immigrants who have not yet naturalized and groups in American society that historically were not considered citizens for reasons of race, and (2) it is the terminology used in government documents, both historical and contemporary. According to the Immigration and Naturalization Act, an alien is "any person not a citizen or national of the United States."

8. While citizenship has been granted infrequently for service by nonmilitary personnel, we rely here on the example of noncitizen soldiers to make our argument that "citizenship for service" is a regular American practice. As we explain in this essay, the policy of granting citizenship to soldiers precedes the founding of the country, and expedited naturalization for military service—in times of war *and* peace—has been in place for over a half century.

9. Since whites who were drafted for the Continental Army sometimes sent slaves as substitutes, by 1779 about 15 percent of the army was African American (Fleming 1997). The history of African Americans in the military has been the subject of much recent scholarship (see Berns 2001, Buckley 2001, Moskos and Butler 1996, Nalty 1986). The acquisition of citizenship status by African Americans after the Civil War, and the subsequent deprivations of concomitant

rights as a result of racism are an important (and much larger) part of the history of the country, but in this essay we focus only on noncitizens who were not denied citizenship because of their race, i.e., the effect of immigrant status on the relationship between citizenship and military service, independent of racial considerations. Obviously, the denial of citizenship—both its status and its rights—because of race was not limited to African Americans. Native Americans did not gain the right to citizenship until the 1920s, and different Asian immigrants struggled to naturalize up until the mid-twentieth century, partially as a result of judicial indecision about who was white or Caucasian (Benn Michaels 1995, Haney Lopez 1996). A discussion of the relationship between citizenship and race is beyond the scope of this essay, but is addressed more extensively in other essays in this volume by Kenneth Prewitt, Jane Junn, and Lisa García Bedolla.

10. In general, the property requirement kept the poor from voting (Kerber 1997).

11. For everyone else, declaration of intent was required until the 1952 Immigration and Nationality Act.

12. Congress, House. Congressman Rainey of Illinois, speaking for the Naturalization of Aliens in Military Service. 65th Cong., 2nd sess., Congressional Record (3 May 1918), 6018.

13. Concerns about the loyalty of aliens, civilians as well as soldiers, arose again in World War II (Vagts 1946), particularly for those immigrants from Germany, Italy, and Japan.

14. Congress, House. Congressman Rogers of Massachusetts, speaking for the Naturalization of Aliens in Military Service. 65th Cong., 2nd sess., Congressional Record (3 May 1918), 6014.

15. State citizenships that were granted before the Constitution was signed were made null and void by its ratification. This is one reason why the Marquis de Lafayette received honorary citizenship of the United States only recently. While he had been made a citizen of eight different states following the Revolutionary War, he was not granted American citizenship in the years immediately following the establishment of the United States. In the summer of 2002, Lafayette was recognized for his service to this country, and is only the sixth individual to receive an honorary citizenship.

16. Despite this legislation, courts upheld in *Takao Ozawa v. United States* (260 U.S. 178 [1922]) and *United States v. Bhagat Singh Thind* (261 U.S. 204 [1923]) that Asian aliens who were veterans were precluded from benefiting from it. In 1935 Congress finally allowed the naturalization of alien World War I veterans who had been denied the right because of their race (Muller 2001).

17. President Ronald Reagan passed a similar executive order in 1987 for aliens and noncitizen nationals who served in the Grenada campaign. However, because he restricted its beneficiaries to those individuals who had active-duty service *in* Grenada, this executive order was voided by the courts. All

other such orders had extended to all veterans, regardless of location of their wartime service.

18. Congress, House. Congressman Allen of Illinois, speaking against the Enlistment of Aliens in the Regular Army. 81st Cong., 2nd sess., Congressional Record (22 June 1950), 9095.

19. Congress, House. Congressman Rich of Pennsylvania, speaking against the Enlistment of Aliens in the Regular Army. 81st Cong., 2nd sess., Congressional Record (22 June 1950), 9098.

20. In the oath of enlistment, an enlistee swears to "support and defend the Constitution of the United States against all enemies, foreign and domestic; that [he or she] will bear true faith and allegiance to the same; and that [he or she] will obey the orders of the President of the United States." Similar language is used in the oath of citizenship, although the citizenship oath mentions service to the United States explicitly, while it is assumed in the enlistment oath. The main difference is that in the citizenship oath, the individual renounces all other allegiances to states in which he or she was a former subject or citizen.

21. Congress, House. Congressman Abernethy of Mississippi, speaking against the Enlistment of Aliens in the Regular Army. 81st Cong., 2nd sess., Congressional Record (22 June 1950), 9099.

22. Congress, House. Congressman Short of Missouri, speaking for the Enlistment of Aliens in the Regular Army. 81st Cong., 2nd sess., Congressional Record (22 June 1950), 9103.

23. Ibid.

24. Race, however, did trump service at many different points in time in American history. For example, regardless of their sacrifices, African American soldiers were not treated as equal citizens after their service.

25. Congress, Senate. Senator Lodge of Massachusetts, speaking for the Enlistment of Aliens in Regular Army. 81st Cong., 1st sess., Congressional Record (10 January 1949), 110.

26. A figure showing the *percentage* naturalized under military provisions of total naturalizations looks almost the same as figure 1.

27. The data on enrollment numbers come from correspondence with Lt. Col. James P. Cassella, U.S. Army defense press officer, Office of the Assistant Secretary of Defense (Public Affairs).

28. www.whitehouse.gov/news/releases/2002/07/20020704-3.html

29. The Ninth Circuit Court had recently ruled that schoolchildren should not have to swear allegiance "under God" every day at school.

30. The "Citizenship for America's Troop Act," sponsored by Senator Barbara Boxer (D-CA) and Representative Martin Frost (D-TX), would exempt soldiers from paying the $300 application fee and would allow them take the required citizenship exam abroad (Bustos 2003). Representative Darrell Issa (R-CA) proposed to grant citizenship to survivors of noncitizen soldiers, even if they were in the country illegally (Wilkie 2003).

31. Indeed, since 1862, over 660,000 alien veterans were granted citizenship, 200,000 of whom were naturalized in 1918 alone (Goring 2000).

32. While this essay focuses on the United States, the practice of granting citizenship for service is not an example of American exceptionalism. Service in the French Foreign Legion, for example, can also lead to French citizenship, although the requirements are not the same as in the United States.

The Impact Of Dual Nationality
on Political Participation

Bruce Cain and Brendan Doherty

Global economic forces and new regional political arrangements are changing our conceptions of citizenship and nationality.[1] More nations now offer opportunities for dual nationality than before. Regional agreements such as the European Union give foreign nationals employment and travel rights that were previously granted to citizens only. So-called "cosmopolitans" go so far as to tout the ideal of borderless societies and question the relevance of national identities altogether. But what are the practical effects of granting individuals multiple nationality rights? Are U.S. citizens with dual nationality, for instance, any different from other citizens in their commitment to civic duties such as voting, or in their willingness to take advantage of opportunities to contact or influence elected officials?

Broadly construed, the cosmopolitan ideal envisions an ever-expanding universe of citizenship rights and responsibilities. Dual nationality is merely a step along the path toward having citizenship rights in every country, or perhaps toward a world where the concept of citizenship loses all meaning. However, the expansion of these opportunities also implies greater responsibilities and costs. It takes time and effort to keep up with the issues of the day in any given country, or to secure an overseas ballot and vote.[2] In short, the dream of expanding nationality potentially runs afoul of the pessimistic predictions of standard political science findings. Previous research has suggested that since political participation is costly, participation rates drop as costs increase. By implication, if dual-nationality U.S. citizens must bear greater costs of being informed and actively participating, then we should expect their participation levels in the United States to be lower than those of traditional single-nationality citizens.

Hence, the basic question in this essay is whether U.S. citizens with dual nationality have similar participation rates as single-nationality citizens, and if they do not, is this simply a function of different de-mographic profiles, or is it consistent with the pessimistic expectations of the cost model? Additionally, how does the voting behavior in the United States of immigrants who come from countries that allow dual nationality compare with that of those from countries without such provisions? In exploring these issues, we draw on data from the 1999 *Washington Post*/Kaiser Family Foundation/Harvard University La-tino Survey that we obtained from the Roper Center for Public Opin-ion Research.

Based on our estimations, we conclude the following. U.S. citizens born abroad in countries that allow some form of dual nationality are less likely to have ever voted in the United States than are those citi-zens born in countries that do not permit dual nationality. Addition-ally, U.S. citizens with dual nationality are less likely to register and to vote in the United States than nondual U.S. citizens who come from the same countries and were eligible to claim dual nationality but did not. Our analysis does not allow us to conclude anything with con-fidence about other forms of political participation. The differences in registration and voting rates cannot be accounted for by demo-graphic factors alone, because the profiles of dual nationality and single-nationality U.S. citizens from countries in Latin America that allow dual nationality are quite similar. This leads us to believe that higher costs, lower perceived benefits, or weaker socialization norms may account for the difference. This raises the interesting policy ques-tion of whether granting more multiple citizenship opportunities in the future might contribute to already declining participation rates.

Dual Nationality and the Theory of Participation

Practical questions about dual nationality have been framed by an ongoing spirited normative debate. Scholars such as Stanley Renshon have advanced arguments against the granting of dual nationality, as-serting that it causes citizens to have divided loyalties. Indeed, critics of dual nationality have long equated it with bigamy, arguing that a person could no more be faithful to two countries than he or she could be to two spouses. They decry the fact that dual nationals are subject to the laws of both countries, and could thus be obliged to serve in each country's military. In light of the fact that approximately 85 per-cent of U.S. immigrants come from countries that allow some form of dual nationality and that many countries have recognized dual nation-ality only in recent years, opponents view dual nationality as something that is dramatically changing the composition of the civic character of the United States and weakening the national fabric by encouraging dual allegiances. In analyzing the debate over dual nationality, Jeffrey O'Brien dubbed those who hold this view "quasi-nationalists."

Scholars such as Peter Spiro advance an alternative vision of citizenship, which Jeffrey O'Brien labels "postnational" (O'Brien 1999; Spiro 1997, 1999) In this view, dual nationality is a logical measure in an increasingly economically and politically interconnected world in which democratic countries are rarely at war with each other. Rather than weakening civic attachments, supporters of postnationalism argue that dual nationality can benefit both the individual and the country by advancing international interdependence and understanding. They contend that maintaining ties to a person's former country does not lead to shallower civic engagement in the United States.

Set against this normative backdrop, previous research has begun to investigate and answer empirical questions about dual nationality. If, indeed, dual nationals are less participatory, more conflicted in their loyalties, or slower to assimilate, these important factors might influence the national debate. But there clearly is a need for more research on these and other topics, as empirical data on dual nationality are difficult to come by (see Bloemraad 2003; Spiro, 1997, 1999; Renshon 2000, 2001; and Hammar, 1985). While there is a consensus that dual nationality in the United States is on the rise, the U.S. government does not ask about it in the census. Thus, empirical research on the subject is based on survey research, draws on related data, or focuses on countries such as Canada that do have reliable data sources on the subject.

Some studies show that the existence of a dual-nationality option increases the odds that immigrants will choose to naturalize (Jones-Correa, 2001a, 2001b; Johnson, Reyes, Mameesh, and Barbour, 1999), but there is conflicting evidence on this point (de la Garza et al. 1996, Yang 1994). Dual citizenship in Canada seems to decrease with the length of residence in the host country, and is related to education and language skills (Bloemraad 2003).

Fewer studies have focused on dual nationality and voting. An article by Michael Jones-Correa (2001a) examined the institutional and contextual variables that affect immigrant naturalization and voting among Latinos. Arguing that allowing dual nationality lowers the costs of participating politically in the United States by allowing an individual to naturalize without having to give up a formal connection to her country of origin, this study found that Latino immigrants from countries that allow dual nationality are more likely to vote in the

United States than are individuals from countries that do not have such a citizenship provision. Similar results have been found by analyses of Current Population Survey voting data for immigrants from other racial and ethnic groups (Ramakrishnan 2002, 2005).

In this essay, we focus on two principal questions. Do U.S. citizens with dual nationality, compared with those from the same countries who could have chosen dual nationality but did not, participate at lower rates, and if so why? And how does the voting behavior in the United States of citizens who come from countries that allow dual nationality compare with that of those from countries that do not? While we agree with Jones-Correa's argument that dual-nationality provisions lower the costs of acquiring U.S. citizenship, we question whether this argument can be extended to political participation in the United States.

The standard participation model predicts that dual nationals will participate less. In essence, that model states the following. The odds of an eligible citizen voting are a function of the likelihood of affecting the outcome of a race, the perceived benefits from the outcome, the costs of voting, and socialized norms that make individuals feel obligated to vote (Downs 1957, Riker and Ordeshook 1968).

$$Pr(V) = F(P, B, C, D, e)$$

Where:

V is the act of voting (participating)
P is the expectation of affecting the outcome
B is the benefit associated with the election outcome
C represents the costs associated with participating
D is the benefits associated with acting according to socialized norms
And e represents other random factors.

How then do dual nationals compare with nondual nationals in this model? At the outset, we can say that P should not differ for dual and nonduals; that is, the odds of voting in an election in which the seat is competitive seat should not be different for dual than nondual citizens. Rather, it is the other factors that we expect may vary.

For the dual national, there are two implicit participation equations: one for the country of origin and the other for the country of residence. Most important, being a member of two countries increases the cognitive duties. The dual national must pay the cost in time and effort—the "bother," so to speak—of keeping up with issues and candidates in both countries. In this sense, we expect that C should be higher for dual nationals than for nondual nationals, and that should, on average, lower the odds of political participation.

It is also possible that B and D could be different for dual nationals as well. If dual nationality does indeed imply divided loyalty, then perhaps dual nationals do not perceive as much at stake in U.S. elections. And for the same reason, it is possible that their socialization into the civic norms that support voting and democratic participation is weaker. While the case for B and D being different for dual citizens than nondual citizens seems to us less plausible than the case for higher costs, we cannot rule out this possibility.[3] This will have some implications for the way we later interpret the coefficients in our analysis.

The standard political science participation model predicts that participation should be lower for dual nationals. To test this, we conduct our analysis at two levels. First, as other scholars have done, we compare the voting behavior of citizens from countries that do allow dual nationality with that of those people from countries that do not. Second, we focus only on people from countries that do allow dual nationality and compare the political participation of those who claim dual nationality to those who could have chosen to hold dual nationality but did not.

Comparing Citizens from Countries That
Do and Do Not Allow Dual Nationality

Our analysis draws on the 1999 *Washington Post*/Kaiser Family Foundation/Harvard University National Survey on Latinos in America. Of the 2,417 self-identified Latinos interviewed, 504 were U.S. citizens who were born outside of the United States. Of these respondents, 267 were U.S. citizens who were born in countries that allow some form of dual nationality,[4] while 237 were born in countries that did not. Citizens born in Cuba accounted for 29.6 percent of the 504 respondents, while 24.8 percent were born in Mexico. Respondents from the Dominican Republic (7.1 percent), El Salvador (5.2 percent), and Peru (4.8 percent) were the next-most-represented countries among the study's respondents.

While a cost model might predict that allowing dual nationality will make it more likely for individuals from those countries to naturalize in the United States, what will be the impact on registration and voting? In light of the arguments about cognitive duties set forth above, we might expect that individuals from countries that allow dual nationality might participate less in the United States than those from countries that do not. While our assumptions about these cognitive duties apply more clearly to those who chose dual nationality in comparison with those who could have chosen such status but did not, which we analyze below, the question of how those from countries that do allow dual nationality compare with those from countries that do not is an interesting one.

We test this with a multivariate logit model predicting the effect of whether a respondent's country of birth allows dual nationality on registration and voting, with dichotomous dependent variables, controlling for income, education, English reading skill, gender, age, years lived in the United States, and years of U.S. citizenship.[5] We use logit models, because the analyses involve dichotomous outcomes such as "registered" or "not registered" and "voted" or "not voted." The results of this estimation are in table 1.

The estimations indicate that whether or not a respondent's country of birth allows dual nationality is a significant predictor of having ever voted in the United States. Controlling for the other variables in our equation, coming from a country that allows dual nationality lowers the probability of having ever voted in the United States. Years in the United States predict a higher probability of registering and voting, and education does so for voting. Age and years of living in the United States each predict a higher probability of having ever voted. The finding that citizens born in countries that allow dual nationality are less likely to have ever voted in the United States than are those from countries that do not allow dual nationality is contrary to prior findings based on the Current Population Survey (Jones-Correa 2001a, Ramakrishnan 2002), suggesting that this issue is still an open question.

Comparing Citizens Who Do and Do Not Choose Dual Nationality

We next focus on the voting and participation levels of those individuals who could have chosen dual nationality and did so compared to those were eligible but did not. Of the 2,417 self-identified Latinos interviewed in the 1999 *Washington Post*/Kaiser Family Foundation/Harvard University National Survey on Latinos in America, 745 were born abroad in countries that allow dual nationality with the United States and had lived in the United States for at least five years at the

Table 1 Logit regression analysis of registration and voting
by Latino U.S. citizens born abroad

	Registered to vote in U.S.	Ever voted in U.S.
	(0 = No, 1 = Yes)	(0 = No, 1 = Yes)
Dual nationality allowed by country of birth	−0.306 (0.265)	−0.556 (0.264)**
Years in U.S.	0.033 (0.018)*	0.044 (0.018)**
Age	0.015 (0.012)	0.020 (0.011)*
Years of U.S. citizenship	0.017 (0.017)	0.041 (0.018)**
Gender (0 = Female, 1 = Male)	0.367 (0.238)	0.096 (0.236)
English skill reading	0.361 (0.439)	0.555 (0.436)
Education	0.781 (0.477)	1.481 (0.477)***
Income	0.237 (0.451)	−0.098 (0.452)
Constant	−1.001 n = 450	−1.951 n = 453

***$p < .01$ **$p < .05$ *$p < .10$
Entries are unstandardized regression coefficients with standard errors in parentheses.
All independent variables were coded from 0 to 1, except age, years in U.S., and years of U.S. citizenship.

time they were questioned.[6] Those respondents were born in the following eleven countries: Brazil, Colombia, Costa Rica, Dominican Republic, Ecuador, El Salvador, Jamaica, Mexico, Panama, Peru, and Uruguay.[7]

Of these 745 respondents, 157 identified themselves as U.S. citizens with dual nationality, 106 as single-nationality U.S. citizens, and 482 as non-U.S. citizens. Respondents from Mexico composed 52.3 percent of this portion of our study, followed by Salvadorans at 18.3 percent and Dominicans at 9.8 percent. Immigrants from Colombia and Peru provided 6.2 percent and 5.9 percent of these respondents, respectively, and the remaining six countries accounted for percentages ranging from 0.4 percent (Brazil) to 3.5 percent (Ecuador) of these respondents. The limited number of dual-nationality citizens from each country precludes us from analyzing variations in their political participation by country of origin.

As discussed above, the lack of any comprehensive data on dual nationality in the United States raises challenges when studying the subject. This inquiry is based on self-reported survey data, and thus we must rely on respondents' declarations of single or dual nationality. What we are attempting to measure is the impact of a person's citizenship status on political participation. Some declarations of dual nationality in our study may not reflect legal status, but rather psychological declarations of allegiance. This is regrettable, but nonetheless these survey data are the best available method of measuring nationality status. We assume that measurement error is randomly distributed throughout the population.

We first examined the impact of dual nationality on whether a respondent was registered to vote in the United States, had ever voted in the United States, and had voted in the 1998 or 1996 congressional and presidential elections. noncitizens are necessarily excluded from the analysis of voting in the United States, leaving us with 263 single- and dual-nationality citizens. The descriptive statistics for our participation variables demonstrate a clear pattern: compared with single-nationality U.S. citizens, fewer dual nationals are registered to vote (84.0 percent to 59.4 percent) and have ever voted in an election in the United States (74.5 percent to 51.0 percent). The differences are also significant in terms of voting in particular elections such as the 1998 congressional election (59.8 percent to 42.3 percent) and the 1996 presidential election (59.8 percent to 30.5 percent), but there may be reliability issues with these measures based on when immigrants were eligible to vote and difficulties in remembering elections from more than a year prior to the survey.

While these tables are consistent with the expectations of the standard participation model, we cannot conclude that the reason might be cost unless we control for other potential explanations. In particular, we need to control for the possibility that dual citizens participate less because they are, on average, more demographically disadvantaged. Looking to the standard political science models again, we see that lower levels of education, difficulties in reading English, lower income levels, having arrived in the United States more recently, and being younger tend to predict lower levels of participation (among the many studies of factors affecting political participation, see Wolfinger and Rosenstone 1980; de la Garza and DeSipio 1992; Pachon and DeSipio 1994; Leighley and Vedlitz 1999; Uhlaner, Cain, and Kiewiet 1989). Many of these attributes relate to a cost model, of course, in

Table 2   Registration and voting by dual nationality

	Dual-nationality U.S. citizens	Single-nationality U.S. citizens	Total
Registered to vote in the U.S.	92 59.4%	89 84.0%	181
Not registered to vote in the U.S.	63 40.6%	17 16.0%	80
Total	155 100.0%	106 100.0%	261
Ever voted in U.S.	80 51.0%	79 74.5%	159
Never voted in U.S.	77 49.0%	27 25.5%	104
Total	157 100.0%	106 100.0%	263
Voted in 1998 U.S. congressional election	66 42.3%	61 59.8%	127
Didn't vote in 1998 U.S. congressional election	90 57.7%	41 40.2%	131
Total	156 100.0%	102 100.0%	258
Voted in 1996 U.S. presidential election	47 30.5%	61 59.8%	108
Didn't vote in 1996 U.S. presidential election	107 69.5%	41 40.2%	148
Total	154 100.0%	102 100.0%	256

the sense that less well-educated people and those with language problems will have more difficulty and thus incur more costs when they vote. Age, years in the country, and years of citizenship measure the stake that people feel in elections and the store of relevant electoral information they have accumulated over time.

One alternative hypothesis is that dual-nationality citizens are different from single-nationality citizens in their participation patterns because they are more demographically disadvantaged. We test this with a multivariate logit model predicting the effect of dual nationality on registration and voting, with dichotomous dependent variables, controlling for income, education, English reading skill, gender, age, years lived in the United States, years of U.S. citizenship, and whether a respondent has voted in his or her country of origin since coming to the United States.

The estimations indicate that dual nationality is a significant predictor of both registration and voting, and that the signs of the coefficients are consistent with the predictions in the political science literature. Controlling for the other factors in our equation, being a dual national lowers the probability of registering to vote and of voting in two of the three equations that predict voting patterns in the United States. Education predicts a higher probability of registering and voting for all four variables, and age does so for registering and two of the three voting variables. Years in the United States predicts a higher probability of having voted in 1998, while years of U.S. citizenship displays a similar relation to having voted in 1996. While it can be problematic to rely on someone's recall of whether he or she voted in an election several years ago, the relationships between dual nationality and the variables for registering to vote and having ever voted in the United States provide support for the predictions of the cost model of participation.

To estimate the effect of dual nationality on these measures of political participation, we calculated predicted probabilities of registering and voting based on dual-nationality status. Keeping the values of control variables at their actual levels, for each individual in the sample, we computed the probability of registering and voting if she were a dual citizen and if she were not. Then we calculated mean predicted probabilities across all individuals to produce an estimate of the impact of dual nationality on participation. The effect of dual nationality lowered the mean predicted probability of registering to vote by 20 percentage points, to 0.62 from 0.82 calculated for single nationality. Similarly, the mean predicted probability for having ever voted in the United States was 0.57 for dual nationality and 0.68 for single nationality, and for having voted in the 1996 presidential election, the mean predicted probability dropped to 0.39 for dual nationality from 0.51 for single nationality. These differences illustrate the substantial impact of dual nationality on political participation.

Next we turn to forms of political participation beyond registration and voting. Are dual nationals more or less likely than other Latinos born abroad to volunteer or work for a Latino political candidate, attend a public meeting or demonstration regarding Latino concerns, or contribute money to a Latino political candidate or organization? These measures gauge participation in activities related to Latino candidates and organizations instead of probing participation in more general political activities, reflecting the focus of the Latino survey that forms the basis of this study. While participation in Latino-related activities may have a great deal to do with factors like where respondents live and whether Latinos are running for office, it provides opportunity for measuring the impact of dual nationality on other forms of political participation. Additionally, by examining participation that, unlike registering and voting, is not dependent upon citizenship, we can include in the analysis noncitizens from the countries that allow dual nationality and who have been in this country at least five years.

Examination of descriptive statistics shows that dual nationals again lag behind single-nationality U.S. citizens in percentage measures of all three indicators of political participation. It is even the case that higher percentages of noncitizens than dual citizens engage in two of these three types of participation: dual nationals reported to have volunteered or worked for a Latino candidate more than did noncitizens, but trailed both single-nationality U.S. citizens and noncitizens in attending meetings/demonstrations and giving contributions.

Do these descriptive findings hold when we control for demographic factors? Using a logit model, we analyzed the effect of dual nationality on each of these three measures of participation and used ordinary least squares regression analysis to predict the effect of dual nationality on an index of the number of these activities engaged in by each respondent. The results of this analysis, controlling again for income, education, skill reading English, gender, age, years lived in the United States, and whether a respondent has voted in his or her country of origin since coming to the United States, are shown in table 3.

In this analysis, dual nationality does not have a significant effect on whether an individual engaged in any of these three types of political participation. The one consistent result is that English reading skill predicts greater participation in two of the three activities and in the participation index, as we would expect. Interestingly, the only other statistically significant findings are that the number of years a person has spent in the United States predicts a higher probability of working or volunteering for a Latino political candidate, and that males are more likely to participate in two of the three activities and have a higher score on the political activity index. In sum, dual nationality does predict lower levels of registration and voting, but it does not appear to have a statistically significant effect on these other forms of political participation, controlling for other variables.

Table 3   Logit and OLS regression analysis of political activities of Latinos born abroad

	Volunteered or worked for pay for a Latino political candidate, or not	Attended a public meeting or demonstration regarding Latino concerns, or not	Contributed money to a Latino political candidate or Latino political organization, or not	Index: # of these political activities undertaken (OLS)
	(0 = No, 1 = Yes)	(0 = No, 1 = Yes)	(0 = No, 1 = Yes)	(0, 1, 2, 3)
Dual nationality	−0.048 (0.404)	−0.162 (0.226)	−0.338 (0.332)	−0.067 (0.062)
Voted in country of origin	0.340 (0.393)	0.232 (0.211)	0.292 (0.302)	0.087 (0.059)
Years in U.S.	0.038 (0.016)**	−0.004 (0.012)	0.013 (0.015)	0.004 (0.003)
Age	−0.010 (0.016)	0.010 (0.009)	−0.008 (0.013)	0.000 (0.003)
Gender (0 = Female, 1 = Male)	0.456 (0.350)	0.344 (0.181)*	0.462 (0.264)*	0.119 (0.050)**
English skill reading	1.027 (0.649)	0.951 (0.335)***	1.199 (0.480)**	0.312 (0.093)***
Education	1.077 (0.681)	0.176 (0.361)	−0.037 (0.519)	0.093 (0.101)
Income	−0.342 (0.670)	−0.353 (0.379)	0.399 (0.506)	−0.037 (0.106)
Constant	−4.503	−2.185	−3.248	0.061
R^2	—	—	—	0.050
Adj. R^2	—	—	—	0.039
S.E.E.	—	—	—	0.656
	n = 706	n = 707	n = 706	n = 706

*** $p \leq .01$ ** $p \leq .05$ * $p \leq .10$

Entries are unstandardized regression coefficients, with standard errors in parentheses.

All independent variables were coded from 0 to 1, except age, years in U.S., and years of U.S. citizenship.

Note: Analysis limited to Latinos who have lived in the U.S. for at least five years and were born in the 11 countries in our sample that allow dual nationality.

Predicting Characteristics by Nationality

Another way to see whether differences between dual nationals and other foreign-born Latinos are negligible is to estimate an equation that distinguishes the three main types in our sample—U.S. citizens with dual nationality, single-nationality U.S. citizens, and noncitizens—in terms of objective characteristics. To explore the distinctions among dual nationals, single-nationality U.S. citizens, and noncitizens, we used multinomial logit regression analysis to compare our base category, dual nationality U.S. citizens, with respondents in each of our other two categories who could have opted for dual nationality but did not. Additionally, as it is possible that the odds of becoming a dual citizen are a function of the length of time the option has been available to nationals of particular countries, we added a variable to our analysis that accounts for the number of years that had passed between the 1999 Latino survey and the year when each country adapted dual-nationality provisions. The countries ranged from Uruguay, which recognized dual nationals beginning in 1919, to Mexico, which first did so in March of 1998.

We also added a variable to control for whether a country used a "top-down" or "bottom-up" approach when they adopted their dual-nationality law. According to Jones-Correa (2001b), "bottom-up" policies are enacted in response to popular pressure from citizens abroad, while the impetus for "top-down" policies comes from government officials with little influence from the community abroad. Countries with dual-nationality provisions adopted in response to "bottom-up" pressure might be expected to see a higher incidence of people choosing dual nationality. Brazil, Costa Rica, El Salvador, Jamaica, Panama, Peru, and Uruguay were classified as "top-down," while Colombia, the Dominican Republic, Ecuador, and Mexico were categorized as "bottom-up."

Table 4 reveals the results of the multinomial logit model that relates the odds that an individual will be a citizen, noncitizen, or dual citizen to that person's demographic profile, and the controls for the length of time the option has been available and whether the option was imposed in a "top-down" or "bottom-up" manner.

A comparison of dual nationals to single-nationality U.S. citizens shows that the differences between them are negligible. Single-nationality U.S. citizens are predicted to be less likely to have voted in their country of origin in recent years than dual nationals and are less likely to declare that they are ideologically liberal. Otherwise, the two categories are not predicted to differ in statistically significant ways. As these are the two groups examined for registration and voting activity, this suggests that our finding that dual nationality predicts lower probability of registration and voting is not a result of demographic differences between the groups.

When we compare dual nationals to noncitizens, we see more dra-

Table 4   Multinomial logit regression analysis of dual nationals, non-U.S. citizens, and U.S.-only citizens (base category: dual citizens)

	Non-U.S. citizens	U.S.-only citizens
Voted in country of origin	0.106 (0.281)	−1.383 (0.467)***
Years in U.S.	−0.083 (0.018)***	0.024 (0.019)
Age	−0.003 (0.013)	0.024 (0.016)
Gender (0 = Female, 1 = Male)	0.059 (0.234)	0.035 (0.303)
English skill reading	−1.322 (0.431)***	0.566 (0.583)
Education	0.112 (0.476)	1.111 (0.592)*
Income	−0.736 (0.479)	0.575 (0.571)
Ideology (0 = Conservative, .5 = Moderate, 1 = Liberal)	−0.140 (0.299)	−0.704 (0.399)*
Party ID (0 = Republican, .5 = Independent, 1 = Democrat	−1.010 (0.339)***	−0.500 (0.428)
Importance of religion in daily life	−0.987 (0.434)**	−0.758 (0.546)
Trust in government	−0.386 (0.430)	0.586 (0.566)
Years country of origin has allowed dual nationality	−0.013 (0.016)	−0.046 (0.030)
Adoption of dual nationality was Top-down = 1 or Bottom-up = 0	0.389 (0.382)	0.284 (0.593)
Constant	4.982	−1.539
Dual nationals n = 121	Non-U.S. citizens n = 362	U.S.-only citizens n = 94

*** $p \leq .01$ ** $p \leq .05$ * $p \leq .10$
Entries are unstandardized regression coefficients, with standard errors in parentheses.
All independent variables were coded from 0 to 1, except age, years in U.S., years of U.S. citizenship, and years country of origin has allowed dual nationality.
Note: Analysis limited to Latinos who have been in the U.S. for at least five years and were born in the 11 countries in our sample that allow dual nationality.

matic differences. Noncitizens are predicted to have lived fewer years in the United States, to have less skill reading English, are more likely to identify themselves as Republicans or Independents as opposed to Democrats, and are less likely to cite religion as a very important factor in their daily lives. Neither the variable that measures the length of time the native country has offered dual nationality nor the "top down" versus "bottom up" distinction is significant. Dual citizens, in short, are virtually identical to single-nationality citizens in demographic characteristics, but are more socioeconomically advantaged than noncitizens.

Conclusion

Our analysis has provided suggestive evidence to two of the main concerns regarding dual nationality and political participation. With respect to this sample of self-identified Latinos who are eligible for dual nationality, we find that U.S. citizens with dual nationality are less likely to register and to vote in the United States than their single-nationality U.S. citizen counterparts are and that the disparity in participation cannot be explained by the usual socioeconomic factors. This result is consistent with a cost explanation, but also with other hypotheses that we cannot rule out: that these dual nationals do not perceive as much at stake in U.S. elections because of conflicted loyalties, are less likely to be socialized into U.S. civic norms, or perhaps are less likely to be mobilized by domestic political organizations (see chapters by Junn and Ramírez and Wong in this volume). Additionally, we find that U.S. citizens who were born abroad in countries that allow some form of dual nationality are less likely to have ever voted in the United States than are those citizens born in countries without dual-nationality provisions.

The relative proximity of the home countries for the dual-nationality citizens in our study raises questions about dual nationals from other parts of the world. The salience of home-country ties and the incentives to maintain citizenship might vary dramatically for those from more distant regions of the globe. We hope that further analysis can explore these dynamics and alternative explanations more thoroughly in the future.

Dual nationality is in many respects a moving target; this study investigates a slice of the situation as it stood in the fall of 1999, just eighteen months after Mexico had enacted its dual-nationality provision. With the recent adoption of such laws by a number of countries, the dynamics of immigration and citizenship may be altering rapidly and dramatically. Dual nationality may allow immigrants to maintain ties to their home countries short of physical return, thus shifting long-observed patterns of circular migration. The number of countries allowing dual nationality suggests that the world is indeed moving away from the quasi-nationalist notion of citizenship toward the post-nationalist conception. This shift is certainly not inevitable, but it does appear to be happening.

So, what do our findings imply for a future of multiple nationalities? Given that there are cognitive and opportunity costs associated with these additional civic obligations, we might expect that citizens with dual nationalities will have less interest and/or ability than single-nationality citizens to participate fully in U.S. political life. That does not mean that dual nationality is a bad idea any more than it was a bad idea to grant eighteen-year-olds the right to vote. In both cases, there is a strong case for why they should have the right to participate fully in U.S. civic life. But at the same time, if the results of this study are borne out by further research, we may have to accept that both eighteen to twenty-one-year-olds and dual-nationality citizens may not be active participants to the same degree as older and single-nationality citizens.

Notes

1. While nationality and citizenship are often used interchangeably, the terms have distinct meanings (Jones-Correa 2001b). As countries vary in their nationality and citizenship provisions, we focus on the broader concept, nationality. Mexico, for example, offers dual nationality that grants certain property rights but not full dual citizenship that would include voting rights from abroad.

2. The cost of obtaining an overseas ballot is a consideration for those who enjoy the rights of full dual citizenship, but not for those dual nationals from countries that do not allow voting from abroad.

3. Other factors that might affect B and D, such as whether respondents live in ethnic enclaves, were not included in the survey on which we base this study and thus are not part of this study.

4. Brazil, Colombia, Costa Rica, Dominican Republic, Ecuador, El Salvador, Jamaica, Mexico, Panama, Peru, and Uruguay. Information on dual nationality provisions in Latin American countries is drawn from Jones-Correa (2001b).

5. While this analysis responds to those of Jones-Correa (2001a) and Ramakrishnan (2002), our focus is on dual nationality provisions and not the impact of institutional rules of the game. Thus, we do not include control variables of state election turnout rates, and closed registration, registration canceling, and mail-in ballot provisions, which we do not believe would be correlated with the included independent variables.

6. While legal residents can apply for citizenship after five years in the United

States, the administrative process is often slow. Thus, we also ran our analysis on only those respondents who had been in the United States for at least six years and then for at least seven years to see if changing this criterion altered our results. While there were minor differences in certain equations, these re sults did not vary substantially from our analysis using the five-year criterion, and the results using any of the three breaking points support our general conclusions about the participation of dual-nationality U.S. citizens.

7. Survey respondents who claimed dual nationality but who were born in countries that do not permit dual nationality with the United States, including forty-five from Cuba, three from Venezuela, and five from Bolivia, are excluded from our analysis. An additional thirty-one non-Latinos claimed to be dual nationals, but since non-Latinos were not asked their country of birth in the survey, we had no group against which to compare them, and thus excluded them from the analysis. Nine other respondents who claimed dual nationality and gave their country of birth as "other", "don't know", or "U.S." were also excluded from the analysis.

Transnational Politics and Civic Engagement
Do Home-Country Political Ties Limit Latino Immigrant Pursuit of U.S. Civic Engagement and Citizenship?

Louis DeSipio

Over the past decade, the number of immigrants naturalizing in the United States has surged. According to the Immigration and Naturalization Service (INS) and the Bureau of Citizenship and Immigration Services, naturalizations grew from an average of 146,000 annually in the 1970s, to 221,000 annually in the 1980s, to 562,000 annually in the 1990s. In the years since 1996—the beginning of the contemporary surge—the number of immigrants naturalizing annually averages 650,000.

The origins of this steady increase in naturalization are several. While there are particular shocks and enhanced incentives that appear periodically (Portes and Stepik 1993, DeSipio 1996a), the underlying cause of the contemporary growth in naturalization is the combination of high interest among immigrants in pursuing U.S. citizenship and steady growth in the long-term immigrant population (Pachon and DeSipio 1994, NALEO Educational Fund 2004). These long-term immigrants have been shown consistently to be more likely to naturalize than are more recent immigrants, particularly among Latinos, who make the largest pool of immigrants to permanent residence.[1] The increase in immigration beginning with the 1965 amendments to the immigration law ensures that there now are large numbers of immigrants with the twelve to fifteen years of legal residence that often precedes naturalization among Latinos (U.S. Immigration and Naturalization Service 2003: Tables M and 54, and *INS Statistical Yearbooks*, previous years).

The rapid increase in the number of immigrants naturalizing should not obscure the fact that there is also an increase in the number of immigrants eligible to naturalize who have not. Data on the emigration and deaths of the legal permanent residents is not maintained, so it is not possible to provide an exact number of citizenship-eligible immigrants. A recent estimate of 2000 census data conducted by the Urban Institute's Jeffrey Passel for the NALEO Educational Fund estimated that there were 7.7 million legal permanent residents in the United States eighteen years of age or above with sufficient residence (generally, five years) to be eligible to naturalize. Of these, 4.2 million were Latinos (NALEO Educational Fund 2004). Legal permanent residents under eighteen years of age can naturalize only as part of their parents' naturalization.

This large pool of immigrants, including a significant share of longer-term immigrants, raises a recurring question for the polity. Will these immigrants join the polity and participate as equals with the U.S. born? The United States has faced this question before, but the cyclical nature of large-scale immigration makes it particularly pressing now. The roots of much contemporary immigration can be traced to the 1965 changes to immigration law. The dramatic effects of that law on the numbers of immigrants were not felt until the 1980s. So, we are now in the era of a mature immigration, where there are large numbers of recently naturalized citizens, many long-term permanent resident immigrants, and an even larger pool of short-term immigrants, many of whom are undocumented. This variety offers an analytical opportunity, exploited here, but also a pressing policy challenge.

In this essay, I want to revisit two existing scholarly literatures on the civic engagement of immigrants and on what differentiates immigrants who naturalize from those who do not. I want to see if the findings of this existing scholarship remain when a newly emerging characteristic in the contemporary immigrant experience is added to the story. Specifically, I want to analyze the impact of transnational political engagements and comparative evaluations of political opportunities in the United States and the country of origin on civic, residential, and political attachment to the United States.

This essay has three parts. First, I briefly review the existing scholarship on immigrant civic engagement and immigrant naturalization propensity and indicate why "transnational" politics might alter traditional patterns of U.S. immigrant political adaptation. Second, I discuss a new data source—the Tomás Rivera Policy Institute (TRPI) 2002 Immigrant Political Participation Survey[2]—that allows me to test the impact of several sets of immigrant characteristics that have been shown to shape immigrant civic engagement and naturalization propensity (demographic, attitudinal and familial, and immigration and settlement), but that also includes a rich battery of questions relating to home-country political engagement and attitudes toward the individual-level political opportunities in each country. Finally, I test three models of immigrant civic and political attachment to the United States.

Immigrant Civic and Political Engagement

The degree to which immigrants engage U.S. politics has long been a topic of scholarly and public policy debate. Fear of permanent immigrant nonincorporation is often balanced in the popular mind by equally ungrounded fears that immigrants will dominate U.S. politics and change its core values (Huntington 2004a, 2004b, as contemporary examples). The reality, of course, has been somewhere between these poles historically and continues to be today. In this essay, I examine three measures of immigrant civic, residential, and political engagement in U.S. politics. Specifically, I assess community organizational involvement among Latino immigrants, long-term residential intentions, and naturalization behaviors. Community organizational activities are open to all immigrants and provide the opportunity to participate in civic life at the local level. All immigrants can plan long-term residence in the United States, but immigrant legal status may significantly shape those plans, particularly for those without legal status. Naturalization, conversely, is open only to legal permanent residents who meet statutory eligibility requirements (for most, five years of legal residence).

Immigrants from Mexico and other parts of the Americas have long participated in the activities of organizations meeting collective needs. The rebirth of Mexican American politics in the late nineteenth century and the first manifestations of Caribbean immigrant politics in this same era took the form of locally driven organizations formed to meet collective needs (Arellano 2000; Gutiérrez 1995, chapter 1; Sánchez Korrol 1994, chapter 5). Some of the major evolutions in twentieth century Latino politics were driven by new organizational formulations.[3]

Despite the critical role that organizations have played in the establishment and evolution of Latino politics in the twentieth century, organizational politics has diminished in importance for the broader field of Latino politics since the 1975 extension of Voting Rights Act (VRA) coverage to Latino communities (DeSipio 2004). The politics of U.S.-citizen Latinos has increasingly focused on electoral politics and community-based organizations often serve as foundations for candidacies and campaigns. The relative decline in the importance of organizational life to politics, of course, is not a characteristic unique to the Latino community (Skocpol 2003), but the decline is more dramatic in the Latino U.S.-citizen population, because organizations played a relatively more important role in the era before the VRA reduced the manipulation and exclusion of Latino voters.

For immigrant Latinos, who are largely precluded from direct participation in electoral politics, organizations retain their more traditional role as a centerpiece of community politics. Despite the importance of organizations to Latino immigrant politics, the majority of immigrants do not participate in organizations (a characteristic also true of U.S.-born Latinos) (de la Garza, with Lu 1999). The dynamics of which among Latino immigrants participates in organizations and who does not is relatively understudied. Sidney Verba, Kay Lehman Schlozman, and Henry Brady (1995, chapter 8; Burns, Schlozman, and Verba 2001, chapter 11) find that Latino immigrants are generally less likely that U.S.-born Latinos as well as whites and blacks to be organizationally involved.

Immigration has steadily increased in the 1980s and 1990s as has naturalization, so there is consistently a higher share of recent Latino immigrants relative to longer-term, nonnaturalized immigrants. A few characteristics of the Latino immigrant population are worth noting. First, Latinos generally, and Latino immigrants specifically, are younger and have lower levels of education and income than non-Hispanic whites. Also, the longer the length of residence in the United States, the higher the likelihood of community organizational participation among Latino immigrants (DeSipio et al. 1998).

Not all permanent residents naturalize. What distinguishes those who do from those who don't? As previously indicated, the single most important predictor of naturalization among immigrants is length of residence: immigrants who reside in the United States longer are more likely to naturalize than those with shorter periods of residence. This is true today and was true of turn-of-the-century immigrants (Gavit 1922; U.S. Immigration and Naturalization Service 2003, table 54). Speed of naturalization, however, varies by nationality and by region of origin. In the contemporary era, Asian immigrants naturalize the fastest and immigrants from the Americas naturalize the slowest. Traditionally, the nationalities with the longest wait between immigration and naturalization are nationals of the two countries that border the United States, Mexico and Canada.

At the individual level, several factors explain diverse rates of naturalization, among them demographic characteristics, attitudinal and associational variables, immigration and settlement characteristics, and inconsistent bureaucratic treatment. Of these, demographic characteristics of immigrants are the most studied and have been shown to have the most reliable and most sizeable impact on naturalization. Income, white-collar employment, professional status, home ownership, years of schooling, and English-language abilities increase the likelihood of naturalization (Barkan and Khokolov 1980, Portes and Mozo 1985, Jasso and Rosenzweig 1990, Yang 1994, DeSipio 1996b, Johnson et al. 1999). The married are more likely to naturalize than the unmarried, and women more likely than men. Immigrants who arrived as young children are more likely to naturalize than are those who arrived as teenagers or adults, controlling for length of residence.

Attitudinal and associational variables have also been shown to shape the likelihood that an immigrant will naturalize. Roots in the United States, attitude toward life in the United States, and social identification as an American each has been shown to have a positive impact on the likelihood of naturalization (García 1981, Portes and Curtis 1987). Immigrants who associate mostly with noncitizens are less likely to naturalize (DeSipio 1996b). Michael Jones-Correa (1998) finds that an "ideology of return [to the home country]" discourages naturalization. Finally, permanent residents who state an intention to stay in the United States are more likely to express an interest in pursuing naturalization and in successfully naturalizing (DeSipio 1996b).

Immigration and settlement experiences also shape naturalization propensity. Immigrants who entered as refugees, skilled workers, or for political reasons are more likely to naturalize (Jasso and Rosenzweig 1990, Portes and Mozo 1985). The higher the sending country's GNP, the lower the likelihood of naturalization (Yang 1994). National-origin differences persist after controlling for other factors shown to influence naturalization. Guillermina Jasso and Mark Rosenzweig (1990) find that immigrants from Mexico are less likely than average to naturalize than nationals of other large immigrant-sending countries. Controlling for sociodemographic, associational, and immigration-related factors, Louis DeSipio (1996b) finds that among Latinos, Cubans and Dominicans are more likely than Mexicans to begin the naturalization process and, once they began the process, to become U.S. citizens. Hans Johnson and colleagues (1999) examine how local governments can influence immigrant naturalization propensity.

The administration of the U.S. naturalization program (now part of the Department of Homeland Security—DHS) is the final factor shown to influence naturalization. Naturalization has traditionally been decentralized, which results in differential treatment of applicants from one INS district office to another (DeSipio and Pachon 1992). INS has recently proposed reforms that will minimize the variation in applicant treatment between naturalization offices (DeSipio, Pachon, and Moellmer 2001), but the legacy of this differential treatment will likely continue to cause confusion among some immigrants and, perhaps, discourage pursuit of naturalization. Potential naturalizees are further confused by repeated changes in the fees associated with naturalization (currently $390).

Incentives to naturalize and resources to assist immigrants seeking to naturalize also change. In the mid-1990s, for example, many immigrants felt besieged and feared losing the rights that had traditionally been extended to permanent residents (DeSipio 1996a). California passed Proposition 187, which denied state education and social service benefits to undocumented immigrants, and Congress passed the 1996 Welfare Reform bill, which eliminated permanent resident eligibility for federal social welfare benefits such as Supplemental Security Income and Aid to Families with Dependent Children. Congress also made it easier to deport permanent residents who committed crimes in the United States. Administrative changes at the Immigration and Naturalization Service (INS) also encouraged permanent residents to pursue naturalization. Permanent residents with green cards more than ten years old had to replace their cards for the first time in the agency's history. INS also repeatedly raised the fee for naturalization in this period. Finally, Latino and immigrant organizations increased the resources available to assist immigrants to pursue U.S. citizenship. Univision and other Spanish-language media promoted the importance of naturalization to Latino audiences.

It is not possible to disaggregate the impact of changes on an individual Latino's propensity to naturalize (DeSipio and Pachon 2002), but the cumulative effect of these pressures and the growing pool of citizenship-eligible immigrants was to move the largest number of immigrants in American immigration history to apply for naturalization.

Over the past decade, scholars of the U.S. immigrant experience have increasingly analyzed the degree to which immigrants, and in some cases their U.S.-born children, engage the politics of their sending communities and countries. This emerging scholarship of immigrant political transnationalism has made important, if sometimes overstated, contributions to our understandings of the mechanisms of immigrant participation in home-community and home-country society and of politics and of immigrant settlement in the United States. For the most part, the case studies of active political transnationalism examine a specific immigrant-sending community (e.g., Levitt 2001) or a specific form of transnational behavior across multiple immigrant-ethnic populations, for example, migrant remittances (de la Garza and Lowell 2002). Some transnational scholarship theorizes about the opportunities for the creation of sustained transnational connections between immigrants and their sending communities (Glick Schiller, Basch, and Blanc-Szanton 1992; Smith and Guarnizo 1998).

The new scholarship of transnational politics has also explored the administrative structures and political implications of sending-country efforts to extend nationality or citizenship to emigrants abroad (de la Garza and Velasco 1997, González-Gutiérrez 1999, de la Garza and Pachon 2000, Jones-Correa 2001b). Scholars have also begun to explore whether transnational political attachments extend into the second generation (Fouron and Glick Schiller 2001, Levitt and Waters 2002). Finally, political theorists have also begun to explore the impact of new transnational political formation among émigrés on traditional conceptions of citizenship (Guarnizo 1997b, Ong 1999). As more émigrés and, perhaps, their children begin to maintain political ties in both the United States and their country of origin/ancestry, traditional country-bound notions of citizenship may have to be recast (Soysal 1994, Bosniak 2001).[4]

This burst of scholarship and the underlying phenomenon that it documents highlights what might be a weakness in existing study of civic engagement and naturalization propensities among immigrants in the United States. While certainly not a new phenomenon, the volume of contemporary immigration and the relative ease of international communication and transportation make it much easier for immigrants to be transnational. The transnational scholarship shows that some subset of immigrants—approximately 20 percent of Latino immigrants and few in the second generation, by my estimate—engage the civic and political life of their sending communities or countries after emigration (DeSipio et al. 2003). Yet, this scholarship does not, for the most part, ask about the consequences of transnational engagement for civic engagement in immigrant-receiving societies, in residential plans of immigrants, or in naturalization.

Transnationalism raises questions about what we know about immigrant civic engagement and immigrant naturalization propensity. One possibility (hypothesis one) is that transnational engagement in the civic and political life of the sending country reduces the likelihood that immigrants will become involved in U.S. civic life or seek naturalization. If the transnational engagement allows a space for immigrants to achieve their political goals in their countries of origin and reduces the bonds that have developed in the past between immigrants and the United States, then immigrants who are transnationally engaged will be less likely to manifest civic or political attachment to the United States, controlling for other factors. A second possibility (hypothesis two) is that the transnational engagement offers a resource for immigrants who have engaged in transnational activities and that they can translate the skills, networks, and interests that they have developed to U.S. civic life and to naturalization.

This hypothesis—that the transnationally engaged will be more likely to be civically engaged in the United States and to naturalize—builds on two notions. The first piece is that political learning is transferable, so skills and interests developed in transnational politics can be applied to U.S. politics (and visa versa). The second is that some people are more likely than others to become engaged in civic and political life. For immigrants, these interests are more likely to first manifest themselves in home-country focused community and civic activities because those are more pressing and more attainable. The interests of these more civically/politically engaged immigrants, however, soon shift to their communities in the United States. Clearly, the null hypothesis is that transnational behavior is irrelevant to immigrant civic engagement or naturalization. If this is the case, then the measures of transnational behavior will not prove significant, and traditional predictors of civic and political engagement will assume their traditional roles.

In the analysis that follows, I test three models of civic and political engagement in the United States among contemporary Latino immigrants. The first model measures Latino immigrant propensity to participate in U.S. civic organizations. The second looks at long-term residential intentions. Finally, the third analyzes naturalization among Latino legal permanent residents eligible for naturalization. These models include factors shown to influence the likelihood of organizational participation and naturalization. I add to these predictors two measures of transnational political behaviors and two measures of attitudes toward political opportunities in the sending country and in the United States.

Data

The analysis is based on the results of a telephone survey with 1,602 Latino immigrants conducted by the Tomás Rivera Policy Institute in

July and August 2002. To ensure that we could analyze between Latino national-origin groups, TRPI targeted the survey to four nationality groups—three of the four largest Latino immigrant populations
(Mexicans, Dominicans, and Salvadorans)[5] as well as Puerto Ricans.
Although Puerto Ricans are not immigrants because of the Jones
Act, TRPI hypothesized that they experience a political adaptation
as migrants that parallels most experiences of immigrants. Puerto Ricans have, for the most part, been neglected in the scholarship on
transnational politics. That said, they are U.S. citizens by birth and,
consequently, are excluded from my analysis of U.S. naturalization
propensity.[6]

The survey includes at least 400 respondents from each national
origin group. In households with more than one eligible adult, TRPI
randomly selected the respondent (using the "most recent birthday"
method) to reduce bias in sample. Respondents were given the opportunity to respond in either English or Spanish, and all interviewers
were fully bilingual. Approximately 94 percent of respondents answered the questionnaire in Spanish. On average, surveys took seventeen minutes to complete once the screening was completed.[7]

Characteristics of respondents' families, as well as the respondents'
demographic immigration characteristics appear in the DeSipio and
colleagues 2003 study. A quick review of these data indicates that the
respondents to the TRPI Immigrant Political Participation Survey are
broadly representative of the immigrant populations from these four
nations. The share of naturalized respondents among those either reporting citizenship or legal permanent resident status also closely resembles the Latino legal immigrant population as a whole.

U.S. Civic and Residential Attachment
among Contemporary Latino Migrants

I test the relationship between transnational political engagement and
U.S. residential and civic attachments using multivariate models of
this engagement. The first model tests for the predictors of engagement in at least one of seven U.S. civic organizations (a church, a labor union, a parent-teacher organization, a sports club, a fraternal
order, a hometown association, or any other club). Approximately
28 percent of respondents reported *no* memberships in any of these
organizations. This is a straightforward test of participation in organizations that immigrants can participate in regardless of legal status
and that are reliable predictors of other forms of political activity. The

second model tests for the predictors of intent to make a permanent home of the United States. Overall, approximately 61 percent of respondents reported that they did plan to make a permanent home of the United States. Although this is probably an underestimate of the actual long-term residential patterns of these migrants, it offers an indication of where immigrants see their long-term future and captures a nascent sense of connection between immigrants and the United States, regardless of immigration status. Finally, the third model focuses on predictors of naturalization. Since naturalization is limited to permanent residents with five years of legal residence, I exclude respondents without legal status and permanent resident respondents with fewer than five years of permanent residence from this model. I also exclude Puerto Ricans. This diminishes the sample somewhat to 710. In the TRPI Immigrant Participation Survey, approximately 28 percent of residents from Mexico, the Dominican Republic, and El Salvador reported that they were not permanent residents or naturalized U.S. citizens. Of the remainder, 62 percent were permanent residents and 38 percent had naturalized.

The models I tested included three components: respondent demographics, respondent immigration and settlement characteristics, and respondent transnational political engagement and evaluations of political opportunities in the United States and the sending country.

As I have indicated, demographic characteristics have long been known to influence naturalization and civic engagement. I include four demographic traits in this model: age,[8] education, household income, and gender. Based on the available scholarship, I anticipate that older, more-educated, and higher-income respondents are more likely to be civically engaged in the United States and to be naturalized. I would also expect these demographic characteristics to be positive predictors of intending to reside permanently in the United States, though there is no scholarship on this question to substantiate this expectation. Latina immigrants have been shown to be more likely to be engaged in community organizations and to pursue naturalization (Alvarez 1987, DeSipio 1996b, Pardo 1998).

I also control for the impact of several immigration and settlement-related characteristics: length of residence in the United States, respondent immigrant legal status, location of the respondent's immediate family, experience of discrimination in the United States, and country of origin. Based on the previous scholarship, I anticipate that migrants who have resided in the United States for longer periods will be more likely to be engaged in U.S. civic activity, more likely to anticipate spending their lives in the United States, and much more likely to be naturalized. Those with legal status or who had naturalized would also be more likely to be civically engaged. Respondents whose immediate families are in the United States or are divided between the United States and the country of origin will be more likely to engage U.S. civic activities and be naturalized than are those whose family members are primarily abroad. Finally, based on some previous research in immigrant responses to discrimination in the United States (DeSipio 2002), I anticipate that respondents who perceive greater levels of discrimination in U.S. society will be more likely to be engaged in U.S. civic activities and to have naturalized. Discrimination here is a learned response that measures understanding of U.S. political institutions. I also include country of origin as a control, but have no prediction as to the effects.

Finally, I include four measures of transnational political engagement: (1) participation in organizations facilitating transnational engagement in the past year, (2) participation in home-country elections or election-related activities in the period since migration, (3) attitudes toward where the respondent's political voice would be more likely to be heard, and (4) perceived levels of influence in the home country and the United States.

If transnational engagement facilitates incorporation in the United States, I would anticipate that these factors would have a generally positive effect on the dependent variables, controlling for the other factors. If, however, transnationalism encourages greater distance from the United States, the variables would be signed negatively.

Organizations, meetings, and sending-country government offices offer a connection between immigrants and their countries of origin. Overall, approximately 70 percent of immigrants/migrants from the four nations under study have engaged in transnational organizational activity in the year before the survey. Dominicans and Puerto Ricans were the most likely to have engaged in these transnational activities and Salvadorans the least likely. Just 60 percent of Salvadorans had participated in transnational organizational activity in the year before the survey.

With the exception of following politics in the news, very few Latino immigrants engaged in transnational electoral or partisan activities. No more than one in nine, for example, had voted in home-country elections. Few had contributed money to candidates or parties in the home country, attended a rally in the United States for a home-country party, or had been contacted by a representative of the home country to become engaged in home-country political or cultural affairs. Overall, just 19 percent had participated in some electoral behavior in the country of origin since migration. Puerto Rican migrants and Dominican immigrants were the most likely to have participated in home-country electoral behaviors, and Mexicans and Salvadorans were the least likely. Nearly 30 percent of Dominican immigrants had been electorally active in the Dominican Republic since immigration to the United States.

The final two variables in the model test respondents' perceptions of political opportunities in the United States and in the country of origin. The first is a question of how much influence the respondent perceives that she or he has on home-country politics. I report it as a three-point scale from "none" to "a great deal." I include this as a control to make sure that the reported transnational behaviors do not oversignify a sense of influence. In other words, it is possible that immigrants who are engaged at home are doing so for family or social reasons and do not perceive their activities to be politically influential. Few respondents believe that they have no influence (less than 10 percent for each nationality group); the majority of each nationality group reports that they have "some" influence on the home nation. Between 24 percent (Puerto Ricans) and 36 percent (Salvadorans) perceive that they have "a great deal of influence."

The final transnational variable asks respondents where they perceive they have more influence—the home country, the United States, or both equally. Nearly 50 percent of respondents report that they have more influence in the United States. Dominicans are the most likely of the four nationality groups under study to report that they have more influence in the home country (21 percent); Puerto Ricans are the least likely (11 percent).

Results

Demographic and immigration characteristics proved more salient in predicting the likelihood of immigrant participation in U.S. civic and community organizational activities than did the transnational measures. These traditional explanatory variables, however, were joined by one of the transnational measures—participation in home-country organizational activity.

Not surprisingly, more-recent immigrants were somewhat less likely to participate in U.S. political organizations. Respondents with families in the United States (whether all or in part) were more likely to participate. As predicted, respondents reporting having experienced discrimination were somewhat more likely to be organizationally involved (by a factor of two). Somewhat unexpectedly, increasing levels of education had a negative effect on the likelihood of civic involvement. Permanent residents and naturalized citizens were more likely to be civically involved than immigrants without legal status.

One of the measures of transnational engagement also proved to be a significant predictor of U.S. organizational involvement controlling for the more traditional predictors. Respondents who reported membership in organizations focusing on the country of origin were more likely to also be involved in U.S. organizations. This suggests, perhaps not surprisingly, that some immigrants are simply more organizationally engaged. It also may suggest that the distinction that I am making between U.S. organizations and home country-focused organizations is not so rigid.

The factors shaping migrants' long-term intentions about whether to reside in the United States or the country of origins are shaped by a combination of immigration and transnational engagement factors. Demographic characteristics other than, possibly, age had little statistically significant impact on a reported intention to stay in the United States—each additional year of age increased the likelihood of reporting an intention to stay in the United States by about 1 percent in the specification of the model that excluded length of residence in the United States.

In terms of immigration characteristics, more recent immigration diminished the likelihood of reporting an intention to stay in the United States (each additional year reduced this likelihood by 4 percent) and respondents with most of their family in the United States were more likely to report an intention to stay as were permanent residents and naturalized citizens relative to migrants without legal status. Salvadorans were more likely than Mexicans to report an intention to stay (by a factor or more than 1.5). Puerto Ricans and Dominicans were about half as likely as Mexicans to report an intention to stay in the United States. Perceived discrimination had no effect on residential intentions.

The transnational factors had a consistent impact. Respondents who reported engagement in home-country electoral activities were approximately 25 percent less likely than those who did not to report an intention to stay in the United States permanently. Involvement in home-country organizational activities was signed negatively but did not achieve statistical significance. Respondents who perceived they

Table 1 Predictors of respondents' involvement in U.S. organizations

Independent variable	Odds ratio	SE
Demographics		
Age	0.998	0.008
Education (grade school or less)		
Some high school	0.873	0.213
HS graduate	0.611**	0.237
Post–high school	0.760	0.254
Household income	1.000***	0.000
Gender (men as control)	1.269	0.164
Immigration characteristics		
Year of immigration	0.965***	0.011
Immigration status (not permanent resident or naturalized citizen) ·		
Permanent resident	2.001***	0.219
Naturalized citizen	1.553**	0.283
Location of family (most in home country)		
Equally divided	1.486**	0.194
Most in the U.S.	1.838***	0.224
Country of birth (Mexico as control)		
Puerto Rico	1.426	0.310
El Salvador	1.058	0.216
Dominican Republic	0.844	0.250
Experience of discrimination in U.S.	2.016***	0.193
Transnational political engagement		
Home-country electoral behaviors	0.970	0.182
Home-country originally behaviors	1.761***	0.086
Home-country political influence (none)		
Some	0.788	0.289
A great deal	0.613	0.311
Where does respondent have more influence (home country)		
About the same	0.865	0.236
More in the U.S.	0.966	0.227
Constant	69.523***	21.716
Total cases	1,051	
Predicted correctly	77.7%	
R-squared	0.239	

*** $p \leq 0.01$, ** $p \leq 0.05$; * $p \leq 0.10$.
Source: The TRPI Immigrant Political Participation Survey, 2002.

Table 2 Predictors of respondents' prediction of long-term residence—
home country or the United States

Independent variable	Full model		Model excluding year of immigration	
	Odds ratio	SE	Odds ratio	SE
Demographics				
Age	0.992	0.007	1.013**	0.005
Education (grade school or less)				
Some high school	1.215	0.180	1.213	0.170
HS graduate	1.134	0.205	1.061	0.190
Post–high school	1.225	0.213	1.236	0.201
Household income	1.000	0.000	1.000	0.000
Gender (men as control)	1.045	0.138	1.057	0.129
Immigration characteristics				
Year of immigration	0.961***	0.009	Excluded	
Immigration status (not permanent resident or naturalized citizen)				
Permanent resident	1.794***	0.202	1.911	0.189
Naturalized citizen	1.720***	0.248	2.215	0.227
Location of family (most in home country)				
Equally divided	1.110	0.172	1.247	0.158
Most in the U.S.	1.814***	0.188	2.153***	0.173
Country of birth (Mexico as control)				
Puerto Rico	0.455***	0.245	0.509***	0.227
El Salvador	1.493**	0.195	1.365*	0.181
Dominican Republic	0.562***	0.215	0.478**	0.200
Experience of discrimination in U.S.	0.983	0.149	1.025	0.139
Transnational political engagement				
Home-country electoral behaviors	0.739***	0.134	0.780**	0.127
Home-country originally behaviors	0.986	0.060	0.963	0.055
Home-country political influence (none)				
Some	0.857	0.242	0.847	0.228
A great deal	0.753	0.261	0.782	0.245
Where does respondent have more influence (home country)				
About the same	0.880	0.203	0.894	0.189
More in the U.S.	1.763***	0.190	1.892***	0.000
Constant	78.188***	17.188	−1.393***	0.388
Total cases	1,051		1,172	
Predicted correctly	64.2%		63.2%	
R-squared	0.179		0.156	

*** $p < 0.01$, ** $p < 0.05$; * $p < 0.10$.
Source: The TRPI Immigrant Political Participation Survey, 2002.

had more political influence in the United States were more likely to report an intention to remain in the United States permanently.

Because expectations about long-term residential patterns are so strongly shaped by one factor—year of immigration—I tested a second specification of this model that excluded this variable. The predictive power of the model declined significantly with this exclusion but did not alter the results. The predictive power of location of family increased in significance and magnitude as did the predictive power of where the respondent thought she or he had more influence. Respondents who believed they had more influence in the United States were nearly twice as likely to report an intention to stay in the United States as those who believed they had more influence in the home country.

The findings of the existing scholarship on propensities to naturalize are largely confirmed. Demographic factors dominate the story, particularly in a model that excludes year of immigration. In the specification including year of immigration, years of education has the most explanatory power. My sense is that education both offers substantive skills that are rewarded in the U.S. economy and the bureaucratic coping skills needed to complete the naturalization application process. In this specification, year of immigration also proves significant, with each additional year reducing the likelihood of naturalization by approximately 12 percent. Women were more likely than men to naturalize. Income was positively signed and significant, but had no substantive impact. Family in the United States also proved to be a positive predictor, but of marginal significance.

Only one of the transnational measures proved to be significant: respondents who perceived they have more political influence in the United States were more likely to be naturalized than immigrants who perceived they had more influence in their country of origin. Considering that the behavioral measures of transnational engagement proved significant in the other models, this finding should offer some solace to critics of U.S. naturalization policy. Immigrants who naturalize are distinguished from those who do not based on individual characteristics and their family relationships (as has, arguably, always been the case) rather than because of newly emerging relationships with their countries of origin.

For reasons discussed earlier, I tested a second specification of the model excluding year of immigration. As with the second specification of the residential intentions model, this specification had less overall predictive value. In this model, age attained statistical significance. The

Table 3 Predictors of respondent naturalization (among legal permanent
residents with five or more years of residence)

Independent variable	Full model		Model excluding length of residence	
	Odds ratio	SE	Odds ratio	SE
Demographics				
Age	1.008	0.011	1.051***	0.008
Education (grade school or less)				
Some high school	1.565**	0.305	1.406	0.273
HS graduate	1.931*	0.349	1.491	0.298
Post–high school	3.827***	0.345	3.048***	0.301
Household income	1.000***	0.000	1.000***	0.000
Gender (men as control)	1.712**	0.224	1.548**	0.197
Immigration characteristics				
Year of immigration	0.879***	0.018	Excluded	
Location of family (most in home country)				
Equally divided	1.494	0.316	2.086***	0.280
Most in the U.S.	1.693*	0.317	3.234***	0.279
Country of Birth (Mexico as control)				
El Salvador	1.105	0.289	0.641*	0.251
Dominican Republic	1.219	0.298	0.729	0.256
Experienced discrimination	1.081	0.245	1.152	0.213
Transnational political engagement				
Home-country election behaviors	1.067	0.220	0.989	0.196
Home-country originally behaviors	0.965	0.099	0.770	0.085
Home-country political influence (baseline = none)				
Some	0.887	0.365	0.699	0.332
A great deal	1.261	0.386	0.835	0.349
Where does respondent have more influence (baseline = home country)				
About the same	0.884	0.343	0.948	0.303
More in the U.S.	1.787*	0.304	1.949**	0.266
Constant	252.177***	36.181	−4.505***	0.685
Total cases	546		611	
Predicted correctly	74.0%		72.8%	
R-squared	0.384		0.269	

*** $p < 0.01$, ** $p < 0.05$; * $p < 0.10$.
Source: The TRPI Immigrant Political Participation Survey, 2002.

highest level of education remains significant, though the magnitude of the impact declines slightly. Location of family members becomes quite significant, with respondents reporting most family members in the United States reporting naturalization more than 3.2 times higher than respondents reporting most family members in the country of origin. In this specification, Salvadoran migrants proved less likely to naturalize than Mexican migrants. As was the case in the first specification, respondents reporting more political influence in the United States were considerably more likely to naturalize than those reporting more in the home country, controlling for the other variables in the model.

Conclusions

As the post-1965 wave of immigration has begun to mature, the United States is, in many ways, in a new phase of its long immigration history. The current wave of immigration is soon to reach its fortieth birthday. Unlike the post–Civil War immigration wave, the roots of an organized opposition to immigration at current levels—either legal or unauthorized—do not have a foothold in the policymaking process or in mass organizing (Tichenor 2002). So, it is reasonable to assume that immigration will continue at current levels, or increase, for the foreseeable future.

Immigrants today have opportunities to sustain or rebuild an engagement with their sending communities and sending countries in a way that was difficult for most in the past. Transportation and communication networks allow for a sustained transnational engagement for many migrants. The volume of immigration and the networks that facilitate it ensure that many immigrants in the United States live and work around many from the same sending communities. Many continue to have family in these communities. Although a political transnational engagement is the exception rather than the rule among most Latino immigrants, it is important to measure whether this nascent transnationalism is reshaping the process of immigrant civic and political engagement in U.S. politics and society.

Although this question can only be answered rigorously with longitudinal data, the evidence from the TRPI Immigrant Political Participation Survey offers some insights. The expanding opportunities for migrants to be involved in the electoral politics of their sending countries does appear to have an independent effect on their perceptions of long-term connection to the United States and, in more cases than not, speeds it. Involvement in these activities reduces respondents' evaluations of the likelihood of their staying in the United States permanently. At the same time, this one form of home-country engagement is balanced by perceptions of influence. Migrants who perceive they have equal or more influence in the United States see their futures here unlike those who perceive that their influence is primarily in the sending country. These impacts appear even after controlling for demographic and immigration/settlement related characteristics previously shown to influence questions of attachment.

With one exception, transnational engagement has little impact on U.S. organizational participation. The exception—home-country organizational behavior—quite likely tells a story not of transnationalism, but of political socialization. Individuals who are organizationally active are likely to be active in many arenas. Finally, transnational engagement does shape naturalization propensity, but in a civically encouraging manner. Those who feel the most influence in the United States are the most likely to have naturalized. This indicates that there remains a political dimension to decisions to naturalize. Home-country electoral or organizational involvement are not statistically valid predictors of naturalization, suggesting that Latino immigrants are not using transnational opportunities in ways that some scholars anticipate of a fully realized dual citizenship.

The final lesson of this survey of Latino immigrant transnational attitudes and behaviors is that this new set of resources for immigrant politics must be accounted for as scholars continue to analyze the contemporary process of immigrant incorporation in the United States. The contemporary scholarship analyzes the story of immigrant social and political adaptation as one that occurs primarily in the United States. While transnationalism is the exception in immigrant communities today, and will probably remain so in the future, it nevertheless offers an opportunity (and a new one, for the mass of immigrants) for political socialization and an outlet for individuals' civic energies. As the number of immigrants grows and the concentrations of immigrants from specific parts of the world deepen, it is likely that some will have political experiences shaped by transnational engagements that are distinct from the majority and that these engagements will lead them to different political and civic outcomes. As the data here suggest, that difference can serve as an encouragement to increase connections to the United States and to U.S. civic institutions. It is also possible, however, to envision a scenario where these transnational engagements act as a further barrier to informal and formal connections between immigrants and U.S. politics.

Notes

I would like to express my appreciation to Ricardo Ramirez, Karthick Ramakrishnan, Taeku Lee, and the participants in the "A Nation of Immigrants: Ethnic Identity and Political Incorporation" conference for comments on an earlier draft of this chapter.

1. I use the terms Latino and Hispanic interchangeably to refer to U.S. residents who trace their origin or ancestry to the Spanish-speaking nations of Latin America. The focus of this project is Latino immigrants and migrants, so all analysis of Latinos presented here refers to people who were born in one of the four nations included in the TRPI survey described later—Mexico, Puerto Rico, the Dominican Republic, or El Salvador.

2. I would like to express my appreciation to the Tomás Rivera Policy Institute for access to these data. The survey was designed by Louis DeSipio, Rodolfo O. de la Garza, Harry Pachon, and Jongho Lee. A more detailed discussion of the design of the survey and the findings related to the relationships between home-country political activities and U.S. political engagement among Latino immigrants appears in DeSipio et al. 2003 (http://www.trpi.org/PDF/Immigrant_politics.pdf, [Accessed June 15, 2004]).

3. These include organizations made up primarily of the U.S.-born—such as the League of United Latin American Citizens (LULAC), the American G.I. Forum, the Young Lords, and the Chicano Movement organizations—as well as immigrant-driven organizations—the Congress of Spanish-Speaking Peoples, the United Farmworkers, and the Cuban American National Foundation.

4. This emerging scholarship of immigrant transnational politics does have some recurring weaknesses, however. First, there is no effort to assess the overall frequency of transnational politics among immigrants. Second, the scholarship of transnational politics often assumes, often uncritically, that such transnational political activity is durable over time and offers immigrants resources they can use to shape not just the politics of their sending communities/countries, but also their communities in the United States. Finally, most analyses focus only on a single sending community or a single country of origin. As a result, it is more difficult to identify general patterns in the exercise or significance of transnational political activity among immigrants.

5. Cuban immigrants were excluded from the survey for two reasons. First, because of Cuba's nondemocratic government, Cubans do not have the same opportunities to participate in Cuban politics that the four nationality groups under study do. Second, the Cuban American-Cuban relationship has been, and continues to be, extensively analyzed (Calvo and Declercq 2000, Croucher 1997, García 1996, Torres 1999, as examples).

6. In a separate analysis, Adrian Pantoja and I have analyzed patterns of transnational engagement among Puerto Rican migrants to see if there is a distinct Puerto Rican pattern of transnational politics driven by the unique relationship of Puerto Rico and the United States (DeSipio and Pantoja 2004).

7. All respondents were at least eighteen years of age and immigrants/migrants from one of the four nations under study. To complete the 1,602 surveys, TRPI completed calls to 10,470 phone numbers. Of these, 4,454 were disconnected, businesses, or had call-screening software in place. Nearly 1,200 potential respondents refused to participate at the point of initial contact. Approximately 2,000 potential respondents were found to be ineligible to participate during the six question screening process (for example potential respondents who were not of Mexican, Dominican, Salvadoran, or Puerto Rican origin). Initial attempts were made to contact an additional 8,207 phone numbers. These numbers remained available in the sample pool at the end of survey. Contact had not been made for such reasons as reaching an answering machine, the phone not being answered, or reaching a busy signal.

8. As is the case in many surveys, a large share of respondents to the TRPI Immigrant Political Participation Survey fail to provide answers to some specific questions, particularly demographic questions on age and household income (14 percent and 16 percent, respectively). The final question that resulted in high nonresponse rates was year of initial migration to the United States (13 percent). As will be evident, these nonresponses reduce the overall sample size by as much as one-third. It is reasonable to assume that these nonrespondents are not randomly distributed. Assuming these respondents are similar to those of other surveys, higher-income respondents and older respondents are more likely to be excluded. These respondents are generally more likely to have higher than average levels of civic engagement and naturalization rates. The respondents who did not offer year of initial immigration were more likely than average to report that they were neither permanent residents nor naturalized U.S. citizens. These respondents are generally less likely to have higher than average levels of civic engagement and would be ineligible for naturalization (and excluded from the model).

Part 3

After Citizenship
*Party Identification
and Mobilization*

Out of Line
Immigration and Party Identification among Latinos and Asian Americans

Zoltan Hajnal and Taeku Lee

Much of the burgeoning literature on contemporary immigrant political incorporation is motivated by careful theory and analysis on how today's political parties compare with those of yesteryear (e.g., see Jones-Correa 1998a; Rogers 2000b; Wong 2000a; Gerstle and Mollenkopf 2001; Ramírez 2002; Lien, Conway, and Wong 2004; Ramírez and Wong, this volume). For the most part, the scholars behind these works conclude that today's parties lack the organizational capacity, the cultural literacy, and perhaps even the political motivation to shepherd new immigrants into the political process and nurture secure attachments with a particular political party. Even before the current spate of works on immigrant political incorporation, other scholars of urban politics have noted that not all immigrant groups from Europe were equally incorporated (see, e.g., Ignatiev 1995, Jacobson 1998), that the willingness of party machines to incorporate new immigrants varied across historical contexts (Mayhew 1986) and with the degree of party competition in a city (Erie 1988), and that nonparty organizations like neighborhood associations, unions, churches, and ethnic voluntary associations were equally vital in incorporating new immigrant groups (Sterne 2001).

Yet, this relative absence of evidence for a strong role for parties in mobilizing new immigrants has not dampened the interest or enthusiasm of politicians, pundits, party activists, and political scientists alike in passing conjecture and reaching conclusions about how Asian Americans and Latinos will come to see themselves in partisan terms. Will Asians and Latinos ally with the Democratic Party on the basis of collective racial interests as African Americans have since the civil rights era (Dawson 1994, Tate 1993)? Or will their party identification be channeled more by economic interests, foreign policy preferences, home-country politics, and liberal and conservative ideological beliefs? Will Asians and Latinos help to reconfigure and reconstitute existing political coalitions? Will they seek to leverage their numbers as swing voters? Or will they simply vote as individuals on an election-by-election, candidate-by-candidate basis?

The variety of opinions on these questions is almost as many as the number of opinion makers. One of the more colorful such examples comes from Peter Brimelow in *Alien Nation,* who concludes that "the post-1965 immigrants are overwhelmingly visible minorities. And these are precisely the groups that the Republican Party has had the most difficulty recruiting. . . . The numbers are indisputable: Current immigration policy is inexorably reinforcing Jesse Jackson's Rainbow Coalition" (196). Interestingly, Brimelow further argues that Latinos contribute prominently to this "scalawag" coalition (together with African Americans, Jews, and "minority whites"), but with respect to Asians, "[t]he truth is this; no one has the faintest idea how the Asians will vote" (197).

In this essay we examine the contemporary relationship between immigration-based groups and the American two-party system by taking the important prior step of properly conceptualizing party identification—whether individuals come to identify with a particular political party and, if so, which party they identify with and why they do so. We first review the conventional "linear" political science model of party identification and enumerate several reasons why the linear approach is not likely to tell us much about partisanship acquisition among Latinos and Asian Americans. These arguments are then tested using the two principal political surveys of Asians and Latinos—the 1989–90 Latino National Political Survey and the 2000–2001 Pilot National Asian American Politics Study. As a statistical test, these multivariate analyses are principally concerned with demonstrating the limits of existing models of party identification to immigration-based populations like the Asian American and Latino communities—a yardstick that the corresponding empirical results easily exceed. The essay concludes with some elements of a fuller account of how such new immigrant groups are likely to develop their partisan attachments and the questions that then arise from their party affiliation.

The Linear Model of Party Identification

While substantial controversy exists over the likely partisan attachments of Asians and Latinos, there is little dispute over how to conceptualize party identification. To date, one view dominates our understanding of party identification. The prevailing view assumes a linear scale of party identification, anchored by a linear scale of ideological orientation, from Republicans on the political right to Democrats on the political left and Independents at the midpoint. As Angus Campbell and colleagues note, "[t]he partisan self-image of all but the few individuals who disclaim any involvement in politics permits us to place each person in these samples on a continuum of partisanship extending from strongly Republican to strongly Democratic. We use the word 'continuum' because we suppose that identification is not simply a dichotomy but has a wide range of intensities in each partisan direction" (1960, 122–23).

This continuum is usually operationalized by the following three items from the American National Election Studies (ANES) (or some similar version of these), used in virtually every study of American voting behavior:

Q1. Generally speaking, do you usually think of yourself as a Republican, a Democrat, an Independent, or what?
Q2. [IF REPUBLICAN OR DEMOCRAT] Would you call yourself a strong (Republican/Democrat) or not a very strong (Republican/Democrat)?
Q3. [IF INDEPENDENT] Do you think of yourself as closer to the Republican or Democratic Party?

Most often, these questions are recoded into a single, unidimensional scale of seven ordered categories, such as the one shown in figure 1.[1]

By this coding, "moderate" Democrats and Republicans are those individuals who identify with these corresponding parties (in Q1) but whose identification is not strong (in Q2). "Weak" Democrats and Republicans are those individuals who choose to identify as an Independent (in Q1) but are willing to acknowledge a partisan bent (in Q3). Other versions of this same seven-category scale refer to "weak" partisans as Democratic or Republican "leaners," with the term "pure Independents" reserved to those individuals who identify as an Inde-

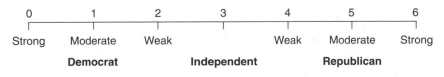

Figure 1 Continuum of party identifications

pendent (in Q1) and reject any partisan inclinations (in Q3). Notwith-standing some debate over the proper scaling of party identification, in almost every such version Independents are placed squarely in the middle of the scale.[2]

This conventional linear model has not gone uncontested. One line of research has been to test how distinct Independents are from parti-sans in their political behavior. Bruce Keith and colleagues (1992) and Arthur Miller and Martin Wattenberg (1983), for instance, demon-strate that in terms of voting behavior there is little to distinguish In-dependent leaners from moderate partisans (cf. Dennis 1992). Others have challenged the unidimensionality of party identification. A third set of studies has focused on the enduring role of childhood and early adulthood socialization in childhood and early adulthood (Campbell et al. 1960, Niemi and Jennings 1991, Beck and Jennings 1991).[3]

In the end, however, the linear measurement scale remains essen-tially unchanged (Green 1988). Indeed, almost every study attempting to understand voter behavior or some other aspect of political behav-ior includes this basic linear model. As Petrocik notes, "[t]he index of party identification is so universally accepted as the variable around which to organize a discussion of political behavior in the United States that it is difficult to find a monograph or research article which does not introduce party identification as a consideration in the anal-ysis" (1974, 31). Similarly, Keith and colleagues conclude that "[w]e see no problems with the traditional measure" (1992, 196).

Immigration, Identity, and the Linear Model of Party Identification

We argue that the linear view of party identification is limited for sev-eral reasons. First, most studies focus principally on the behavioral implications of identifying as an Independent (e.g., Wattenberg 1990, Bartels 2000). In particular, the guiding question tends to be that of how Independents vote and whether segments of this nonpartisan pop-ulation act like dyed-in-wool partisans on election Tuesday. To these questions, there is ample good evidence. Without contesting it, we sub-mit that the focus on behavioral implications ignores the vital prior question of why some choose to identify with a political party and others do not. Similar to Campbell and his colleagues (1960), we ar-gue that there is a meaningful distinction between identifying with a party (agreeing to the statements "I am a Democrat" or "I am a Re-publican") and acting like a partisan (voting for a candidate on the basis on one's party identification). As the authors of *The American*

Voter put it, party identification is a "psychological identification which can persist without legal recognition or evidence of formal membership and even without a consistent record of party support" (Campbell et al. 1960, 121).[4]

The act of identifying with the labels "Democrat," "Republican," and "Independent" itself is an important social and political fact worthy of social scientific explanation. Our focus on social identity is similar to that taken by Donald Green and his colleagues in their recent *Partisan Hearts and Minds* (2002), with two important differences. First, Green and colleagues focus primarily on one's self-classification as a Democrat or a Republican, to the neglect of nonpartisanship as a potentially meaningful category vis-à-vis one's social identity as well. A person may take the label of "Independent" as a significant source of personal pride, a reflection of one's self-esteem, and a marker of consequential group boundaries. Furthermore, a person's ambivalence (i.e., answering "not sure" to the typical question), detachment (i.e., stating that they do not think in partisan terms), or noncompliance (i.e., refusing to answer the question) tells us a great deal as well about their sense of political identity and attachment of political institutions.

Second, Green and colleagues examine one's party identification qua social identity in isolation, that is, without regard to other primary social identities that might inform and influence a person's political orientation. We are explicit about the fact that the multiplicity and interactive nature of social identities is central to a complete account of party identification. Charles Merriam, one of the founding fathers of political science and earliest theorists on political parties articulated such a more contingent approach to the social group bases of party identification almost a century ago:

> It is also possible to make a study of the party system by viewing the various social forces and elements out of which the party is made, and by showing how these factors are combined to produce the Republican or Democratic or other party result. We may look at the various groupings, of class, race, religion, section, in their relation to parties. . . . We may see how the party becomes a going concern, an institution, an attitude; how party allegiance becomes part of the political heritage of many persons. . . . We may, in short begin the analysis of the party by examining its composition in terms of political and social forces, rather than of historical evolution or of political mechanism. (1922, 1–2)

The most significant limitation, however, in the conventional models of party identification is that there is a deep assumption of a single, linear, unidimensional scale. As Campbell and his colleagues contend, "[t]he partisan self-image of all but the few individuals who disclaim any involvement in politics permits us to place each person in these samples on a continuum of partisanship extending from strongly Republican to strongly Democratic" (1960). A corollary to this assumption is that one's party attachments are anchored by a single, linear, unidimensional ideological continuum from strong liberals to strong conservatives (where strong liberals are the most likely group to identify as strong Democrats, strong conservatives are the most likely group to identify as strong Republicans, and staunch moderates are the most likely group to identify as pure Independents). Rather than viewing the growing tendency of Americans to identify as Independents as politically meaningful, some scholars instead decry Independents as "an unstable vote . . . that is basically unpredictable over time, and introduces into elections an increased volatility that today's fluid politics do not need. . . . Its volatility and malleability does little to ease the concern of those who value stability and order in American politics" (Crotty 1983, 37).

This assumption of linearity, paralleled by a linear ideological spectrum, is especially inapt for Asian and Latino party identification on several grounds. The core empirical analysis in this essay is aimed at showing the potentially misleading and incomplete portrait of Asian and Latino party identification that results from such a narrow linear conception. For one thing, not all groups are equally familiar with the terrain of American politics. In particular, the relationship of immigration-based groups like Asians and Latinos with the U.S. party system and with choices like "Democrat" or "Republican," "liberal" or "conservative" is likely to be filled with uncertainty. How Asians and Latinos gain their literacy and orientation about politics in the United States will depend, among other things, on the extent to which they have developed a sense of political efficacy, trust in political institutions, and an understanding of liberal-to-conservative ideology. There are ample grounds, based on the sociological literature on immigration, to expect this process to be a bumpy one. Rather than a left-right ideological spectrum, political opinions may instead be rooted in religious and cultural values or in issues of greater interest vis-à-vis the politics of one's home country or the politics of immigrants in the United States.

Before turning to this analysis, there is yet one final limitation to many typical studies of party identification. Namely, they tend to simply ignore race and ethnicity, both theoretically and empirically. Often, African Americans, Latinos, and Asian Americans are excluded from the analysis. Bruce Keith and his collaborators in *The Myth of the Independent Voter,* for instance, note that "[b]ecause blacks are the most disaffected of any major population group, omitting them also avoids complications if one examines relationships between alienation and independence" (1992, 32). Latinos and Asian Americans did not even receive mention in their study. This omission is further justified on the grounds that Independents are a largely white phenomenon, that since "the increase in Independents was confined to the white population . . . most of our analysis in subsequent chapters excludes blacks" (1992, 26).

Rather than exclude racial and ethnic minorities because they are too small in number or too homogeneous in their partisan attachments and behavior, we instead argue that bringing our understanding of the processes of racial formation and immigrant acculturation is a vehicle to better understand how people—African American, Asian American, Latino, and white—come to identify (or not to identify) with a particular political party. To some extent, this focus on race and immigration is not new (see, e.g., Finifter and Finifter 1989, Cain et al. 1991, Pachon and DeSipio 1994, Lien 2000, Wong 2000a). Others have examined the effects of immigrant status, age of entry, and time in the United States on party identification (Cain et al. 1991, Wong 2000a, Welch and Sigelman 1993, Uhlaner and Garcia 2001, de la Garza et al, 1992). For the most part, however, these scholars continue to adopt the conventional, linear approach, with the prevailing assumption that nonwhites identify with a party for the same reasons as whites.

Pattern and Disorder in Latino and Asian Party Identification

What then, does this linear measurement model tell us about the party attachments of Asian Americans and Latinos? The general facts of Asian American and Latino partisanship based on previous studies are fairly clear-cut. Hispanic Americans identify with the Democratic Party more often than they do with the Republican Party by a roughly two-to-one margin (Alvarez and García Bedolla 2001, Uhlaner and Garcia 2002, de la Garza 2004). With Asian Americans, there is a modest but growing preference for allying with the Democratic Party over the Republican Party, but at far more modest margins than for Latinos. According to one review of twelve national, state-level, and metropolitan-level surveys in the 1990s, the edge does not go consistently to the Democratic Party until the 1998 off-year elections (Lien 2001).[5] In terms of the split between Democratic and Republican Party identification, Asian Americans and Latinos fall in between whites (who are the group most likely to identify as Republicans) and African Americans (who are the group most likely to identify as Democrats).

With both Asian Americans and Latinos, there are several critical caveats to these general facts about the direction of partisanship. Among other things, the patterns of party identification vary substantially by ethnic/national origin groups—among primary Latino subgroups, Cubans being the most likely to identify as Republicans and among primary Asian subgroups, Vietnamese (and by some accounts, Koreans) being the most likely to identify as Republicans (Cain, Kiewiet, and Uhlaner 1991; de la Garza et al. 1992; Uhlaner and Garcia 2002; Lien, Conway, and Wong 2004). Moreover, party identification varies by immigrant status (foreign born and generation), the number of years lived in the United States, and naturalization as citizens. Lastly, we also know that issues and interests matter—most obviously in the arena of foreign policy interests as an explanation for why Cubans, Vietnamese, and Koreans tend to identify as Republicans more often than do other Latino and Asian subgroups.

These stylized facts about Asian American and Latino party identification, however, are grounded in some conventional assumptions about partisanship. First, it assumes that the central question of interest is the pairwise comparison between the Democratic and Republican parties. This obviates other potentially consequential features of the relationship between these immigration-based groups, such as whether or not Asians and Latinos even think in partisan terms, how certain they are about their stated partisan preferences, and whether ideology serves as a guide to one's partisanship. The potential limitations of this linear account of partisanship can be most easily and powerfully demonstrated in the different ways we might describe how Latino partisanship patterns have changed over time.

In the biennial National Election Studies time series, for instance, the portrait we draw of the partisanship patterns of Latinos depends critically on how we count Independents who lean toward one party or another. If respondents are crudely classified by self-identification as "Democrat," "Independent," or "Republican," the resulting relationship over time looks fairly stable. Across the range of years for which there is a sufficient number of Latino respondents to draw reasonably valid year-to-year estimates (i.e., from 1978 to 2002), roughly half of all Latino Americans identified as Democrats, with about one in six identifying as Republicans and one in three identifying as Independents.[6] If those Independents who lean toward a party are counted as partisans, an entirely different portrait emerges. Now there is a marked shift over time among Latinos, especially in their identification with the Republican Party. Under this categorization, the proportion of Latino respondents to the American National Election Study (ANES) who identify as Republican rises from less than 15 percent in 1978 to almost 38 percent by the 2002 series.[7]

As James Gimpel and Karen Kaufman's (2001) analysis of exit poll data show, this shift carries potentially meaningful implications for how Latinos vote. Pooling network exit polls of presidential elections from 1976 to 2000, Gimpel and Kaufman find that in the 1976 election between Jimmy Carter and Gerald Ford, Latinos voted overwhelming Democratic over Republican, 82 percent to 18 percent. By the most recent 2000 election between Al Gore and George W. Bush, this gap had slimmed to a margin of a 62 percent Democratic vote and a 35 percent Republican vote among Latinos. The National Association of Latino Election Officials (NALEO) most recent 2004 Latino Election Handbook similarly observes an increasing trend toward registration with the Republican Party among California Latinos since the year 2000.

At the same time, other studies argue that Latino Americans are actually growing more Democratic. Matt Barreto and Nathan Woods (2005), for example, find that the proportion of registered Latino Democrats to registered Latino Republicans in Southern California increased substantially between 1992 and 1998. Moreover, there is good evidence that California's divisive ballot initiatives (especially Propositions 187 and 209) have had a galvanizing and mobilizing effect in the Latino community, inducing noncitizens to naturalize, nonvoters to mark their ballots, and nonpartisans to identify with the Democratic Party (Segura, Falcon, and Pachon 1997; Pantoja, Ramírez, and Segura 2001; Ramírez 2002). And yet other studies suggest that Latino partisanship is sensitive to the party-specific issue positions and agendas (Alvarez and García Bedolla 2003, Nicholson and Segura 2005). Our purpose here is not to mediate these contentious claims, but to underscore the difficulties embedded in coming to a coherent view of Latino party identification.

Beyond this question of categorization, our understanding of Latino and Asian American party identification is also constrained by the conventional assumption of linearity. This can be demonstrated quite vividly by the proportion of Latinos and Asian Americans who find the pairwise choice of identifying with the Democratic or the Republican Party either irrelevant or inadequate. In the 1984 Institute of Governmental Studies survey of Californians (the first academic poll with a reasonably large sample of Asian Americans) and the 2001 Pilot National Asian American Politics Study (PNAAPS, the first nationally based multicity, multiethnic, and multilingual academic survey of Asian Americans), roughly one in two respondents opted for some choice other than Democratic or Republican.[8] This same point is made by comparing responses to the party identification measures in the ANES against that in the 1993–94 Multi-City Study of Urban Inequality (MCSUI; see Bobo et al. 2000). There is a subtle change in question wording in the MCSUI from the standard ANES item, where respondents to the MCSUI are asked "Generally speaking, do you usually think of yourself as a Republican, Democrat, Independent, *or something else* [our emphases]." This change produces a dramatic number of respondents, especially among Asians and Latinos, who indicate that they have no preference among these choices. More than 45 percent of Latinos and almost 58 percent of Asians surveyed in the MCSUI indicated such a lack of preference. From the standpoint of most conventional approaches to party identification, then, about half of these immigration-based groups would likely be coded and discounted as "missing data."

This difference between the ANES and the MCSUI is, significantly, reflected in the contrasting aims of the sampling designs. The ANES is a stratified random sample that seeks to replicate the national adult citizen population, with limited oversamples of historically difficult-to-reach populations and, until recently, only English interviews. In contrast, the MCSUI's sampling design focuses on large metropolitan areas that tend to be immigrant centers, offers a limited range of non-English interviews (Spanish, Mandarin, Cantonese, and Korean), and explicitly oversamples areas with concentrated racial and ethnic minority populations and areas with a disproportionate number of low-income households. Thus, the ANES sample is biased toward assimilated and acculturated Latinos, while the MCSUI concentrates on the population least likely to fit the standard models of party identification and most likely to be uncertain and ambivalent about partisan choice (see, e.g., Lee 2001a).

Modeling Party Identification

Thus far, we have demonstrated some limitations that result from conceiving of Asian American and Latino party identification as a linear and ordered choice. This mostly descriptive and negative account makes the point that how we measure party identification has consequences for what we make of it substantively. It also makes the point that nonpartisanship (whether identifying as an Independent, being indifferent or uncertain about their preferences, or not thinking in partisan terms) is at least as interesting an aspect of party identification among these immigration-based groups as the direction of one's partisanship (identifying as a Republican or a Democrat). Two important elements of our empirical test remain. First, we have yet to test, in a systematic way, whether ideology—understood as a linear, ordered category from strong liberals to strong conservatives—has the same defining role to play in shaping the party identification of Asian Americans and Latinos that it has with white Americans. Second, our argument that party identification is an unordered choice holds a strong implication for how we ought to conduct that systematic test of the role of ideology.

Our strategy for these remaining elements is straightforward. We test for the role of ideology with a very streamlined multivariate model of party identification. Recall that there are two distinct elements to the test of whether ideology anchors the partisan attachments of immigration-based groups—the degree to which ideology is predictive of party identification and the degree to which this relationship, if predictive, is linear. This latter element is tested for by including separate variables for each category of ideological attachment, where strong ideologues (liberal and conservative) are distinguished from weaker ideologues (liberal and conservative) and from staunch moderates. If the typical view of party identification is correct, then the following should be the case: that strong liberals should be most likely to identify as a Democrat, weaker liberals should be somewhat less likely to identify as a Democrat, followed next in descending likelihood of identification by moderates, then weak conservatives, and lastly, by strong conservatives. The mirror relationship should hold in the opposite for the likelihood of identifying as a Republican.

Beyond ideology, we control for some immigration and ethnicity specific factors that are likely to differentiate party identification patterns within the capacious pan-ethnic rubrics of Asian American and Latino (see Jones-Correa and Leal 1996, Lien et al. 2004). With immigration, we differentiate between those individuals not born in the United States from "generation 1.5" individuals (those who migrated to the United States as a child), those who are second generation, and those who are third generation or higher in the United States. We also control for the number of years a person has lived in the United States. Note that with generation 1.5 individuals, there is a reasonable expectation that partisanship acquisition follows the same pattern of socialization that children born in the United States might adapt. Similarly, one might expect socialization effects to vary with length of tenure in the United States.

With ethnicity, we control for the ethnic/national origin of respondents as well. As numerous studies of Asian Americans and Latinos have demonstrated, the diversity of political orientations within such diverse pan-ethnic categories is considerable. Important dimensions of phenomena like partisanship acquisition might be either amplified or obfuscated by treating all persons within such categories as identical. Lastly, we also examine a person's age (both in biological years and as the squared values of those years, to capture potential nonlinearities in age effects), educational achievement, family income, and gender. In addition to being typical demographic correlates of public opinion, age, education, income, and gender are also key indicators of social status. To the extent that the Democratic Party is often viewed as defending the interests of the indigent and the Republican Party is viewed as safeguarding the privileges of the affluent, these markers might structure the party choices of Asians and Latinos.

In addition to specifying a model that appropriately tests for the linearity (vis-à-vis ideology) of partisanship, we also need to use a statistical estimator that allows an individual's partisan choice to be unordered. The most common statistical estimator used to test competing models of party identification is the ordered probit (e.g., Franklin and Jackson 1983), which assumes that the dependent variable is ordinal but does not assume that the differences between gradients are identical—that is, with the typical "0" to "6" party identification scale, ordered probit does assume that the difference between a strong Republican ("0") and a Republican leaner ("2") is identical to that between a Republican leaner ("2") and a Democratic leaner ("4") or that between a Democratic leaner ("4") and a strong Democrat ("6").

The estimator we use is multinomial logit, which allows us to capture the effect of each independent variable on each pairwise combination among possible party identification categories (see Aldrich and Nelson 1984). That is, rather than modeling party identification as a continuum from Democrat to Independent to Republican, multi-nomial logit allows us to estimate the relative probability of identify-ing between each pair of choices—Independent or Democrat, Repub-lican or Independent, Democrat or Republican. Because multinomial logit is an explicit nonlinear statistical estimator, the parameter esti-mates can be somewhat of a challenge to interpret. To make the result clearer, we transform these parameter estimates into odds ratios that allow for assessments of relative magnitude—the relative odds of, say, identifying as a Republican or an Independent, given a one-unit change to our independent variable of interest, say, of being Cuban or non-Cuban. Lastly, multinomial logit also allows us to test for the na-ture of choice between other kinds of unordered categories. Specifi-cally, in the case of Asian Americans, we will use it to compare be-tween categories of "nonpartisanship"—between those who do not think in partisan terms, those who are unsure about their partisan-ship, and those who identify as Independents.

Data Description

This account of party identification is examined using data from the primary political surveys of the groups in question—the 1989–90 La-tino National Political Survey (LNPS) and the 2000–2001 Pilot Na-tional Asian American Politics Study (PNAAPS). The LNPS com-pleted 2,817 face-to-face interviews with Latinos between July 1989 and April 1990. Of this sample, 1,546 respondents were Mexican, 589 Puerto Rican, and 682 Cuban. Roughly 60 percent of the Latino sample chose Spanish as their preferred language of interview (de la Garza et al. 1992).[9] There are alternative surveys of the Latino popu-lation that might have been used—such as the 1999 *Washington Post*-Kaiser-Harvard University-Latino Survey, the 2000 Knight-Ridder Latino Voter Study, and the 2002 Pew Hispanic Center National Sur-vey of Latinos. These alternatives enjoy the benefit of being more re-cent (an important benefit, given the rapidity of demographic change in the Latino community), but they suffer other limitations. Each of these other surveys has a more limited number of political attitude items and makes cost-sensitive choices in the sample design and inter-view method (only the LNPS is a face-to-face interview). The Knight-Ridder survey only interviews those Latinos who pass a likely voter screen, thus filtering out the vast proportion of Latinos who are non-citizens, unregistered to vote, or otherwise indicate a low likelihood of voting. The Knight-Ridder and *Washington Post* surveys only differentiate between liberals, conservatives, and moderates, with no shades of ideological attachment in between. And the Pew Hispanic Center survey does not even ask respondents about their ideological beliefs.

For Asian Americans, there is little question over which data to use. The PNAAPS is the primary multicity, multiethnic, and multilingual survey of Asian Americans, fielded over ten weeks after the November election (see Lien et al. 2001, 2004). Six primary Asian ethnic groups—Chinese, Filipinos, Japanese, Koreans, South Asians, and Vietnamese—and five major metropolitan centers of large Asian American populations—Los Angeles, Honolulu, the Bay Area, Chicago, and New York—are represented. Interviews were conducted over the telephone and Chinese, Koreans, and Vietnamese were given the choice of a non-English language of interview. The resulting sample yielded 1,218 adult Asians, which included 308 Chinese, 168 Korean, 137 Vietnamese, 198 Japanese, 266 Filipino, and 141 South Asian Americans.[10]

Ideology and Unordered Choice

Table 1 shows our findings on the basic structure of Latino party identification—as modeled by ideological beliefs, immigration status, ethnic background, and status-related demographic factors. The categories of party identification that are examined here are "Democrat," "Republican," and "Independent." Unlike many other studies, we have chosen not to separate out partisan leaners among the Independents, because we view the choice to identify firstly as an Independent as meaningful in its own right and also because the results do not differ markedly by reserving the category only for "pure Independents." Table 1 also, unlike most presentations of multinomial logit regressions, presents estimates for every pairwise combination of the three categories. Technically, a "baseline" category against which other alternatives are compared must be chosen for the model to be statistically "identified," and in many cases, there are strong theoretical grounds for choosing that optimal base category. In our case, the theory argues that each pairwise choice is significant. Hence tables 1 and 2 show the results from two separate estimates—first, with "Independent" and then with "Democrat" as the base category.

Table 1 clearly shows that the effect of an individual's ideology on party identification is both selective and relatively modest.[11] Moderate and strong conservatives are both more likely to identify as Independents than Democrats and more likely to identify as Republicans than

Table 1 Multinomial logit model of Latino partisanship

	Pr(Rep) v. Pr(Ind)		Pr(Dem) v. Pr(Ind)		Pr(Rep) v. Pr(Dem)	
	MNL	RRR	MNL	RRR	MNL	RRR
Strong liberal	−.15	.86	.33	1.39	−.48	.62
	.42		.36		.34	
Moderate liberal	−.37	.69	−.09	.91	−.28	.76
	.24		.21		.20	
Weak liberal	−.10	.90	−.08	.92	−.02	.98
	.26		.23		.22	
Weak conservative	−.28	.76	−.33	.72	.05	1.05
	.22		.20		.19	
Mod. conservative	.21	1.23	−.53	.59	.74	2.09
	.20		.19		.17	
Strong conservative	.10	1.11	−.78	.46	.88	2.41
	.30		.28		.25	
Foreign born	.88	2.42	−.10	.90	.99	2.68
	.27		.24		.24	
Generation 1.5	−.25	.78	.16	1.18	−.41	.66
	.26		.23		.21	
Second generation	.05	1.04	.29	1.33	−.24	.78
	.25		.20		.22	
Years in the U.S.	−.02	.98	−.002	1.00	−.01	.99
	.01		.009		.01	
Cuban	1.59	4.90	−.74	.48	2.33	10.27
	.20		.21		.17	
Puerto Rican	.33	1.39	.72	2.05	−.39	.68
	.21		.18		.17	
Age	.03	1.03	.13	1.13	−.10	.91
	.02		.02		.02	
Age-squared	—	1.00	—	1.00	.0008	1.00
	.0000		.0009		.0002	
	.0003		.0002			
Education	.05	1.05	.06	1.07	−.01	.99
	.02		.02		.02	
Family income	.03	1.03	−.01	.99	.04	1.04
	.02		.02		.02	
Male	.00	1.00	−.36	.70	.36	1.43
	.15		.13		.12	
Constant	−2.06		−2.61		.54	
	.62		.56		.53	
Chi-sq (d.f. = 34)					756.59	
P-value					.000	
Pseudo R-squared					.178	
Number of observations					2102	

Note: The cell entries in the columns labeled "MNL" are in italics when their relationship to Latino and Asian partisanship exceeds conventions of statistical significance ($p < 0.05$).

Democrats. None of the other ideological categories holds a statistically significant relationship. By contrast, immigration- and ethnicity-related factors are more consistently predictive. Foreign-born Latinos are more likely to identify as Republicans (whether the pairwise choice is between Republican and Independent or between Republican and Democratic) than Latinos who are third generation or higher. Generation 1.5 Latinos appear most likely to identify as Democrats over Republicans. With ethnicity, Cubans are more inclined toward the Republican Party than Mexicans for each pairwise combination and Puerto Ricans are more likely than Mexicans to lean toward the Democratic Party.[12]

There are also significant effects among the demographic status variables we examine. Men are more likely to identify as Republicans or Independents than they are to identify as Democrats. Wealth biases toward identifying as Republican rather than a Democrat. The effect of education and age is nonlinear. More-educated Latinos are more likely to identify as a Republican or as a Democrat than as an Independent. Both younger and older Latinos are more likely to identify as a Republican or an Independent than they are to identify as a Democrat.

As the results from table 1 suggest, one of the most important features of both Latino and Asian American opinion is that underlying patterns vary substantially by ethnic subgroup. If the model in table 1 is estimated separately for Cubans, Puerto Ricans, and Mexicans (results not shown), several ethnicity-specific patterns in the relationship between ideology and party identification emerge. For Cubans, conservatism only predicts the choice between identifying as a Republican and a Democrat. For Puerto Ricans, only extreme conservatism predicts the choice between identifying as an Independent rather than a Democrat.[13] The closest approximation to a linear relationship obtains with Mexican Americans: weak conservatives are more likely to identify as Independents than Republicans; strong liberals are likelier to identify as Democrats than as Independents; weak, moderate, and strong conservatives are more likely to identify as Independents than as Democrats; moderate and strong conservatives are more likely to identify as Republicans than as Democrats; strong liberals are more likely to identify as Democrats than as Republicans.[14]

The unordered patterns of party identification are quite distinct for Asian Americans. Table 2 replicates the same model for Asians as that shown in table 1 with one exception—PNAAPS does not allow us to distinguish "weak" ideologues from "moderate" ideologues. Thus, table 2 shows the coefficients and odds-ratios for "weak" liberals and

Table 2   Multinomial logit model of Asian partisanship

	Pr(Rep) v. Pr(Ind)		Pr(Dem) v. Pr(Ind)		Pr(Rep) v. Pr(Dem)	
	MNL	RRR	MNL	RRR	MNL	RRR
Strong liberal	.38	1.46	.70	2.02	−.32	.72
	.63		.48		.53	
Weak liberal	.45	1.56	*.97*	*2.65*	−.53	.59
	.42		*.34*		.34	
Weak conservative	*1.08*	*2.95*	−.25	.78	*1.33*	*3.79*
	.40		.36		*.34*	
Strong conservative	.89	2.44	.10	1.10	.79	2.21
	.64		.62		.54	
Foreign born	.02	1.02	−.44	.64	.46	1.58
	.81		.67		.70	
Generation 1.5	.79	2.20	.33	1.39	.46	1.59
	.67		.61		.58	
Second generation	.40	1.49	.26	1.29	.14	1.15
	.68		.53		.59	
Years in the U.S.	−.02	.98	−.02	.98	−.00	1.00
	.02		.02		.02	
Filipino	*−1.75*	*.17*	*−2.08*	*.12*	.33	1.39
	.66		*.60*		.40	
Indian	*−2.17*	*.11*	*−2.29*	*.10*	.12	1.13
	.73		*.63*		.50	
Korean	*−1.13*	*.32*	*−1.73*	*.18*	.60	1.83
	.66		*.61*		.38	
Japanese	*−2.93*	*.05*	*−2.66*	*.07*	−.27	.76
	.82		*.68*		.61	
Vietnamese	*−1.66*	*.19*	*−3.75*	*.02*	*2.08*	*8.03*
	.70		*.69*		*.53*	
Age	.08	1.08	−.01	.99	.09	1.09
	.06		.05		.05	
Age-squared	−.000	1.00	.001	1.00	−.001	1.00
	.001		.001		.001	
Education	−.12	.89	*−.14*	*.87*	.02	1.02
	.07		*.06*		.06	
Family income	*.22*	*1.25*	.06	1.06	*.16*	*1.18*
	.10		.09		*.08*	
Male	.32	1.38	.29	1.34	.03	1.03
	.30		.26		.25	
Constant	−.41		4.58		−4.98	
	1.92		1.63		1.58	
Chi-sq (d.f. = 36)					128.50	
P-value					.000	
Pseudo R-squared					.137	
Number of observations					480	

Note: The cell entries in the columns labeled "MNL" are in italics when their relationship to Latino and Asian partisanship exceeds conventions of statistical significance ($p < 0.05$).

conservatives and "strong" liberals and conservatives (as compared against the base category of firm moderates). Curiously, the principal effect is among weak ideologues: weak conservatives are more likely to identify as Republicans than as Independents and more likely to identify as Republicans than as Democrats; weak liberals are more likely to identify as Democrats than as Independents. Extreme ideological beliefs appear statistically unrelated to party identification.

Compared to this mixed, somewhat unusual story about ideology, the ethnicity-specific differences are striking and strong. Chinese Americans are least likely to identify as Independent (than as Republican or Democrat) compared to all other ethnic groups. Vietnamese Americans are more likely than any other group to identify as Republican rather than as Democrat. Among the remaining variables we examine, well-educated Asians appear more likely to identify as Independents than as partisans (cf. the relationship between partisanship and education for Latinos in table 1) and family income is an important marker of difference between Republicans and both Independents and Democrats. There are no gender or age effects, and none of the immigration-related measures of interest has a statistically significant effect on Asian American party choice.[15]

As we noted earlier in this essay, one of the most distinctive features of Asian American party choice is the degree to which Asians appear to reject the choice set between identifying as a Republican and a Democrat. Approximately half of the respondents to the PNAAPS choose a response category other than these two. Thus, a significant question to ask about Asian American party identification is how "nonpartisans" differ from one another. The PNAAPS allows us to distinguish between three categories of nonpartisanship—respondents who identify as Independents, those who are unsure how to respond, and those who volunteer that they do not think in partisan terms. If this categorization of nonpartisanship is modeled using the same set of explanatory variables used in tables 1 and 2, the core finding is that identification as an Independent is much more distinct from either of the other two nonpartisan categories than they are from one another. That is, detachment and ambivalence are rather similar in kind as forms of nonpartisanship, and notably dissimilar to Independents. Ideology is unrelated with nonpartisanship.[16]

Toward a Theory of Party Identification

These results nudge us a bit closer to a more complete and accurate account of party identification generally, as well as of the relationship of Asian Americans and Latinos to partisan politics in the United States. The bulk of our empirical evidence challenges the assumptions underlying the prevailing approach to the study of Asian American and Latino party identification. As a positive account of whether these immigration-based groups identify with a party, and if so, which one and why, our analysis is admittedly thin. Elsewhere (Lee and Hajnal 2005), we argue that the key to developing such a more complete and accurate account entails incorporating the processes of racial and ethnic identity formation and immigrant political adaptation into our existing models of party identification. This insight is elaborated theoretically and empirically, and extended to other groups (notably, African Americans and white Americans) as well.

To wind up this essay, we outline some key features of this more general account. We argue that beyond ideology are two defining characteristics of Latino and Asian American identity and immigrant experience germane to party identification: uncertainty about politics and assimilation into social life in the United States. The upshot of the first defining characteristic is that the greater the uncertainty about what party politics means in an American context (and therefore, uncertainty about liberal-conservative ideology as a marker for one's political orientation), the greater the likelihood of identifying as a nonpartisan. We expect this for many reasons. A significant proportion of Asians and Latinos are born and educated outside the United States and face persistent residential, cultural, and linguistic segregation and widespread stereotyping and discrimination (Lee 2000, Bobo et al. 2000, Massey 2000, Santa Ana 2002). As Jane Junn, Kathryn Pearson and Jack Citrin, S. Karthick Ramakrishnan, and others in this volume have argued, the assimilation of Asians and Latinos into democratic life in America has been far from seamless and "straight-line." And as Ricardo Ramirez and Janielle Wong (also in this volume) amply show, traditional partisan elites have only a limited role to play in reaching out to and mobilizing these immigration-based groups. Ultimately, we argue that rather than choose between parties that they know little about or support a party they do not yet trust, substantial numbers of Asians and Latinos may hedge their bets and identify as nonpartisans.

The second major defining characteristic of Asian and Latino social adaptation guiding our expectations is that, for communities of color, one's primary political identity is often anchored by one's primary ethnic group identity (Padilla 1984). Here we elaborate on Dawson's (1994) account of racially linked fate by specifying the separable links in this chain between racial/ethnic and political identification. With Asians and Latinos, moreover, uncertainty and ambivalence are characteristics not only of partisan identity formation, but also ethnic identity formation. Thus we expect party identification to vary not only with the strength of Asian and Latino identity, but also with the underlying factors that potentiate or impede that identity in formation—such as in-group social interaction, experiences with discrimination, perceptions of the discrimination facing one's coethnics, and civic engagement and organizational activism. Each of these kinds of experience and perception reflect learning about how race and ethnicity are lived in the United States, both generally and specific to Asian Americans and Latinos (see Padilla 1984, Espiritu 1992, Jones-Correa 1998, Saito 1998, Wong, 2001).

Ultimately, these two factors—uncertainty and ambivalence in political identity formation and assimilation or resilience in ethnic identity formation—bring us back to a long-standing debate about party identification. Specifically, a general bone of contention among scholars of parties remains between those who emphasize the critical role of parental socialization and those who emphasize the value of rational comparison between political parties. Our account takes seriously the immigration-specific and ethnoracial contexts in which partisanship acquisition is likely to occur for Asian Americans and Latinos. To do so, we argue, requires extending the reach of both social psychological accounts beyond parental socialization and information-based accounts beyond the limiting choice set of Republican or Democratic ideologies and issue agendas. We work toward a more encompassing theory of party identification, moreover, without resorting to facile normative assumptions about the democratic perils of nonpartisanship or untested empirical assumptions about the political apathy and ineptitude of immigrant-based ethnic electorates.

Notes

We thank the Russell Sage Foundation for their generous support of this work.

1. "Moderate" Democrats and Republicans are those respondents who identify as a Democrat or Republican in Q1 but who do not identify strongly in Q2. "Weak" Democrats and Republicans are those respondents who iden-

tify as an Independent in Q1 but who will acknowledge that they lean toward a party in Q3.

2. Fiorina (1981) argues that the assumption of equal intervals between categories is faulty. Keith et al. (1992) and others propose a five-point scale with weak and moderate identifiers collapsed together. Claggett (1981) and Shively (1979) argue that partisanship is two-dimensional, party acquisition and partisan intensity.

3. This view has been criticized, especially from rational choice perspectives that urge examination of macroeconomic conditions, candidate preferences, issue positions, and vote choice in any given election (Franklin and Jackson 1983, Allsop and Weisberg 1988). But others counter that party identification remains an enduring, stable self-classification and (when measurement error is considered) largely exogenous to candidate evaluations, issue positions, and vote choice (Green, Palmquist, and Schickler 2002; Green and Palmquist 1990; Beck and Jennings 1991).

4. Significantly, if we are to speak of party identification as a cause of anything, it cannot be conflated with partisanship (i.e., it cannot be measured behaviorally, as the putative "effects" of the cause).

5. In part, the ambiguity about Asian American partisanship results from the sensitivity to survey sampling methodology, context effects, and "house" effects (variance by polling firm). In the comparison of two exit polls in California following the 1996 general elections, one survey, conducted by the Voter New Services, found that the proportion of Republicans far outweighed the proportion of Democrats (48 percent to 32 percent); the other survey, conducted by the *Los Angeles Times,* reached the opposite conclusion about Asian party identification—44 percent of respondents identified as Democrats, only 33 percent as Republicans (Lien 2001, 154–55).

6. Such a comparison shows at best subtle changes at work. The proportion of Latinos who identify with the Democratic Party diminished perceptibly from 51 percent in 1978 to 45 percent by 2002, while the proportion who identify with the Republican Party inches upward from just under 14 percent to just above 18 percent.

7. Over the same years, the proportion of Democratic identifiers declines from about 68 percent in 1978 to 53 percent by 2002, with pure Independents declining from 18 percent in 1978 to just 9 percent in 2002. Between 1978 and 2002, there were 18,888 valid responses from whites, 2,913 from African Americans, and 1,290 from Latinos in the cumulative National Election Studies (NES) file. There is a strong bias likely in the Latino sample, especially based on a very limited variation in the language of interview. From 1980 on, the NES conducted a very limited proportion of its interview with Latino respondents in Spanish. In the preelection surveys, Spanish interviews were conducted only in 1980, 1984, 1988, and 1992 and only for 16 percent of the valid cases; in the postelection years, only from 1978 through 1994 and only for 11 percent of the valid cases. As Lee (2001a) shows, there is a strong bias in the self-

reported party identification of Latino Americans by language of interview: based on the Latino National Political Survey (LNPS), the distribution of partisanship among English-language interviewees is significantly more Democratic than among Spanish-language interviewees.

8. In the Pilot National Asian American Political Survey (PNAAPS), Asian Americans avoid partisan labels in diverse ways—13 percent identify as Independents, 16 percent indicated that they were "not sure" of their party identification, and almost 20 percent volunteered that they did not think in partisan terms.

9. The full sample includes 598 non-Latino subjects. The overall response rate for the Latino sample was 74 percent.

10. Vietnamese and Asian Indians were oversampled to generate a sufficiently large number of respondents for analysis. Other details of the survey methodology can be found in Lien et al. 2001.

11. There are two columns of statistical results for each pairwise comparison: one column with parameter estimates and their corresponding standard errors (labeled "MNL") and another column with the correspondent log odds-ratio, or "relative risk ratio" (labeled "RRR"). The base category for the "Pr(Rep) v. Pr(Ind)" and "Pr(Dem) v. Pr(Ind)" columns is "Independent"; the base category for the "Pr(Rep) v. Pr(Dem)" column is "Democrat."

12. The relatively greater explanatory power of these immigration- and ethnicity-related factors can be demonstrated by conducting likelihood ratio tests between the unrestricted and restricted models, where ideology dummy variables are excluded in one instance and immigration/ethnicity variables are excluded in the other instance.

13. Ideology has a positive, but nonsignificant effect on the pairwise choice between Democratic and Republican partisan identification.

14. The separate analyses by ethnic group also reveal differences in immigration-specific and demographic status factors. Foreign-born, second-generation, and both the youngest and oldest Cubans, for instance, are more likely to identify as Independents than as either Democrats or Republicans. For Chicanos and Puerto Ricans, by contrast, being foreign born makes one more likely to be partisan than Independent. Immigrant Chicanos and Puerto Ricans are also more likely to be Republicans than Democrats.

15. Unlike the LNPS, the sample size of the PNAAPS does not permit us to disaggregate our analysis by ethnic subgroup. The results from table 2 suggest that at least for Chinese and Vietnamese Americans, and possibly more groups, there are distinct differences at work.

16. Consistent with the results shown in table 2, Chinese Americans are much less likely to identify as Independents than they are to be unsure of their partisanship or report not thinking in partisan terms. In addition, the longer an Asian lives in the United States and the more highly educated she is, the more likely she is to identify as an Independent than choose one of the other non-partisan categories.

Nonpartisan Latino and Asian American Contactability and Voter Mobilization

Ricardo Ramírez and Janelle Wong

An inclusive political system is arguably one of the hallmarks of a democratic society. Yet Asian Americans and Latinos, two of the fastest growing segments of the American population, consistently demonstrate the lowest turnout rates of the major ethnic or racial groups (Jamieson, Shin, and Day 2002). According to the Current Population Survey, 43 percent of Asian American citizens and 45 percent of Latino citizens of voting age turned out in the 2000 presidential election, compared to 62 percent of non-Latino whites and 57 percent of non-Latino blacks (Jamieson, Shin, and Day 2002). Research on Asian American and Latino political participation is critical for understanding the prospects for and limits to full participation in the United States among the country's increasingly diverse population.

One critical factor to consider when examining voter turnout among Asian Americans and Latinos is political mobilization (Rosenstone and Hansen 1993; Verba, Schlozman, and Brady 1995; Leighley 2001). Although voter mobilization is among the most important functions of political parties during campaigns, *nonpartisan* mobilization by community organizations may be especially important for understanding the political participation of Latinos and Asian Americans for the following reasons: First, finite campaign resources compel partisan organizations to use modern campaign technology to target as many partisans as possible, yet at the same time focus only on those who are likely to vote. This mobilization approach has unintended consequences for participation patterns. By neglecting to contact all voters, certain segments of the electorate are not exposed to the most direct elite mechanisms for increasing voter turnout. As a consequence, there is an increasing share of forgotten electorates, such as young voters, immigrant voters, and non-English-speaking voters, which further depresses turnout. Many of these forgotten voters include sizable number of Latinos and Asian Americans.

Second, local party organizations, often cast as critical institutions for the political incorporation of European immigrants in the past, do not mobilize contemporary immigrants in a consistent or committed fashion today.[1] Progressive era reforms, changes in party structure, and the rise of candidate-centered campaigns have led to a decline in political machines and party strength in United States politics (Ceaser 1978, Erie 1988, Wattenberg 1994). In turn, partisan mobilization efforts are the exception, rather than the rule (Skocpol 1999, Ramírez 2002, Barreto et al. 2003, Wong 2004). Personal contact by neighborhood party activists is largely a thing of the past. In the breach, nonpartisan community groups such as advocacy organizations and ethnic voluntary associations are mobilizing populations that include a large proportion of immigrants, such as Asian Americans and Latinos (Green and Gerber 2004, Ramírez 2005, Wong 2004). Unlike parties, nonpartisan organizations should be more likely to expand the scope of targeted voters, given broader organizational goals of informing and empowering local communities. Finally, although they are less often the targets of mobilization compared to non-Latino whites (Gershtenson 2002; Leighley 2001; Frymer 1999; de la Garza, Menchaca, and DeSipio 1994), studies also show that mobilization efforts directed toward other racial minority groups, such as blacks and Latinos, are likely to have a very positive effect on their political participation (Leighley 2001).

One of the most critical aspects of any mobilization effort is contact. To deliver a mobilization message, such as encouraging individuals to get out the vote, contact must first be made with members of the targeted group. It is commonly believed that self-reported contact patterns are structured by various strategic decisions of political elites to contact certain individuals, especially those who are likely voters, and not others. In addition, reception to contact is assumed to vary by individual—some people are easier to contact than others. For example, some people are more likely to be away from their home phones during the times phone contact is attempted. Some may be more reluctant than others to pick up their phones even when they are at home. Furthermore, those who are easier to contact may also demonstrate voting habits that are distinct from those who are more difficult to contact (Gerber and Green 2000). In fact, previous studies confirm that those who are easier to contact are also more likely to vote (Gerber and Green 2000, 2001).

An understudied empirical question is whether specific factors determine which individuals are contactable. The first part of this essay examines whether those who are contacted are qualitatively different from those who are not successfully contacted, and whether certain factors explain the variation in contact rates, or "contactability," of population subgroups. Are forgotten electoral groups too difficult to target and mobilize? What can "real-world" voter mobilization efforts tell us about patterns of contactability among Asian Americans and Latinos?

The next part of the essay focuses on the effects of different nonpartisan mobilization strategies by community organizations on vote turnout among Asian Americans and Latinos. Using survey data, various studies have found a significant relationship between contact and voting. For example, past studies have relied on the use of survey questions that ask respondents whether they have been contacted and encouraged to vote by a party or other organization and whether they have voted (Rosenstone and Hansen 1993; Verba, Schlozman, and Brady 1995; Leighley 2001; Lien, Conway, and Wong 2004). However, studies based on analysis of survey data are limited. First, researchers must rely on respondents' self-reporting to gauge whether contact actually occurred, as well as self-reported turnout. More important, researchers cannot be certain that higher rates of turnout among those who indicate that they have been mobilized are really attributable to contact, or whether they result from other factors (Green and Gerber 2004, Gerber and Green 2001, 2000).

Organizations, like parties, are most likely to target high-propensity voters (Rosenstone and Hansen 1993, Leighley 2001). Drawing on recent surveys of Asian Americans and Latinos, we find that, in general, voters who are homeowners, married, native born, have higher education, and have higher incomes are more likely to report receiving any type of mobilization request (partisan and/or nonpartisan). Therefore, organizational bias toward the most likely voters may explain higher turnout among those who have been contacted. According to Jan Leighley, "it is virtually impossible to estimate the effect of mobilization on participation while giving sufficient consideration to the extent to which they are interrelated. Individuals and institutions are likely to mobilize those who are likely to participate and mobilization always predicts participation successfully" (2001, 161). In addition, surveys do not allow researchers to control for the type or quality of contact (Green and Gerber 2002).

To address these problems, recent studies have emphasized the im-

Table 1   Self-reported mobilization of Latino and Asian American voters

	No GOTV		Any GOTV		Partisan GOTV	
	Asian	Latino	Asian	Latino	Asian	Latino
Gender						
Female	57	68	43	32	38	18
Male	52	68	49	32	43	20
Age						
18–29	59	64	41	36	32	22
30–39	59	68	41	32	36	18
40–49	55	63	45	37	42	23
50–59	49	69	51	31	49	20
60 and over	46	74	54	26	50	14
Education						
Some HS or less	77	75	23	25	19	14
HS grad	69	67	31	34	26	19
Some college	48	67	52	33	45	21
College grad	46	63	54	37	50	21
Income						
Up to $24,999	68	74	33	26	27	16
$25,000 to $49,999	53	63	47	37	43	22
$50,000 to $79,999	41	63	59	38	56	22
$80,000 and above	32	64	68	36	61	24
Not reported	61	73	39	27	33	15
Marital status						
Married	54	67	46	33	43	19
Not married	55	69	45	31	37	19
Nativity						
Native born	37	63	63	37	58	23
Foreign born	60	76	40	24	35	13
Homeowner						
Homeowner	43	65	57	35	53	21
Not homeowner	67	73	33	27	27	16
Party ID						
DEM	47	65	54	35	48	20
GOP	45	73	55	27	49	17
IND/OTHER	51	70	49	30	42	18
DK/RF	67	79	33	21	30	15

portance of implementing a randomized experimental design in studies of voter mobilization. Researchers have begun to work closely with community organizations to study the effectiveness of Get Out the Vote (GOTV) efforts. By design, this approach is not subject to concerns that arise with self-reported contact and self-reported turnout, or the endogeneity of mobilization and turnout. In addition to their

Nonpartisan GOTV		Dual GOTV	DK
Asian	Latino	Latino	Latino
16	5	1	5
23	5	4	3
19	7	6	1
16	6	3	5
20	6	4	4
21	4	5	3
22	3	3	6
7	3	3	5
8	8	3	4
22	4	4	4
25	6	6	4
15	6	2	3
18	6	5	4
23	7	5	4
32	2	6	4
16	4	2	6
19	5	4	5
19	6	3	3
28	6	5	4
16	4	3	4
23	5	4	5
15	5	3	3
22	6	5	4
24	4	2	5
26	4	4	4
12	4	0	2

Sources: Tomas Rivera Policy Institute, 2001 Post Election Survey; Pilot National Asian American Political Survey, 2001.

Note: Income categories for Asian Americans are (1) up to $29,999; (2) $30,000 to $59,999; (3) $60,000 to $79,999; (4) $80,000 and above; (5) not reported.

For Asian Americans, mobilization questions included: "During the past 4 years, have you received any letter, e-mail, or telephone call from a political party or candidate organization or other political group about a political campaign?" (Partisan) "In the past 4 years, did someone you know try to request you to vote, or to contribute money to a political cause, or to engage in some other type of political activity?" (Nonpartisan)

For Latinos, mobilization questions included: "Over the past year, were you asked to register or vote by a candidate for office or a person working for a candidate, a representative of a political party, or someone in your community?" "Were you contacted by the Democrats, Republicans, both parties, or by representatives of other parties?" "Other than someone from the political parties or candidates, were those who contacted you community organizers or people working with non-profit organizations, union members, people from churches or religious organizations, or someone else?"

contribution to the understanding of the effectiveness of different voter mobilization efforts, these studies caution against broad assumptions that pervade the literature on the positive effects of all voter mobilization efforts. Beyond the general effects of Get Out the Vote efforts, Ricardo Ramírez (2002, 2005) and Alan Gerber and Donald Green (2001, 2004) have shown that type and quality of contact matter. The effectiveness of voter mobilization from one effort to another may depend on the message being conveyed to the treatment population, who administers the contact, as well as the possibility that certain types of voter mobilization may be more effective in certain types of elections (e.g., presidential vs. off-year) and among those less likely to vote or be contacted (e.g., youth, Latinos, etc).

Experimental Research Setting and Design

Los Angeles County is the most populous county in California with 28 percent of the state's 33.9 million residents and 26 percent of the state's 15.7 million registered voters. A total of 12 percent of the county's population is made up of Asian Americans, and about one-third of the state's Asian American population resides in Los Angeles County. Latinos account for 44.6 percent of the county's resident population, but only 21.5 percent of its registered voters and 20 percent of votes cast in the November 2000 election. Thus, the large concentration of both Asian Americans and Latinos, lower than average registration and turnout rates,[2] and the potential for increased political clout make Los Angeles County an ideal test case for measuring the impact of substantive nonpartisan mobilization efforts among Asian Americans and Latinos. (See table 5 in the appendix to this essay.)

The Asian American Mobilization Effort

Before the November 5, 2002, national election, a randomized voter mobilization experiment was conducted in Los Angeles County. The up-to-date vendor-generated list of approximately 16,000 registered Asian Pacific American voters (Chinese, Korean, Indian, Filipino, and Japanese) included residents of high-density Asian Pacific American zip codes in Monterey Park, Alhambra, Walnut, Diamond Bar, Torrance, Gardena, and Artesia. These voters were randomly assigned to treatment and control groups. Of the total, 27 percent were assigned to treatment group 1 (attempt to contact by phone), 20 percent were assigned to treatment group 2 (attempt to contact by mail), and the remaining (53 percent) were assigned to the control group (no treatment).

The Chinese sample is further distinguished by residence in the East San Gabriel Valley and the West San Gabriel Valley, because the political culture in each locale is distinct. In particular, the West San Gabriel Valley is characterized by a more homogenous Asian American population (mostly Chinese American), a more active ethnic press, a greater degree of Asian American political representation in elected offices, and more political mobilization and education campaigns by local community organizations. In terms of other descriptive characteristics, the treatment group is evenly divided in gender, and the mean age of the group is forty-seven years old. Consistent with other studies (Lien, Conway, and Wong 2004), the group leans Democrat, and a large proportion also declines to state party affiliation. The majority of the group registered within the last decade, with 36 percent of the group registering in just the past two years. In addition, most of those in the treatment group do not exhibit a long voting history.

A few days before election day, the treatment groups received a phone call or mailing from the Center for Asian Americans United for Self-Empowerment (CAUSE), a nonpartisan Asian Pacific American political empowerment organization, encouraging them to vote. Fifty-six volunteers worked on the project; forty-nine were Asian Pacific American and thirty-four were bilingual in English and an Asian language.[3] Each volunteer received two hours of training, and the Get Out the Vote phone campaign was monitored at all times by the director of the project.

The Latino Mobilization Effort

In partnership with the 2002 *Voces del Pueblo* voter mobilization efforts of the Educational Fund of the National Association of Latino Elected Officials (NALEO),[4] a field experiment was conducted before the November 5th, 2002, election. This mobilization effort attempted to reach 405,058 Latino voters in low-propensity precincts through live calls, direct mail, and robo calls (conducted by an automated phone bank) in six sites nationwide.[5] To date, this is the largest, systematic, multistate mobilization effort of the Latino community. This mobilization effort is unique in that NALEO will maintain a database of voters who they will target over a span of several elections. As a field experiment, it is also unique. First, it is the largest GOTV field experiment on Latinos. Also, while it shares the strength of recent field experiments that use a randomized nonpartisan treatment and control group, it is further strengthened by the fact that this experiment was conducted by a well-established organization with name recognition at the grassroots level and among political elites. For the purposes of this article, we focus on the Los Angeles County efforts.

In 2002 NALEO obtained a list of registered Latinos living in high-

Latino-density, low-propensity precincts in Los Angeles and Orange County.[6] Individuals were then randomly assigned to treatment and control groups. Between October 24 and November 4, fifty-one bilingual paid volunteers attempted to contact the live-call target groups in both counties. Short training sessions were conducted before the phone canvassing to give callers instructions on what to say over the phone. Each phone canvasser was given a "scripted message" to follow but was encouraged to conduct the call in a more conversational style. In practice, this conversational approach was the norm among phone canvassers. A total of 781.33 logged hours were worked in their attempt to contact 52,315 Latinos in Los Angeles and Orange counties.[7]

It is important to make the distinction between "assigned" and "attempted" contact. This is relevant for Los Angeles County and Orange County, because the live-call phone bank operation did not attempt to call all households or voters that were assigned to receive such contact. The phone banking operation sorted the voters assigned to receive a live call by precinct. Unfortunately, attempts were not made to call some precincts assigned to this treatment. Voters in 398 precincts were originally "assigned" to be contacted (with a random sample of 2,498 voters assigned to the control group). However, "attempts" were made to call only 169 (42.5 percent) of these precincts. In the end, of the 83,129 voters who were assigned to be contacted by a live phone call, calls to only 35,853 (43.1 percent) were actually attempted, whereas calls to 47,276 (56.9 percent) of those assigned to the treatment were not attempted.

The inability to attempt to call all those assigned to receive a live call meant that the vast majority of the Los Angeles *Voces* population, 51.1 percent, consisted of individuals receiving two treatments (robo call and direct mail), followed by those receiving all three treatments (live call, robo call, and direct mail), 33.3 percent. For the purpose of determining the impact of contactability, we draw on those individuals in treatment groups 1 to 4 where there was an attempt made to reach them by phone.

After the election, voter turnout records were reviewed to compare turnout rates for the treatment and control groups for both the Asian American and Latino mobilization experiments. Vote turnout was verified through cross-checking voter identification numbers with turnout data from the Los Angeles County registrar of voters.

Contactability among Asian Americans and Latinos

An important issue that may affect partisan and nonpartisan mobilization efforts is that some of the intended contacts may be unsuccessful not because the targeted voter is not home or because the telephone number is wrong. Instead, it is possible that the language preference of certain voters may preclude them from receiving the message. Fortunately, Asian Americans who were contacted by phone received the message in English or "in-language" (i.e., non-English language of respondent). These included Korean, Mandarin, Cantonese, Tagalog, Japanese, and Hindi.[8] Similarly, all of the *Voces del Pueblo* (VDP) live-call volunteers were bilingual. This ensured a higher rate of relaying the GOTV message. Therefore, in addition to coding the live-call outcome, VDP volunteers also recorded the respondent's language preference.

Figure 1 presents the results of the phone call attempts among Asian Americans and Latinos, respectively. Successful person-to-person contact of Asian Americans was made with 36 percent of the treatment group. Person-to-person contact among the remainder of the group was not successful in large part because of wrong numbers (20 percent) and targeted individuals not being home (35 percent). The latter group was split between those who did not answer and did not have an answering machine (15 percent of total); those who were not home, but a message was left for them with the person who did answer the phone (3 percent of total); and those who were not home, but a message was left for them on their answering machine (17 percent of total). Approximately 6 percent of the sample was not contacted for reasons not specified by the caller. Callers left a message only on the third attempt at contact. In some cases (3 percent of total), callers were instructed by whoever answered to "call back later" on the third and final attempt at contact. About one out of every four Asian Pacific Americans who was contacted by phone during this study preferred to speak a language other than English. Furthermore, preference for speaking a language other than English ranged from 5 percent among Indian Americans who were contacted successfully to over 60 percent of Korean Americans who were contacted successfully.

Among Latinos, 28 percent received successful person-to-person contact. The remaining Latinos consisted of 29 percent who were not home, 20 percent where the telephone listed in the voting records no longer corresponded to the voter, 1 percent who had moved, and 22 percent where no contact was recorded on the records. Among the

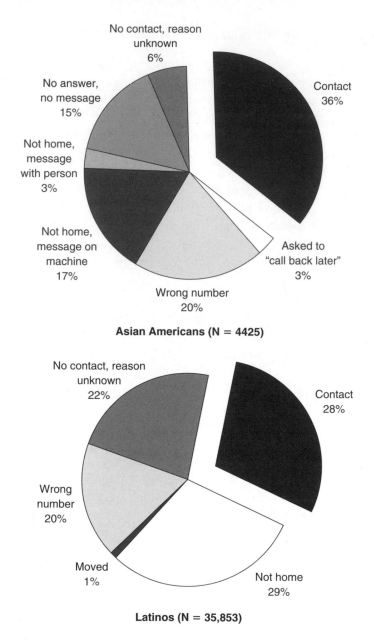

Figure 1 Result of phone call attempts, Asians and Latinos
Sources: Asian American GOTV (2002) and *Voces Del Pueblo* (2002).

successful contacts, nearly half (46 percent) prefer to speak Spanish. Interesting, but not surprising, was the language of preference by age group. The older the age group, the greater the percentage of those who preferred to speak Spanish. Evidently, the choice of language matters when contacting different segments of the Asian American and Latino electorate.

Demographics and Behavioral Influences on Contactability

It is largely assumed that those who are more predisposed to vote are more likely to be targets of mobilization and also more easily contacted. If this is true, then there should be distinct patterns of contactability based on a mix of demographic characteristics (e.g., age, nativity, etc.) and political behavior (e.g., date of first registration, vote history, etc.).

Nativity

There is no consensus of the effects of nativity on political participation. Earlier studies found that U.S. native-born Latinos participate at higher levels (DeSipio 1996b, Cho 1999). Using more recent data that accounts for the dramatic influx of naturalized Latino voters, other studies have found that after controlling for length of residence (Highton and Burris 2001, Wong 2001) and the political context of the state,[9] the native born participate at lower rates than their naturalized counterparts. More specifically, Latino immigrants in California had relatively high levels of voter turnout in response to the racially divisive ballot propositions of the 1990s (Ramírez 2002; Pantoja, Ramírez, and Segura 2001; Ramakrishnan 2005). If California's political context has significant positive impact on long-term voting rates of naturalized Latinos, then theories of immigrant participation may need to adjust accordingly.

It is important to understand whether Asian and Latino immigrants self-report differing levels of mobilization attempts (see table 1; self-reported contact is higher among native-born than naturalized Latinos, 37.1 percent vs. 24.2 percent). It is equally, if not more, important to determine whether contactability of immigrants varies from that of native-born Asian American and Latinos. There was virtually no difference, among Asian Americans, in rates of contact among naturalized and native-born registered voters. Unexpectedly, contactability among naturalized Latino registered voters was higher than among the native born (37.6 percent vs. 34.9 percent). To the extent that this

Table 2   Result of attempted phone contact, 2002

	Contact		Not home	
	Asian American	Latino	Asian American	Latino
Nativity				
Native born	36.7	27.6	24.2	28.8
Naturalized	36.5	29.1	23.5	28.7
Age group				
18–29	29.8	28.5	26.1	28.8
30–39	29.1	24.6	24.6	29.2
40–49	35.6	27.0	25.2	27.2
50–59	38.4	29.3	24.4	30.1
60+	42.5	30.0	18.3	28.4
Reg party affiliation				
Dem	37.1	28.0	23.4	28.5
GOP	35.1	26.0	25.7	30.4
Other	37.4	27.8	22.6	28.4
Decline to state	35.9	21.1	21.9	30.9
Vote history				
0 to 2 elections	34.0		22.9	
3 to 4 elections	35.9		24.5	
5 or more elections	41.9		25.1	
0 of 4		25.5		28.7
1 of 4		31.0		28.8
2 of 4		35.7		27.8
3 of 4		43.0		22.8
Reg cohort				
Pre-1994	37.4	23.7	25.0	27.9
1994–1996	33.4	23.5	23.2	28.6
1997–2000	35.3	28.7	21.4	28.6
Newly reg (2001–2002)	38.6	32.2	26.3	30.0

Sources: Asian American GOTV (2002) and *Voces Del Pueblo* (2002).

pattern can be generalized to Latino immigrants elsewhere, this pattern of contactability contradicts the expectations by scholars and political operatives.

Age

For the Asian American sample, greater age is associated with a higher likelihood of contact. This is consistent with the literature that predicts a higher rate of participation as registered voters grow older. Conversely, the pattern of self-reported contact among Latinos (see table 1), was replicated among the VDP Latino voters, where contact was more successful among eighteen- to twenty-nine-year-olds compared to thirty- to thirty-nine-year-olds. The nonlinear finding for age is somewhat surprising, but this may be the result of higher rates of la-

| Wrong number/No contact | | Outcome unknown | |
Asian American	Latino	Asian American	Latino
31.4	21.9	7.7	21.5
34.9	19.1	5.1	23.1
37.9	21.1	6.1	21.4
40.0	24.1	6.2	21.9
34.5	21.5	4.7	24.2
30.5	19.8	6.6	20.8
33.9	18.2	5.3	23.4
33.3	21.0	6.1	22.4
33.0	21.4	6.1	22.1
33.9	22.4	6.1	21.2
37.5	22.9	4.7	25.1
37.3		5.8	
32.9		6.7	
26.6		6.3	
	23.8		21.9
	18.0		22.1
	12.0		24.2
	8.9		24.1
30.0	24.6	7.5	23.7
38.4	26.0	5.0	22.3
37.1	20.3	6.2	22.3
30.5	17.6	4.6	20.0

bor participation in jobs with nontraditional hours by the thirty- to thirty-nine-year-old Latinos.

Ethnicity

Does contact receptivity vary by ethnic group? We test this proposal using the Asian American sample. Japanese Americans and Indian Americans (South Asian) are the most receptive to contact; approximately 42 percent of each group we attempted to contact were actually contacted. Japanese and Indian Americans demonstrate slightly higher average income and education levels relative to most other Asian American groups (Lai and Arguelles 2003). Furthermore, as a group, Japanese Americans include a smaller proportion of immigrants, and Indian Americans report relatively high levels of political interest compared to other Asian ethnic groups (Lien, Conway, and Wong 2004). These factors may be related to their propensity to pick up the phone. Chinese Americans in the East San Gabriel Valley (36.7 percent), Korean Americans (33.2 percent), and Chinese Americans in the West San Gabriel Valley (33.2 percent) prove slightly more difficult to contact. Filipino Americans (30.3 percent) demonstrate the lowest contact rates. In general, the contact rates among different Asian Pacific American ethnic groups appear fairly consistent, though some groups are slightly easier to contact than others.

Political Behavior Influences

Given parties' interest in winning elections, it makes sense that they would largely focus on the voter history of potential targets of mobilization. They are most likely to target those with a long voting history and those who are partisans. The two most direct measures of likelihood of voting and partisan preferences are prior voting history and registered party affiliation. Some interesting similarities among Asian American and Latino contactability emerge at the bivariate level. Democrats and Independents/Others were just slightly more likely to be contacted than their GOP counterparts. Is it possible that despite higher levels of socioeconomic status among Republicans, they are harder to reach? This may suggest that lower rates of contactability should not be assumed to only exist among poorer individuals. One possible explanation for why Republicans are less likely to be contacted is that they screen their calls more than Democrats and Independents/Others.

Another common pattern between Asian Americans and Latinos is that contactability rises with the frequency of voting. Also, those who registered to vote more recently have the highest rates of contact, most likely because the administrative records are less prone to be outdated. Among Latinos, new registrants were almost 10 percent more likely to be reached than those who first registered to vote before 1994. However, one deviation from the similar patterns exists among Asian Americans where contact was more successful among those who registered before 1994 than those who registered between 1994 and 2000. The differences between the registration cohorts are not very dramatic, but we might expect that Asian Americans who have been registered for a long period of time to exhibit a high degree of political engagement, making them good targets for phone contact.

The Personal and Political: Mutually Reinforcing Determinants?

It is important to examine the bivariate relationship between contactability and specific demographic and political behavior variables. With this in mind, the following caveats should be considered: First, we should not treat all noncontacts the same. Noncontact among some groups is driven more by wrong numbers, whereas in other cases it is because the person was not home. Second, categories are not mutually exclusive, and in some cases are mutually reinforcing. Demographic characteristics are correlated with voting behavior and, therefore, any inferences that we make regarding contact rates and prior vote history must consider the distribution of demographic characteristics among the population. To control for this, we examine the determinants of contactability using logistic regression. The models include three demographic characteristics (i.e., gender, nativity, and age), as well as three behavioral characteristics (party registration, voter history, and date of first registration).

The multivariate analysis in table 3 helps delineate the effects of demographic and behavioral characteristics on contactability.[10] For Asian Americans, women are more likely to be reached than men once other factors are taken into account. Similar to the Latino sample, contact is less successful among Republicans than nonpartisans or Independents, all else being equal. As we might expect, however, those who are older and who have a long and consistent voting history are more likely to be contacted than those who are younger and exhibit little experience with voting. Controlling for other factors, contact is more successful among more recent registrants.

For Latinos, as was the case with the descriptive findings in table 3, certain demographic and behavioral characteristics have unexpected effects on contact rates. For example, women, Republicans, and those ages thirty to thirty-nine are less likely to be reached, controlling for other factors. Conversely, naturalized voters, more active voters, those sixty years of age or older, and those who registered to vote more recently were more easily reached by NALEO's 2002 GOTV effort in Los Angeles County.

Contact and Vote Turnout

Analysis of the Asian American sample (table 4) reveals important differences in the effects of contact by ethnic group and, among Chinese

Table 3 Logistic regression results for predicting contactability, 2002

	Successful contact B (SE)	
Variables	Asian American	Latino
Women	.148* .066	−.053* .025
Naturalized	−.076 .072	−.024 .033
Age 30 to 39[a]	−.110 .116	−.124** .037
Age 40 to 49	.159 .106	−.045 .044
Age 50 to 59	.279* .112	.054 .052
Age 60 or over	.435* .105	.146** .050
Democrat[b]	−.098 .079	−.018 .030
Republican	−.165* .086	−.133** .044
Voted 3−4 elections[c]	.192 .105	
Voted 5 or more elections	.456* .096	
Voted 0 of 4 elections[d]		−.288** .027
Voted 2 of 4 elections		.187** .068
Voted 3 of 4 elections		.431 .233
1st registered to vote pre-1994[e]	−.026 .100	.040 .049
1st registered to vote 1997 to 2000	.210* .100	.213** .035
1st registered to vote 2001 to 2002	.398* .119	.479** .041
Constant	−.979 .129	−.917** .046
Predicted percentage correct	63.56% n = 4,103	71.87% n = 33,372

*Significant at $p < .05$; **Significant at $p < .01$ (two-tailed tests)
[a] Excluded category is "Age 18–29."
[b] Excluded category is "Other Party" or "Decline to State."
[c] Excluded category is "Voted 0–2 elections."
[d] Excluded category is "Voted 1 of 4 elections."
[e] Excluded category is "Registered 1994–96."

Table 4   Estimated effects of contact on turnout among
Asian Americans by ethnic group

Chinese East San Gabriel Valley
Turnout differential (26.2−27.3)/contact rate (36.7) = −3.0%
95% Confidence interval = −10.6 to 9.8

Chinese West San Gabriel Valley
Turnout differential (37.4−32.0)/contact rate (33.2) = 16.3%
95% Confidence interval = −2.8 to 29.9

Filipino
Turnout differential (39.1−39.0)/contact rate (30.3) = 0.3%
95% Confidence interval = −12.1 to 11.0

Indian
Turnout differential (36.0−32.9)/contact rate (42.0) = 7.4%
95% Confidence interval = −3.7 to 17.5

Japanese
Turnout differential (50.8−52.0)/contact rate (42.1) = −2.9%
95% Confidence interval = −18.9 to 8.6

Korean
Turnout differential (29.2−30.1)/contact rate (36.1) = −2.5%
95% Confidence interval = −14.1 to 9.1

Americans, by region. The results show that although contacting Chinese Americans in the East San Gabriel Valley has virtually no effect on turnout −3.0, the estimated effects of contact among Chinese Americans in the West San Gabriel Valley is 16.3 percent. Again, the political context in the West San Gabriel Valley is distinct from that of the East. The West is home to more Chinese American candidates, and the ethnic press is very active around political issues there. Perhaps these factors—a relatively high number of coethnic candidates and elected officials, including two California State Assembly members, an ethnic press active around local and state politics, and a high level of mobilization efforts by community groups—contribute to both the higher level of turnout in general among Chinese Americans and the greater effectiveness of the Get Out the Vote phone contacting efforts in the West compared to the East San Gabriel Valley. In fact, the effects of turnout among Chinese Americans in the West San Gabriel Valley were greater than among any other group in the study.

Perhaps the Chinese American population in the West San Gabriel Valley is more politicized in general than other Asian Pacific American ethnic groups and therefore more easily "activated" to vote through mobilization. Note that the political context in the West San Gabriel Valley is distinct from that of the East. The West San Gabriel Valley is characterized by more coethnic electoral representation. For instance, there are two Asian American members of the California State Assembly representing West San Gabriel Valley, Carol Liu and Judy Chu. Furthermore, the ethnic media in the West San Gabriel Valley devotes a good deal of coverage to Asian American candidates and politics. Finally, local Asian American community organizations tend to focus more of their political empowerment efforts on residents in the West San Gabriel Valley compared to those in the East. The evidence therefore suggests that Asian Americans in the West San Gabriel Valley are more likely than those living in the East to be engaged in civic life through community organizations and exposure to an active local ethnic media, with a Get Out the Vote effort channeling some of this existing civic energy toward the voting booth.

The effect of contact on turnout varies somewhat among the other ethnic groups in the study. Among Indian Americans, the estimated effect of contact is 7.4 percent. In contrast, contact appears to have no effect on whether or not Filipino Americans, Japanese Americans, or Korean Americans turn out to vote. The sign associated with the estimated effect of contact for two of these groups is actually negative. These preliminary data suggest that the effects of contact are likely to vary according to ethnicity and region.

As was the case with Asian Americans, analysis of the effect of the live calls among Latinos in Los Angeles reveals significant and positive effects of mobilization for Latino voter turnout. We base our analysis on the contact and turnout rates of the assigned treatment groups. Because the phone banking was divided up by precincts and calls to entire precincts were not attempted, we cannot shift the unattempted voters to other treatment groups. This is because there may be unobserved (positive or negative) precinct-specific effects of the unattempted calls on turnout that we cannot account for. Thus, while the contact rate of the attempted live calls in Los Angeles was nearly 28 percent, the contact rate of the assigned to receive live calls in Los Angeles County was 12 percent. Disentangling the effects of actually receiving a phone call requires a somewhat more elaborate statistical analysis. Overall, actually receiving a live call from the local phone banks raised turnout among Latinos in Los Angeles County by 4.6 percentage points—an effect that is statistically significant at the .01 level. This rate of productivity is very similar to what has been observed in other phone banks staffed by committed volunteers.

Conclusions

Get Out the Vote efforts often target the most likely voters in order to mobilize the most people with the fewest resources. At least in California, parties and nonpartisan mobilization efforts may unintentionally neglect "reachable" segments of the Latino population if they focus solely on voting history age and party affiliation. In fact, campaigns could get more "bang for the buck" (in terms of contact rates) if they targeted naturalized voters and the newly registered. Asian Americans are often neglected by mobilization efforts altogether (Wong 2004). In fact, less than 1 percent of those Asian Americans in this study indicated that they had been contacted by another group about the election. Yet, this study clearly shows that Asian Americans are reachable, especially those who are older, have a long voting history, and are newly registered. Further, those who are naturalized are no more difficult to reach than those who are citizens by birth.

It could be that for those who can be reached more easily, higher contact rates may not produce the same number of voters at the poll when compared to other segments of the population. Also, given the uncertainty of the voter preferences of these two groups, parties may not be willing to gamble on voters who did not undergo the standard partisan socialization process or on those whose future participation is uncertain. Nevertheless, the effects of these factors on contact rates have normative implications on the strategic nature of partisan and nonpartisan mobilization efforts. One implication is that some long-standing practices by parties that are based on assumptions about who is easiest to reach and mobilize must be challenged. For example, in part because they are mobile and do not turn out at high rates, most parties do not focus their energies on young people. However, we find that for some groups (Latinos), the youngest are easier to reach than their middle-aged counterparts. Among Asian Americans, the youngest registered voters are no harder to reach than those who are thirty to fifty years old. Furthermore, they are also more likely to turn out once contacted (Wong 2004). Another implication is that parties and community organizations should not assume that all groups are equally easy to contact. If they want to be effective, organizations, partisan or otherwise, should consider devoting more resources to those who are hard to reach, such as Latinos who have not voted before.

Further, our research shows that contact does lead to turnout. For Asian Americans, the effects of contact on voter turnout among Asian Americans depend on both ethnic and regional distinctions *within* the

Asian Pacific American community. The effects of contact are much higher among some ethnic groups than others. Furthermore, even within a particular ethnic group like Chinese Americans, the turnout effects of contact depend on geography. The effects are much greater among Chinese Americans who live in the West San Gabriel Valley than among those who live in the East San Gabriel Valley. These differential effects of contact may be attributable to the distinct political context that characterizes each area.

Of the three modes of communicating with Latino voters, only live phone calls produced a statistically significant increase in voter turnout. The inefficacy of direct mail and robotic calls is consistent with results from other experimental campaigns. What remains unclear is the extent to which direct mail and robotic calls targeting low-propensity Latino voters would be more effective in presidential elections. For the present, it appears that the most effective way to mobilize low-propensity Latino voters is through phone banks staffed by volunteers.

Appendix

Table 5   Experimental design

Asian Americans

Total number	Treatment group I (Attempt to contact by phone)	Treatment group II (Attempt to contact by mail)	Control group
16,383	4,425	3,232	8,726
100%	27%	20%	53%

Latinos

	Live calls		No live calls	
	Mail-yes	Mail-no	Mail-yes	Mail-no
Robo-yes	25,532	924	56,725	4,143
Robo-no	858	858	4,212	4,189

Notes

1. Research by Steven Erie (1988) and Gerald Gamm (1989) has shown that the mobilization of European immigrants during the early twentieth century was only done in a piecemeal manner until the dawn of the New Deal era.

2. Latino turnout for 2002 general was 39 percent, compared to the non-Latino turnout of 45 percent and countywide turnout of 44 percent (Tomas Rivera Policy Institute, unpublished analysis of Los Angeles Registrar of Voters data)

3. The volunteers were recruited from an undergraduate "Asian American Politics" class at the University of Southern California, Asian Pacific American student organizations, and students working at CAUSE-Vision21.

4. The NALEO Educational Fund is the leading organization that empowers Latinos to participate in the American political process, from citizenship and voting to public service.

5. These included Los Angeles County, Orange County, California; Houston, Texas; Denver Metropolitan Area; New York City; and the state of New Mexico. These urban areas present NALEO with the opportunity to reach many Latinos efficiently and measure the impact of their efforts.

6. The criteria for selecting precincts required that 70 percent of the registered voters in the precinct be Latino (based on Latino surname lists), but with an average turnout rate of less than 50 percent.

7. We are unable to gauge the number of hours logged for calls made to the Latinos in Los Angeles versus Orange County calls because it was run as a single phone bank for both counties.

8. A small proportion of the Filipino, Indian, and Japanese samples were contacted by volunteers who spoke English only, because they tend to have a higher proportion of English speakers compared to other Asian Pacific American groups in the study. The Chinese and Korean samples were only contacted by bilingual speakers.

9. Race-targeting ballot initiatives have been credited for the mobilization of Latino immigrants to naturalized and become involved in electoral politics.

10. The dependent variable is a dichotomous variable where it equals 1 if contacted, and 0 otherwise.

Part 4

Portents for the Future

Politics among Young Adults in New York
The Immigrant Second Generation

John Mollenkopf, Jennifer Holdaway, Philip Kasinitz,
and Mary Waters

Attempts by new immigrant ethnic groups to gain entry into a political establishment dominated by earlier ethnic groups has been a central story in the politics of New York and many other large old American cities. Established groups have viewed these attempts as threatening to destabilize prevailing electoral arrangements and even jeopardizing their hold on elected offices and the benefits that flow from them. For their part, many newcomers thought that unresponsive incumbents deserved to be challenged, though some newcomers certainly sought upward mobility within the existing framework (Shefter 1994, chapter 6). These interactions between older and newer ethnic groups could be conflictual and extended, but they typically ended up by providing newcomers with a voice in the political system, though often after they gave up some of their ideals. In the process, "immigrant groups" and "racial groups" became "ethnic voting blocks" (Morawska 2001b; Browning, Marshall, and Tabb 2003).

A rising group sometimes made political headway by threatening to defect from a dominant electoral coalition that wished to harness its votes. More often, a gradual generational succession allowed younger cohorts from the new group to win office alongside an older generation from the earlier ethnic groups, gradually displacing them over the long haul—though Irish politicians still hold office in New York City. To overly simplify the complex process of ethnic succession in New York City politics, the Irish and Germans began to overtake the WASP dominance of Democratic politics in the second half of the nineteenth century, the Jews and Italians then challenged Irish dominance from the 1930s through the 1950s, and blacks and Puerto Ricans finally did the same to white ethnics beginning in the late 1950s.

While newly naturalized first-generation immigrants provided some votes for these electoral challenges, new immigrant ethnicities only became firmly politically established after enough of their children—the second generation—emerged into adulthood and became a substantial part of a new electoral majority that evolved to accommodate them. The mobilization of a new ethnic identity in urban politics must often await the arrival of the second generation because the first generation is still oriented toward the home country and struggling to find their place in the new one. (As of 2004, half of New York's immigrant adults—1.4 million people—remain noncitizens.) The New Deal electoral coalition emerged in the 1930s, partly on the basis of first- and second-generation immigrant voters, as did Fiorello LaGuardia's victories in New York City. In exchange for the electoral support they needed to retain office, older political elites allowed members of the new immigrant ethnic groups to achieve some influence. Younger immigrant groups threw themselves into these efforts not only because some could achieve political upward mobility, but also because the older elites developed platforms that spoke to the general needs of immigrant ethnic groups. In this light, David Dinkins's election as New York's first African American mayor in 1989 was part of a long-running story (Mollenkopf 2003).

This process continues to today. While party organizations and party identification are not what they used to be in New York or anywhere else, the Democratic Party remains an effective gatekeeper to elected office in the city (Mayhew 1986). As such, it continues to shape the political incorporation of new immigrant groups. As one of the nation's two largest destinations for new immigrants, New York stands at the forefront of the dramatic demographic changes being wrought by decades of international migration. Like other immigrant gateway cities such as Los Angeles, Miami, and even Chicago, New York is on the threshold of a new epoch of ethnic succession (Logan and Mollenkopf 2003). The era of the civil rights activism and minority empowerment that characterized such cities between 1950 and 1990 is giving way to an era defined by the attempts of new immigrant ethnic groups to break into political establishments now populated not just by white ethnics, but by native-stock African American and Hispanic politicians.

New York is particularly interesting, because it has received immigrants from the Caribbean and Europe as well as Latin America and Asia. As a result, political incumbents of every race are seeing their native-stock component of their ethnic constituencies shrink, while the immigrant stock share is growing. Puerto Rican or Jewish elected officials may claim, for example, to speak for all Latino or white ethnic voters, but they face competition from first- and second-generation Dominicans and Russians who would like to take their place. This situation poses two basic questions: How are members of these new groups attempting to break into New York City politics, and how are the incumbent political elites reacting to them? This essay uses a unique new data set on second-generation immigrants to address the first question. While interesting in themselves, the answers will have increasing relevance to other parts of the country as the impact of immigration is felt more widely in American politics.

The Demographic Context

In the fall of 2004, only a fifth of New York City's residents were native-born white people with two native-born parents, but such people occupy more than half of the city's public offices, including the mayoralty.[1] Because they are older, more likely to be citizens, and more likely to speak English than first- or second-generation immigrant groups, native-stock whites make up a larger share—about 29 percent—of the city's voting-age citizens and even more—33 percent—of the voters in the November 2004 presidential election. As a result, native-stock whites compose the single largest racial-ethnic voting block in the city. In the context of divisions among other groups, this electoral plurality has enabled native-stock whites to win the offices of mayor, public advocate, Brooklyn and Staten Island Borough presidents, and twenty-six of the fifty-one city council seats. Native-stock whites are thus the most overrepresented group compared to their share of the electorate or population. However, native-stock blacks and Puerto Ricans also hold more council seats (27.5 and 19.6 percent respectively) than their shares of the electorate (15 percent and 9 percent) or population (12.5 and 9 percent).[2] First- and second-generation immigrants, conversely, hold far fewer offices than their share of voters or population, leading to the emergence of a new kind of "representation gap" (Logan and Mollenkopf 2003).

Naturalized immigrants and their native-born children are nonetheless a growing part of the city's electorate. Half of all New Yorkers now live in a household headed by immigrants. As first-generation immigrants naturalize and their native-born children come of age, the foreign stock component of the New York City electorate is growing rapidly. In the 2000 Census, 44.5 percent of New York's foreign-born adults had naturalized and tens of thousands of their native-born children reached eighteen. As a result, 1.2 million (27 percent) of New

York's 4.5 million noninstitutionalized voting-age citizens were for-eign born and 1.4 million more (32 percent) were native-born people living in households headed by a foreign-born person.

Immigrants and their family members thus clearly make up a sub-stantial share of the 3.7 million names on New York City's list of reg-istered voters and the 1.5 million voters in the 2001 mayoral election. (Analysts may not have paid much attention to this fact, because poll-ing firms, exit polls, and even CBS/*New York Times* surveys generally do not ask where respondents were born!) Much-needed research on first-generation immigrant political participation is now getting under way (see, for example, Mollenkopf and Minnite 2001; Mollenkopf, Olson, and Ross 2001; Wong 2005; Ramakrishnan and Espenshade 2001.) In New York, the 2001 mayoral election exit poll suggested that immigrants cast a quarter of the votes, a figure confirmed by Lor-raine Minnite's New Americans Exit Polls in 2000, 2002, and 2004. Fi-nally, the voter supplement of November 2004 Current Population Survey suggests that first-generation immigrants made up 27 percent of the city's voters in the 2004 presidential election, while native-born voters with an immigrant parent made up another 16 percent. First-and second-generation immigrants thus make up about 43 percent of the city's voters and 56 percent of its population.

After the 1990 Census, the New York City Council was enlarged and redistricted, allowing the first West Indian and Dominican can-didates to win seats. In the wake of a more modest redistricting in 2003, the city council now has two West Indians, two Dominicans, and one Chinese/Taiwanese member. (No white immigrant has won yet, but Russian candidates have mounted spirited campaigns in Brigh-ton Beach, Brooklyn.) Immigrant stock representatives thus now hold about 10 percent of the council seats, despite being almost half of the electorate. This contrast between demographically declining groups holding a strong political position and growing groups still holding a relatively weak position have created fertile conditions for new kinds of conflict and competition.

As in other American cities, native-stock incumbents—of all races—do not want new immigrant challengers to take over their positions simply because the populations of their districts are changing. New immigrant candidates have a hard time mounting these challenges in part because their new immigrant ethnic bases remain relatively young, are lacking in citizenship, and have lower income, education, and property ownership relative to older, more established ethnic con-stituencies. Moreover, first- and second-generation immigrants come

from so many different backgrounds that they rarely coalesce into co-
hesive pan-ethnic voting blocks in the manner of African Americans.
The single biggest national origin group, Dominicans, accounts for
only about 6 percent of the city's population and 4.7 percent of its
voting-age citizens, so they can only realistically contend for political office on an ethnic basis in the few places where they are concentrated (Marwell 2004). As a group, the Anglophone Caribbeans
constitute a slightly larger share of the city's population—8 percent—
and electorate—5.5 percent—and they too have successfully sought
office in central Brooklyn. Given the racial and ethnic diversity of New
York's immigrants and the relatively small size of any one national origin group, however, these gains are hard to replicate outside zones of
concentration.

The attitudes of immigrants may also hinder their political empowerment and, indeed, the political mobilization of young people from
many different backgrounds (see Ramírez and Wong in this volume).
New political constituencies become mobilized only when their members see a good ideological or material reason for doing so and when
political entrepreneurs with solid group connections emerge to mobilize them. Most first-generation immigrants in New York do not see
why they should participate in local politics, primarily because they
are focused instead on achieving economic success in an unfamiliar,
sometimes unfriendly environment, while vesting their hopes in their
children. Most are too busy to spend much time on politics. Some may
naturalize more for pragmatic than ideological or political reasons
(Singer and Gilbertson 2000). They formed their political orientations
in their home countries, many of which lack a democratic tradition.
At the same time, immigrant blacks, Latinos, and Asians who do become naturalized and get involved in the local political process often
bring political skills and attachments from home and tend to vote
at higher rates than either their native-stock counterparts or their
second-generation children.

Over time, however, the bulk of the immigrant-stock electorate will
be made up of the children of immigrants. Unlike their parents, they
grow up as New Yorkers. Second-generation immigrants make up an
increasing share of every succeeding age cohort of young people who
reach eighteen and are entitled to vote. The city's native-born whites,
blacks, and Puerto Ricans tend to be older and often are beyond child-
bearing age or have comparatively few children. Immigrant families
are younger and larger. More than half of those who were eighteen in
2000 lived in households headed by foreign-born people; three of ten

were born in the United States or are naturalized citizens who arrived as young children. Over time, they will constitute a new majority. Their attitudes about politics and the political system, the degree to which their political behavior will differ from similar young people from native backgrounds, and the kinds of citizens they will become, will have a large impact on the contours of immigrant political participation in New York, the future of the city's politics, and indeed how the immigrant second generation in other parts of the country thinks about politics.

Studying Political Behavior in the Immigrant Second Generation in New York

The "representation gap" has had a profound impact on immigrant stock youngsters. In particular, they perceived the mayoralty of Republican Rudolph W. Giuliani (1993–2001) as being unfriendly to minority and immigrant communities, and during this period they experienced dramatically increased pressure from the police department (Jacobson 2001). In recent decades, many incidents of violence inflicted on first- and second-generation young people, especially males, by white residents or the police, have taken place. This led many young people to become cynical about politics, alienated from the political system, and angry at Mayor Giuliani. National surveys have indicated that many young Americans hold such feelings about politics and are less likely to vote or participate in other political activities than their elders. Until now, however, we did not know how these outcomes varied across different groups of young people in New York City, what factors appear to contribute to these attitudes, and why some young people nevertheless become engaged in civic life.

To answer such questions and many others, we undertook a study of the Immigrant Second Generation in Metropolitan New York (ISGMNY), based at the Center for Urban Research at the City University Graduate Center.[3] This study examined experiences with the educational system, labor market, and social and political worlds of a range of young people aged eighteen to thirty-two in one of the nation's most diverse metropolitan areas. Our study groups included second-generation immigrants growing up in the United States whose parents migrated from (1) the Dominican Republic, (2) Colombia, Ecuador, or Peru, (3) the Anglophone West Indies, (4) China and the Chinese diaspora, and (5) Jews from the former Soviet Union.[4]

We included people who were born abroad but who arrived by the age twelve and grew up here. To distinguish them from their native peers, we also interviewed similar numbers of African Americans, Puerto Ricans, and whites with native-born parents. This allows us to compare two Latino immigrant groups with Puerto Ricans, West Indians with African Americans, and Chinese and Russian Jews with native whites.[5] We completed telephone interviews with 3,415 respondents and did a further in person, in depth interview with 333 of them. Together, the groups being examined here make up about 64 percent of the city's population and 68 percent of its voting-age citizens. As already noted, native stock whites, blacks, and Puerto Ricans are the largest ethnic groups in New York City. First- and second-generation Dominicans, South Americans, West Indians, Chinese, and Russians are, respectively, 6 percent, 3 percent, 8 percent, 4.4 percent, and 3.8 percent of the city's population, or more than a quarter taken together.

Data on these second-generation and native minority young people allow us to explore the roots, dimensions, and consequences of the political attitudes and practices among young people in New York City and analyze why some are more engaged in politics than others despite the political cynicism that is widespread in this generation. We focus on the 2,790 respondents (after weighting) in our sample who grew up in the New York metropolitan area and who currently live in the city. (A number of the whites and blacks in our sample grew up in other parts of the United States and moved to New York City to pursue their careers. Because their political perspectives may have been largely formed elsewhere, we exclude them here. Since we are focusing on New York City politics, we also exclude those living in the New York and New Jersey suburbs.) Because some of our second-generation people were born outside the United States but moved here as small children, some have not become citizens. Our analysis of voting patterns uses a further subset of 2,426 citizens in New York City.

Although these individuals constitute good samples of their specific groups, they do not add up to a representative cross section of all young New Yorkers, because our study focused on understanding eight important groups. However, these groups encompass 80 percent of the young adult population. (In multivariate analysis, we weight each person back to their incidence in the initial population sampled, so that the size of our sample for the group does not bias the analysis.) Subsequent analysis has borne out our initial conviction that group membership and group characteristics have a considerable impact on individual trajectories, even after controlling for family background characteristics.

A Political Profile of Young People in New York City

It is well known that political participation and political attitudes among the young are strongly shaped by the socioeconomic position and politics of their parents. If the political profile of young New Yorkers were to be fully explained by such factors, then we would expect that those with better off families would be the most likely to participate, the most likely to have positive evaluations of the political system, and the most likely to take relatively conservative positions, with those from the poorest families falling at the other end of the spectrum. Given the groups in our study, we would expect the whites and perhaps Russians to fall at the former end of the spectrum, with the Dominicans, Puerto Ricans, and Chinese at the other end of the spectrum, with African Americans, West Indians, and South Americans in the middles, since that is the way that the incomes and education of their parents are distributed. We might further expect that the native-born groups from each racial and ethnic background would be more likely to participate than those of immigrant backgrounds, and perhaps have more positive evaluations of American political institutions, since they would have been socialized politically completely within an American setting.

In fact, we found a different and more complicated pattern. While native whites on one end and Puerto Ricans on the other end generally do conform to this model, the other groups do not. In particular, race plays a major role. African Americans and West Indians both join whites in being the most engaged in politics and civic participation—indeed they outdistance whites on the latter score—while Russians and Chinese are relatively uninterested in politics and uninvolved in civic life. Moreover, it appears that the black and Latino immigrant second generation, far from being less interested in politics than their native peers, are equally or more engaged.

By way of preface, we note that the young people with whom we talked have a generally low opinion of politics and the government institutions with which they have had contact. Overall, a majority of every group agrees somewhat or entirely with the statement that "most elected officials don't care what people like me think." Not surprisingly, figure 1 shows that whites and Russian second-generation

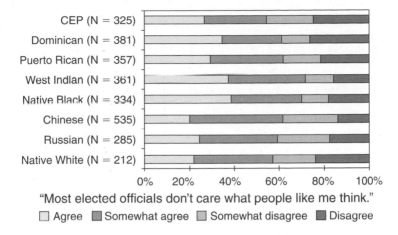

Figure 1 Political alienation by group
Source: ISGMNY respondents who grew up in metro New York and live in New York City.

respondents are least likely to feel this way, along with young people from Colombian, Ecuadoran, or Peruvian backgrounds (hereafter CEP), while West Indians and African Americans agree most strongly. The Puerto Ricans, Dominicans, and Chinese fall in between.

This pattern suggests that race, rather than class background or immigrant status, may motivate this distribution of opinion (with Chinese appearing closer to blacks than to whites in this case). Similarly, the groups also agree that "New York City police generally favor whites over blacks and other minorities," with two-thirds to three-quarters of each minority group agreeing and another 25 percent or so "somewhat" agreeing. Even among whites, Russians, and Chinese, a bit less than half agree, with another third agreeing "somewhat." The main distinction again appears to be racial, with black groups agreeing most, white groups agreeing least, and Latino groups in between, with Chinese being more like whites than blacks in this instance.

When we asked our respondents to elaborate on these concerns, they told us that they think New York City politicians are hypocrites who tell voters what voters want to hear at election time and then do whatever most furthers their career after gaining office, mostly by helping powerful or wealthy interests. As one African American woman said,

> They care in the beginning, to get that position. Then they don't care any more, because the lower class people are not the ones that are pushing him to where he needs to go. He's there now. Now he's gonna ride the purse strings of the rich and famous to get everything else he wants. So

they care until they get to the point they don't need you any more. They'll say anything, that they're gonna help you, help your community, build this, build that. They only care until they get what they're looking out for.

This sentiment was echoed by a Puerto Rican woman:

The politicians want to make it seem like they care about your issues so they listen to what you have to say around election time. Once they're elected, théy really don't come back to your community.

However alienated our respondents are from their elected officials— and they have a pervasive dislike of politics—they, like many other New Yorkers, favor an activist government. Many agree that "the government in Washington should see to it that every person has a job and a good standard of living" and more agree somewhat. Indeed, only among native whites do as many as one in five disagree with the proposition, while African Americans, the group with the largest share of parental employment in public service, are most strongly in favor. Latinos are again in the middle, though they are closer to blacks than whites. One interesting departure from this trend is that West Indian second-generation young people are substantially less support- ive of relying on government than African Americans, while the Chi- nese and Russians are much closer to whites than to black or Latino second-generation youths.

Our respondents show less enthusiasm for New York City politics. Figure 2 indicates that most do not find New York City politics inter- esting. Here, Latino groups show the least interest and the Russians and Chinese are only slightly less disinterested, while native blacks and whites show the most interest, and West Indians also show more interest than the other second-generation groups. Normally, political alienation might be expected to lead to political disinterest. That is clearly not the case here, because the most alienated groups, African Americans and West Indians, are also among the most interested in New York City politics. Conversely, the least alienated group, native whites, also shows a comparatively high level of interest. While West Indians trail not far behind native blacks, Dominicans, CEP, and Puerto Ricans all have low levels of interest (despite moderate levels of alienation), while Chinese and Russians have low levels both of alien- ation and interest in politics.

It is striking that Puerto Ricans have the lowest incomes and griev- ances similar to those of African Americans, yet are considerably less alienated and less interested in New York City politics than African

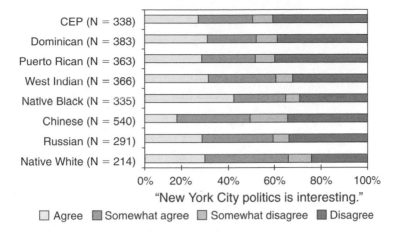

Figure 2 Interest in New York City politics by group
Source: ISGMNY respondents who grew up in metro New York and live in New York City.

Americans. Beyond their skepticism about politicians, our respondents offered a number of other theories about why young people are disinterested in politics. They believe that young people cannot make any difference. As one Russian bluntly put it:

> I believe the younger generation knows that whatever the public officials are saying is a bunch of bullshit and it is not really worth their time to go out and vote because nothing is going to change anyway.

A Puerto Rican woman put a slightly different twist on the same thing:

> A lot of young people today plain don't care. "What have I got to vote for? I'm not gonna waste my time." I've heard that.

People this age are also busy getting established in life or going out and having fun. They have not yet acquired the kinds of responsibilities that might motivate them to engage in politics. One Dominican man explained that young people don't vote because

> They got better things to do and it won't affect them directly. Wait 'til they get older and they want to see things change. Then they feel lit. Young people nowadays just want to have fun and hang out. Worry about it later when they work and get all these taxes taken out of their paycheck.

Not surprisingly, voting rates in the 1996 presidential election closely track levels of interest in New York City politics. Table 1 shows that African Americans were most likely to vote, followed closely by native whites. West Indians showed the next highest rate, showing their affinity with African Americans. Chinese and Russians are far at

Table 1 Presidential election voting

| | Voted 1996 | | |
	Yes	No	Total
CEP	65.0%	35.0%	143
Dominican	61.5%	38.5%	161
Puerto Rican	64.2%	35.8%	193
West Indian	73.9%	26.1%	142
Native Black	82.5%	17.5%	240
Chinese	42.1%	57.9%	190
Russian	51.2%	48.8%	84
Native White	81.9%	18.1%	138

Source: ISGMNY citizen voting-age respondents (in 1996) who grew up in metro New York and live in New York City.

the other end of the spectrum, reflecting their lack of interest in politics. Again, Latinos fall in between, with little distinction between native Puerto Ricans, Dominicans, and CEP. This pattern also does not conform to a standard socioeconomic model. Two disadvantaged— and skeptical if not alienated—groups, African Americans and West Indians, show high rates of participation, while two relatively advantaged groups, Russians and Chinese, participate at much lower levels.

Our in-depth interviews gave some indications of why native blacks and West Indians are more apt to vote than others. These respondents told us that it was important for blacks to develop electoral clout in a white-dominated world and that others had made great sacrifices so that they could do so. An African American put it this way:

> If you don't vote, you can't bitch and moan about what the government is doing to you. It is not only a way to get what you want, it is your obligation. Think of all the people who struggled and fought and died just for you to be able to walk into a school and pull down two levers.

A West Indian man elaborated:

> One of the things that is great about this country is that you can raise your voice . . . by voting. A lot of other countries either came late or still have not gotten to the point where citizens actually have a voice in what goes on in the country and who leads them. It's very American. And as a black person, it is about what it took to give you that. . . . It is very easy to take for granted, but people died. People spilled blood for me to be able to walk into a booth and pull a lever. It's five minutes out of my day. I can do it.

Other groups have both less feeling that political representation was important to the success of their group and less connection to the political system. Robert Huckfeldt and John Sprague (1995) showed that one's community situation has an impact on one's political behavior. This is evident among our respondents. Consider this juxtaposition of the views of a twenty-seven-year-old Chinese man and a white woman. The Chinese man noted that

> Most of the Jews and the blacks already know English when they get here. The Chinese community, only half. There's a percentage that don't speak English and I think the Chinese families are more passive. They don't have the language and they're less inclined to put themselves in the spotlight.

But as the white woman explained,

> I guess there are milieus where there's the social expectation that you will vote and milieus where there isn't and I happen to be in one where people vote so I vote. I'm actually wondering if it runs any deeper than that.

It is well known that participation in neighborhood and civic organizations constitutes the foundation of political engagement (Putnam 2000). Religious participation is another important precursor to civic engagement (Verba, Scholzman, and Brady 1995). Our study confirms that such paths lead some young second-generation and native minority New Yorkers into greater levels of political participation and awareness. Our quantitative survey asked our respondents about membership and participation in religious institutions and civic organizations such as neighborhoods associations, PTAs, political clubs, and other organizations.

The distribution of organizational participation across our groups mirrors their interest in local politics. African Americans once more come out on top, with the highest mean score on organizational participation, followed by West Indians. The highest income group, native whites, conversely, has a lower mean score than any other group except the South Americans. Blacks and West Indians are also the most likely to participate regularly in their churches. Examination of the qualitative data suggests that the whites and Russians belong to professional associations; African Americans and West Indians belong to community-oriented organizations like sports leagues, church activities, and PTAs; and the Puerto Ricans and other immigrant groups are involved in ethnic-specific organizations and sports teams.

Fewer than one-tenth of our respondents belong to a political club, but African Americans, Dominicans, and West Indians are once more at the upper end of this distribution, while Russians, whites, and CEP are at the lower. In every group, more than half the respondents belong to some organizations, and these memberships connect them to relevant social worlds but not usually to the political system. This suggests that social network patterns, as well as attitudes and group grievances, shape political mobilization.

A plausible way to interpret these patterns of political attitudes and political participation across our study groups might be to say that members of second-generation groups who feel that they can make it without much discrimination from the white mainstream—specifically the Russians and Chinese—do not need to advance their interests through politics, while groups that do feel this threat and are connected to the civil rights movement—specifically African Americans and West Indians—do engage in politics as a way to advance or protect their group interests. Similarly, West Indians come from nations with democratic traditions, while the one-party regimes of China and the former Soviet Union did not foster political engagement among the first generation parents. The Latino case remains ambiguous, however. The low socioeconomic status of these groups works against participation, but they have also faced some degree of discrimination, which might work in favor of participation.

Multivariate Analysis

The scholarly literature on voting in America is, after all, mostly based on the experience of nonurban whites, since they make up the bulk of the national electorate and those questioned in such surveys as the National Election Studies. It would not be surprising if urban minority and immigrant groups, or even the native whites living among them, behaved and thought somewhat differently than this population. Statistical analysis readily confirms that factors that have a large impact among middle-class whites, such as age, gender, income, and education, do not explain as much about political attitudes and behavior among our respondents.

For example, using age, gender, education, and the log of weekly earnings for all of our respondents who were voting-age citizens at the time of the November 1996 presidential election to predict answers to the question about whether government officials care about people like the respondent produces an adjusted R^2 of only .024, with only more education being statistically associated with less alienation. Adding information about the racial or ethnic group background of the respondent lifts the adjusted R2 only to .033, with blacks and West Indians both significantly more alienated than native whites. Similarly, these four individual characteristics (age, gender, education, and income) do a poor job of explaining how many different groups respondents belong to (R2 of .030), although all four are statistically significant or nearly so. Native blacks are once again the only group statistically more likely to have more different types of memberships than whites.

To explore the likelihood of voting in the November 1996 presidential election, we began with the same four factors. Although the effect of these variables is in the expected direction (being older, female, better educated, and having higher earnings make one more likely to vote) and are statistically significant, this model also explained a relatively small amount of voting behavior. (The Cox and Snell R2 was .178 and increases to .210 when racial and ethnic backgrounds are included, suggesting that the groups behave differently even after taking basic individual characteristics into account.) African Americans remain strongly more likely to vote than whites, and West Indians remain about as likely, while Chinese and Russians are significantly less likely to vote than whites in this elementary model. (The Latino groups are also less likely to vote than whites, even after controlling for individual factors, but the difference is statistically significant only for Puerto Ricans.) In short, above and beyond age, gender composition, education, and income, something else about the overall situation of our young second-generation and native minority groups is driving their political attitudes and behavior.

If individual factors only begin to explain civic participation and voting, what other factors might tell us more? In particular, why are blacks not only the most alienated, which might be expected, but the most likely to vote, which might not be? Why are second-generation immigrants, especially Chinese and Russians, so unlikely to participate? To answer these questions, we explored whether having a child or being married; watching ethnic media and using a language other than English at home; labor force participation, including working at a unionized job; belonging to organizations and participating in church; parental concern with prejudice; respondents' own experiences of prejudice; and the use of various public facilities growing up explained more about participation. After examining such factors, we could then see whether group differences persisted even after they were taken into account.

Our results were as interesting for what did not explain political outcomes as for what did. For example, despite the fact that becoming a teen parent has a palpable negative impact on many other aspects of respondents' lives, it did not matter for their voting behavior. Nor, after taking respondents' education and earnings into account, did their parents' level of education or growing up in an intact family significantly shape their likelihood of voting. What our respondents said about problems as crime, neighbors not being willing to help, and so on in the neighborhoods where they grew up also had no relationship to their likelihood of voting. Finally, even when their parents told our respondents that they could not trust whites or needed to worry they would face prejudice, that did not make them any more or less likely to vote.

Other variables did contribute to the construction of a more robust model of political participation, however. Table 2 presents the results of an analysis of how our respondents' connectedness to the rest of the world influence voting. As expected, both having a job and getting higher earnings have clear positive effects on voting. Three other measures of social context are also important. Being a New York City resident favors voting. This is most likely because New York City politics dominates the media in the metropolitan area and more people are aware of what is going on and have some stake in the outcome. Using a library while growing up is not only a measure of civic education but also a measure of parental expectations about school performance. Finally, belonging to more types of groups is also significantly associated with voting. In short, being involved in institutions that tie the individual to the larger society around them promotes political engagement.

One's race and immigrant status both play a strong role. Being a member of one of the two black groups (or acknowledging African ancestry as a member of one of the Hispanic groups) has a strongly positive relationship to voting, while being the member of any second-generation group has a strongly negative impact. Conversely, even though they are eligible citizens, Puerto Ricans and those from the other second-generation backgrounds are much less likely to vote, especially the Chinese and Russians. This remains true even after taking a host of individual and organizational factors into account. At first sight, it may seem counterintuitive that the Chinese and Russians are least likely to vote, since these two second-generation groups are the most likely to be getting good college educations and entering professions. So, what is it about these group experiences that works for or against political participation?

Table 2   Binomial logistic model of voting (model extended to groups)

	B	S.E.	Wald	df	Sig.	Exp(B)
Age	.187	.013	213.029	1	.000	1.206
Female	.358	.091	15.361	1	.000	1.431
Education	.175	.020	79.256	1	.000	1.191
Working	.392	.104	14.282	1	.000	1.479
Log weekly earnings	.046	.018	6.658	1	.010	1.047
NYC resident	.303	.145	4.375	1	.036	1.353
Used library	.242	.078	9.625	1	.002	1.274
Belongs to groups	.187	.038	24.403	1	.000	1.206
CEP	−.473	.219	4.658	1	.031	.623
DR	−.495	.195	6.437	1	.011	.610
PR	−.411	.136	9.170	1	.002	.663
WI	−.177	.166	1.146	1	.284	.837
NB	.470	.127	13.626	1	.000	1.600
CH	−1.218	.291	17.548	1	.000	.296
RJ	−1.275	.423	9.087	1	.003	.279
Constant	−7.670	.436	309.579	1	.000	.000

Cox & Snell R^2 = .229; model predicts 71.8% of cases correctly.
Source: ISGMNY citizen voting-age respondents (in 1996) who grew up in metro New York and live in New York City.

Our respondents gave us important clues about the sources of these group differences. Blacks and West Indians are exposed to more racial hostility and discrimination from others, particularly whites, and are acutely aware of their history of racial subordination. They know that their movement toward political equality (indeed parity, if one considers that blacks hold more city offices than their share of the voting-age citizen population or the total population) has been achieved through the civil rights movement. Many African Americans work for government agencies or nonprofit organizations funded by government, while many West Indians work in the health-care sector or other social services also heavily dependent on public funding. Their group interests are deeply embedded in local politics. In short, they are part of the political establishment and see politics as a critical ingredient for protecting their interests, regardless of whatever differences West Indians and African Americans may have on specific questions like reliance on public assistance or who should represent West Indian neighborhoods.

The Chinese and Russians are in a rather different position. Unlike African Americans and West Indians, they both see themselves as outsiders to the political system and do not see political activity as particularly relevant to getting where they want to go. The dominant white mainstream does not regard the children of Russian Jewish immigrants as an outsider group, however. The Chinese also face less discrimination than the other groups, and, when they do experience it, it often comes from other minority and immigrant ethnic groups. Many regard politics not only as a corrupt world, but also as one that is a waste of time in terms of career advancement. Finally, the parents of both groups came from authoritarian one-party states. Both groups heard stories from their parents about how attracting the attention of the authorities could lead to bad outcomes.

However low the rates of political participation in New York City —and they are not high by the standards of white, middle-class suburbs—the city's political system is now producing new political leaders from immigrant backgrounds and greater inclusion of new immigrant minority groups among elected officials than are comparable jurisdictions like the city of Los Angeles (Logan and Mollenkopf 2003). As such, it is a fascinating laboratory for understanding the emergence of a new phase of urban democracy. Although we cannot say what the ultimate outcome will be, several things are clear from the evidence offered here. First, the racial and ethnic alignments inherited from previous generations continue to frame the political position or "opportunity structure" facing the new groups. West Indians seem likely, whatever their differences with African Americans, to make common cause with them, voting at relatively high rates for the same kinds of liberal citywide and national candidates, especially black candidates. Similarly, though their rates of participation and representation are significantly lower, Dominicans and even South Americans will merge with the gradually waning Puerto Rican population to form a larger Latino vote. But the Chinese and Russian second generation appear unlikely to adopt the high levels of political engagement of native whites, if for no other reason than that they think they will get little out of it.

Second, it seems likely that the older African American and Puerto Rican political traditions will be transformed as the new second-generation immigrant minority groups meld into them. No longer can these traditions point to the Civil Rights movement of the 1950s and 1960s as seminal events. Instead, native-born minority officials, together with emerging young second-generation political leaders, will have to forge a new rhetoric that encompasses the immigrant experience without being limited to it. Our qualitative interviews provide some grounds for optimism: when asked whether it was important to be represented by members of their own group, our respondents overwhelmingly replied that the ability of political leaders to relate to the problems of their communities was far more important than their particular ethnic background. Finally, however, our study suggests that these efforts face a major obstacle in the troublingly high level of alienation from and skepticism about local politics among all of these young people. Whether they will become more politically engaged as they grow older and take on more responsibilities in their lives, as some of them told us, will do much to define the future political terrain of the nation's largest city.

Notes

1. The estimates of ancestry and race for New York City and its electorate are drawn from the voter supplement of the November 2004 Current Population Survey, which interviewed households totaling 2,413 persons in New York City. As a result, the confidence interval around given number may be several percentage points.

2. It took African Americans and Puerto Ricans decades of political struggle to achieve this position. African Americans now serve as comptroller (the city's second most important office), the Manhattan and Queens Borough presidents, and council members in ten districts. The comptroller is actually a second-generation West Indian, but only rarely highlights his ancestry. Puerto Ricans serve as the Bronx Borough president and council members in eight districts. African American and Puerto Rican political power is thus far more modest than that of native-stock whites, but has largely achieved parity with voting strength in local legislative districts.

3. We thank the Russell Sage Foundation, the Andrew W. Mellon Foundation, the Rockefeller Foundation, the Ford Foundation, the United Jewish Appeal-Federation, and the National Institute of Child Health and Human Development for their support. The findings reported here reflect the views of the authors, not these organizations.

4. We interviewed about 400 respondents from each background and over-sampled Chinese to learn both about those whose parents came from the mainland and those from Taiwan or Hong Kong. Our Russian sample was restricted to about 300 respondents.

5. For an example of this study's research findings, see Waters, Kasinitz, and Mollenkopf 2002.

Plus Ça Change, Plus C'est la Même Chose?
An Examination of the Racial Attitudes
of New Immigrants in the United States

Tatishe Mavovosi Nteta

> If there were no black people here in this country, it would have
> been Balkanized. The immigrants would have torn each other's
> throats out, as they have done everywhere else. But in becoming
> American, from Europe, what one has in common with the other
> immigrant is contempt for me—it's nothing else but color. Wher-
> ever they were from, they would stand together. They could all
> say, 'I am not that.' So in that sense becoming an American is
> based on an attitude: an exclusion of me.
> —Toni Morrison, "On the Back of Blacks"

The influx of new immigrants since 1965 has led to a burgeoning literature in the social sciences that contrasts the political incorporation
of a new wave of immigrants, from Asia and Latin America, with previous waves of immigrants from Europe in the nineteenth and early
twentieth centuries. "Indeed, whether it is stated explicitly or not, today's discussion of immigrant incorporation is rife with comparisons
to what we know, or imagine that we know, about the experiences of
the pre-1924 immigrants" (DeWind and Kasinitz 1997). The central
debate in the literature revolves around the question of whether new
immigrants are incorporating at the same rate and in the same fashion
as previous waves of immigrants when examining naturalization rates,
level of partisanship, vote choice, identity-based organizing, and immigrant candidates and campaigns across time (Jones Correa 2002, de la
Garza and DeSipio 1997 Gerstle and Mollenkopf 2001, Wong 2002).

Lost in the debate regarding the comparative analysis of immigrant
incorporation has been the role of race in the political incorporation
of earlier European immigrants. As Toni Morrison points out, an important, if not necessary, process in the sociopolitical incorporation of

European immigrants was the acceptance and internalization of America's negative racial attitudes and norms regarding African Americans. These attitudes included the belief in the inherent biological inferiority of African Americans, support for racial segregation in all realms of public life, the denial of political equality to African Americans, and the subsequent distancing from African Americans among early European immigrants. Similar arguments regarding differentiation can be found in the work of scholars in the literature on whiteness (Roediger 1991, Jacobson 1998, Ignatiev 1995, Guglielmo 2003), all of whom point to the salience of the strategy of differentiation from African Americans as a central explanatory variable in the incorporation of Europeans in earlier waves of immigration.

This essay examines the role of race in the sociopolitical incorporation of new immigrants today. Do "new" immigrants engage in a strategy of differentiation from African Americans in an attempt to achieve full sociopolitical incorporation? To uncover if new immigrants are differentiating and distancing themselves from African Americans I look at one aspect of the strategy of differentiation: the expression of negative racial attitudes toward African Americans.[1]

Here I examine two sets of research questions. The first set of questions is descriptive in nature and asks what are the racial attitudes of new immigrants toward African Americans? Do these attitudes differ from native-born Asians, African Americans, Latinos, and whites? Here the focus is on racial stereotypes regarding African Americans, specifically stereotypes regarding the innate intelligence of African Americans and the supposed proclivity of African Americans to prefer welfare and engage in criminal activity. The second set of questions is more explanatory in nature and asks whether existing theoretical models of racial attitudes, used primarily to account for white racial attitudes toward African Americans, can help account for the attitudes of new immigrants. More specifically, do theories of contact, context, and group conflict help to account for negative racial attitudes among new immigrant groups, or are these theories only relevant to native-born whites? If not theories of contact, context, or group conflict, what model(s) better account for the racial attitudes of new immigrants?

The central argument of this essay is that new immigrants, in line with early European immigrants, are engaging in a process of differentiation from African Americans as expressed in the negative stereotyping of African Americans to achieve sociopolitical incorporation. However, existing theories of white racial attitudes that focus on contact, context, and group conflict fail to account for the racial attitudes of new immigrants because of the inability of these theoretical models to take into account the racial position of new immigrants, the exclusion of salient independent variables, and the disavowal of the impact of the process of immigrant incorporation. Immigrant-centered characteristics connected to sociopolitical incorporation better explain negative stereotyping among new immigrants, because the development of these characteristics reflect the process by which immigrant groups have historically incorporated norms revolving around race.

Racial Differentiation in the United States

What is differentiation? Differentiation was the process by which early European immigrants engaged in and expressed a variety of negative behaviors and attitudes toward African Americans. These attitudes and behaviors demonstrated their antipathy to African Americans as well as their acceptance of the existing racial structure that placed African Americans at the bottom of the racial order and whites at the top of this order. Moreover, these attitudes and behaviors were based in large part on those held by Anglo-Saxon whites, and social incorporation meant the increased adoption of attitudes and behaviors held by the native-born white population. Most important among these were the expression of negative and overzealous racial attitudes concerning African Americans relative to the native born, engaging in violent acts against African Americans, including riots against African American communities, restricting African Americans from various industries through the use of union leadership and intimidation, opposition to beneficial policies for African Americans, restriction of African American mobility in the housing market through the creation of neighborhood associations and housing covenants, and support for political parties and candidates that expressed opposition to African American interests, rights, and equality.

Thus, to be incorporated and accepted as American and white (and the benefits that were associated with such status), early European immigrants needed to boost their status position by distancing themselves from African Americans and to demonstrate their attachment to the norms, values, and practices of American society by supporting the existing racial landscape.

The question may naturally arise as to why differentiation succeeded as a strategy of sociopolitical incorporation for Irish, Italian, Polish, and Jewish immigrants. Three factors emerge as important in the successful use of differentiation as a strategy to achieve sociopolitical incorporation: the consolidation of political power through control of urban machines, the economic power expressed through control of unions and apprenticeships, and the alliance with the Democratic Party by these immigrant groups. The lesson learned from the experiences of these immigrant groups, and the Irish in particular, is that, in order for differentiation to be a success, immigrant groups must not only control the tools by which differentiation is achieved, but also provide incentives to the members of the dominant society to abandon their perception of immigrant groups as alien and inferior.

By the early twentieth century, immigrant groups, particularly the Irish, used the political resources at their disposal to gain control of urban machines in New York, Chicago, Boston, San Francisco, and Philadelphia (Erie 1988). With power over urban machines came control over thousands of patronage jobs, including police departments, fire departments, and housing authorities, which led to the use of these departments in sanctioning the process of differentiation from African Americans through the lack of protection of African Americans from acts of violence and housing segregation directed against their communities and citizens. Noel Ignatiev (1995), speaking of the connection between Irish control of police departments, relations with African Americans, and incorporation notes,

> the Irish cop is more than a quaint symbol. His appearance on the city police marked a turning point in Philadelphia in the struggle of the Irish to gain the rights of white men. It meant that thereafter the Irish would be officially empowered (armed) to defend themselves from the nativist mobs, and at the same time to carry out their own agenda against black people. (164)

By controlling the institutions responsible for protecting the rights of African Americans, these immigrant groups were able to engage in differentiation from African Americans with impunity and take an important step toward sociopolitical incorporation.

The second factor that led to the successful use of differentiation to achieve sociopolitical incorporation was the control over unions by these European immigrant groups. A core characteristic of the strategy of differentiation from African Americans is to exclude African Americans from industries dominated by these immigrant groups to bolster the status differential between the two groups and solidify their claim to being American and white. The exclusion of African Americans from the workplace was achieved in large part through control over labor unions by these groups, which vociferously opposed the inclusion of African Americans in various trades through the threat of or use of the strike as well as violence against African Americans who were hired in these industries (Roediger 1991, Massey and Denton 1993, Ignatiev 1995).

Finally, partisan politics also played a significant role in differentiation, as the Democratic Party allowed these immigrant groups to demonstrate their commitment to both the nation and its racial landscape. With the growing numbers of European immigrants arriving during the nineteenth and twentieth centuries, the Democratic Party saw an opportunity for electoral gain through the political mobilization of these groups. Using the lure of support for an inclusive notion of whiteness for all European groups (and the benefits and rights associated with inclusion as American and white) and opposition to nativism, the Democratic Party was able to garner the overwhelming support of these immigrant groups, particularly the Irish. "The Democratic emphasis on natural rights within a government 'made by the white men, for the benefit of the white man' appealed to Irish Catholics in large part because it cut off questions about their qualifications for citizenship" (Roediger 1991, 144). This alliance with the Democratic Party helped to undermine the perception of these immigrant groups as alien and inferior as well as providing a national forum for these immigrant groups to communicate their antipathy toward African Americans through support of Democratic candidates and policies that sought to keep African Americans in a subservient position.

Racial Attitudes and American Public Opinion

Today, scholarly attention on race relations is still focused on uncovering theoretical explanations of white racial attitudes toward African Americans, in line with the belief that America's racial problems are in essence attributable to white America. The literature on white racial attitudes has provided a number of theoretical explanations for the content of racial attitudes, including context, contact, and perceptions of group conflict/competition.

The first set of research findings focuses on contextual factors that lead to distinct racial attitudes toward African Americans. The most prominent theories have been the "power-threat" or "real-conflict" theories (Key 1949, Blumer 1958, Glaser 1994). These theories argue that the racial attitudes of a superordinate group (whites) become more hostile and negative when the size of a minority group (African Americans) increases, as a result, in large part, to perceived threats to socioeconomic position and political power that bolsters feelings of vulnerability among whites. These theories have been tested primarily in counties and metropolitan areas with large African American populations, and the overwhelming conclusion is that size of the African American population is connected with negative racial attitudes among whites (Glaser 1994, Taylor 1998).

A second set of research findings argues that social contact influences the content of white racial attitudes. Individuals who are exposed in some way to direct/personal contact with a member of a minority group will tend to espouse more positive racial attitudes relative to individuals who do not experience this contact (Bledsoe et al. 1995, Ellison and Powers 1994, Welch and Sigelman 2000). Thus, individuals who live or work in racially heterogeneous communities or workplaces will tend to hold more positive racial attitudes toward African Americans, in large part because of the ability of this contact to counteract the negative stereotypes of African Americans (Dyer et al. 1989, Lee 2000, Hum and Zonata 2000, Oliver and Wong 2002).[2]

The third set of research findings regarding the content of white racial attitudes revolves around perceptions of group conflict. This theoretical school argues that whites who strongly identify with their own racial group perceive high levels of conflict/competition between racial and ethnic groups over socioeconomic resources, political power, and/or status; or view African Americans as a threat to the current balance of resources, power, and status are likely to espouse more negative racial attitudes (Blumer 1958, Bobo 1999, Jackman and Muha 1984, Jackman 1994).

Although the primary focus in the literature on racial attitudes is on the attitudes of whites, increasingly attention has been focused on the racial attitudes of Asians, Latinos, and blacks (African, Caribbean, and Latin American) toward African Americans.[3] The most extensive analysis of the content of the racial attitudes of Asians, Latinos, blacks, and whites is Lawrence Bobo and colleagues' *Prismatic Metropolis* (2000). Using the 1993–94 Los Angeles Survey of Urban Inequality (LASUI), a survey that includes a large and representative sample of Asians, Latinos, whites, and blacks, they find that Asian and Latino respondents tend to believe that African Americans are poor, welfare dependent, and affiliated with drugs and gangs, while Latinos also are likely to believe that African Americans tend to practice racial discrimination.

Another study (Kim and Forman 2003) employs the LASUI to examine the content of the racial attitudes of Asians toward African

Americans and Latinos as well as the impact of four factors (social background, partisanship, social psychological factors, and contextual factors) on these attitudes. Nadia Kim and Tyrone Forman conclude that Asians direct more negative attitudes toward Latinos relative to African Americans and that Asians, relative to whites, hold more stereotypical attitudes toward African Americans and Latinos. In their multivariate analysis, they find that Koreans espouse more negative racial attitudes than the Chinese or Japanese do and that males, immigrants, Republicans, and light-skinned Asians also tend to have more negative racial attitudes.

Finally, Taeku Lee (2000) uses a combination of national, state, and local surveys on race relations and racial policies to examine the attitudes of whites, African Americans, Latinos, and Asians toward racial intermarriage, interracial friendships, neighborhood composition, racial discrimination, racial inequality, racial stereotypes, and racial policy preferences. With the focus of his article on Asians, Lee finds that the racial attitudes of Asians are characterized by heterogeneity, compared to the attitudes of whites and blacks, and that this greater heterogeneity results from the salience of ethnicity, length of residence, geographic region, nativity, and immigrant generation.[4]

What accounts for the racial attitudes of immigrants? Although the literature on incorporation does not directly deal with racial attitudes of immigrants, a central aspect of the process of incorporation of immigrants is the internalization and expression of the values, beliefs, and norms of the dominant society by new ethnic and racial groups. These values, beliefs, and norms can be said to include norms, values, and beliefs regarding race and race relations. If the espousal of negative racial attitudes regarding African Americans is an important part of the process of sociopolitical incorporation among immigrants, as I have suggested, immigrant-centered characteristics such as ethnicity, skin color, English proficiency, length of residence, contact with whites, and level of civic participation rather than contact, context, and group conflict, should help to account for the racial attitudes of new immigrants.[5]

Data and Findings

The data for this study come from the 1992–94 Multi-City Survey of Urban Inequality (MCSUI). The MCSUI was conducted from 1992 to 1994 in Atlanta, Boston, Detroit, and Los Angeles and contains two surveys, a survey of households and a survey of employers in each city. Households were selected based on a multistaged, stratified, clustered area-probability design, and in Boston and Los Angeles, Latinos, Asians, African Americans and low-income respondents were oversampled.[6] The survey employed face-to-face interviewers and was administered in English (Atlanta, Boston, Detroit and Los Angeles), Spanish (Boston and Los Angeles), Korean, Mandarin, Chinese, and Cantonese (Los Angeles only). There are a total of 8,916 respondents: 2,953 whites, 3,179 African Americans/blacks, 1,128 Asians, and 1,378 Latinos. There are 2,787 foreign-born respondents: 210 blacks, 324 whites, 972 Asians, and 1,778 Latinos.[7]

The dependent variable measures stereotypical attitudes toward African Americans through an index of items found in the MCSUI. In line with the literature on African American stereotypes, the index contained items that measure the belief that African Americans are involved in drugs/gangs/crime, unintelligent, and welfare dependent (Schuman et al. 1997, Gilens 1996, Bobo 2001).

Do the racial attitudes of today's immigrants, primarily from Asia and Latin America, reflect those of the Irish, Italian, Polish, and Jewish immigrants in regard to the use of the strategy of differentiation? A central indicator of differentiation was not only the expression of antipathy toward African Americans by European immigrant groups, but also the expression of an extreme antipathy toward African Americans when compared to the attitudes of Anglo Saxon whites. Table 1 examines the mean support for African American stereotypes among native and foreign-born Asians, blacks, Latinos, and whites, where −1 indicates complete belief in stereotypes and 1 indicates complete opposition to negative stereotypes. Across all stereotype items, the native born exhibit, relative to the foreign born, more "positive" attitudes toward African Americans. As table 1 demonstrates, foreign-born respondents exhibit more negative racial attitudes concerning African Americans relative to native-born respondents across the range of items that measure racial stereotypes. The clearest example of the relationship between nativity and racial attitudes is found in mean support for the index of stereotype items. This finding is replicated when examining nativity and race, with Latino, Asian, white, and black immigrants exhibiting more negative attitudes relative to their native-born brethren across the range of stereotype items.[8] The data presented in table 1 indicates that the foreign born, relative to the native born, exhibit more negative attitudes toward African Americans, indicating differentiation from African Americans.

Table 1   Mean scores for African American stereotypes among all respondents

	Intelligent	Welfare	Crime	Index
All respondents:				
Native born	−.1767	−.3494	−.6068	−.2416
	(4,414)	(4,427)	(4,308)	(4,412)
Foreign born	−.3995	−.7425	−.6680	−.6395
	(2,488)	(2,524)	(2,422)	(2,552)
Latino respondents:				
Native born	−.4615	−.6059	−.6855	−.5929
	(338)	(340)	(337)	(339)
Foreign born	−.4974	−.8752	−.7484	−.7921
	(1,556)	(1,603)	(1,518)	(1,616)
Asian respondents:				
Native born	−.5455	−.5672	−.7364	−.6090
	(132)	(134)	(129)	(133)
Foreign born	−.6730	−.9001	−.7389	−.8171
	(795)	(821)	(743)	(842)
White respondents:				
Native born	−.3426	−.3842	−.5800	−.2978
	(1,795)	(1,809)	(1,757)	(1,820)
Foreign born	−.2690	−.4433	−.5396	−.3045
	(290)	(291)	(278)	(289)
Black respondents:				
Native born	.0189	−.2689	−.6147	−.1206
	(2,167)	(2,164)	(2,102)	(2,140)
Foreign born	−.0348	−.4673	−.4573	−.2293
	(201)	(199)	(199)	(205)

Note: Sample size in parentheses.
Each variable scaled −1 to 1, with −1 indicating a negative view of African Americans and 1 indicating a positive view of African Americans.

Traditional Models of Differentiation

Do existing models of white racial attitudes, specifically contact, context, and group conflict, help to account for the attitudes of native-born whites and immigrants?[9] Table 2 tests the utility of contact, context, and group conflict models on native-born whites and immigrant groups, where the dependent variable is an index of racial stereotypes regarding African Americans measured 0 to 1, with 0 indicating

Table 2 OLS regression models for African American stereotypes—traditional models

	Native whites	All immigs.	Asian immigs.	Latino immigs.	White immigs.
Los Angeles	−.04*	−.07+	.15	−.06	.06
	(.016)	(.042)	(.092)	(.054)	(.079)
Boston	.02	.02	.13	.02	.04
	(.017)	(.050)	(.080)	(.064)	(.079)
Male	.00	−.04+	−.03+	−.03+	−.00
	(.013)	(.019)	(.020)	(.015)	(.050)
Age	.06*	.00	−.03	−.01	−.02
	(.027)	(.040)	(.044)	(.032)	(.109)
Education	.04	−.00	−.04	−.03	.02
	(.026)	(.037)	(.041)	(.033)	(.092)
Income	.01	−.00	.03	.01	−.07
	(.022)	(.030)	(.031)	(.029)	(.093)
Working	.02	−.02	−.04+	−.01	.04
	(.015)	(.021)	(.024)	(.017)	(.050)
Republican	−.02	.00	.02	.02	−.01
	(.015)	(.022)	(.023)	(.021)	(.075)
Ideology	−.06*	−.03	−.00	−.05	.08
	(.028)	(.038)	(.043)	(.030)	(.093)
Race of interviewer	−.05**	N/A	−.12*	−.04*	.03
	(.017)		(.055)	(.018)	(.051)
Contact	.06+	.03	−.01	−.04	.198
	(.033)	(.074)	(.095)	(.057)	(.167)
African American neighborhood	.03	.04	−.12	−.00	.04
	(.029)	(.067)	(.138)	(.035)	(.149)
Group conflict	−.11***	.02	−.01	.05+	.05
	(.024)	(.037)	(.044)	(.029)	(.094)
Latino		.00			
		(.047)			
White		−.05			
		(.066)			
Black		−.07			
		(.075)			
Asian		−.13+			
		(.072)			
N	632	284	184	393	62
Constant	.524	.549	.356	.418	.462
R²	.101	.245	.126	.052	.194
Adjusted R²	.082	.200	.060	.020	−.020
Standard error	.15658	.14355	.12777	.14370	.16718

+p < .10 *p < .05 **p < .01 ***p < .001

Note: Figures listed are unstandardized regression coefficients and standard errors. All variables coded 0–1.

support of negative stereotypes about African Americans and 1 indicating full opposition to these stereotypes.

Contact. Contact is measured through various items that sought to uncover the extent of contact with African Americans for each respondent in their social network and place of employment. The literature on white racial attitudes argues that contact with African Americans is likely to lead to higher levels of opposition for negative stereotypes of African Americans among whites, because contact with African Americans undermines many of the supposed characteristics associated with these stereotypes. Table 2 tests the utility of the theory of contact among native whites and immigrant groups. As table 2 demonstrates, among white respondents, contact with African Americans does lead native white respondents to oppose negative stereotypes regarding African Americans. However, when examining the attitudes of immigrant groups, contact across immigrant groups is not a significant predictor of attitudes toward African Americans in line with initial expectations regarding the inability of contact to account for the racial attitudes of immigrant groups.

Context. Context is measured using an index of items that tapped the racial composition of the respondent's neighborhood derived from the sampling strata used by the authors of the MCSUI. In line with expectations of the literature on white racial attitudes, living in a predominately African American neighborhood should lead to the support of negative attitudes toward African Americans because of the supposed threat that larger African American populations could have on control over economic and political power within the neighborhood. Surprisingly, context is not a significant predictor of attitudes toward African Americans among native-born whites, as seen in table 2. Similar to native-born whites, context is not a significant predictor for any immigrant group under study.

Group conflict. Group conflict is measured using an index of items that examined the perception of racial group competition in the arenas of both local politics and employment. The literature on white racial attitudes argues that individuals who see high levels of competition and conflict with African Americans are likely to express negative racial attitudes toward African Americans. Table 2 tests the utility of group conflict for native-born whites and immigrant groups. Perceptions of group conflict are a significant predictor for native-born whites and Latino immigrants. In line with expectations, native-born whites who perceive high levels of competition and conflict express support for negative stereotypes of African Americans. Interestingly, among

Latino immigrants, perceptions of group conflict and competition lead to the expression of opposition to negative stereotypes regarding African Americans.

The results for native Whites and Asian, Latino, and white immigrants indicate that the existing theoretical models, particularly contact, context, and group conflict have more success in accounting for the attitudes of native-born whites relative to new immigrant groups. This is especially true for Latino immigrants, when examining the size of the explained variance (R-squared). For Latino immigrants, these models account for only 5 percent of the variation in racial attitudes toward African Americans. In short, for the majority of immigrant groups, contact, context, and group conflict have no significant impact on the racial attitudes of immigrants toward African Americans. However, do immigrant-centered characteristics associated with sociopolitical incorporation, specifically ethnicity, length of residence, English proficiency, civic participation, and contact with whites better account for the racial attitudes of new immigrants toward African Americans? The next section deals with this very question.

Immigrant-based Models of Differentiation

Do immigrant-centered characteristic connected to sociopolitical incorporation help to better account for the racial attitudes of new immigrants? Table 3 tests the effect to ethnicity, length of residence, skin color, English proficiency, civic participation, and contact with whites on the racial attitudes of new immigrants toward African Americans.

Ethnicity. Ethnicity is measured by response to the ethnic category offered by the MSCUI interviewers among Latino and white immigrants and in response to the question regarding the language spoken at home among Asian immigrants.[10] The expectation derived from the disparate literature on immigrant racial attitudes is that ethnic groups that have had contentious relations with African Americans relative to those groups that do not have these relations are likely to express more negative views of African Americans. These groups include Koreans, Puerto Ricans, and Mexicans (Morawska 2001a, Kim and Forman 2003, Lee 2000). Table 3 uncovers little support for the influence of ethnicity on racial attitudes toward African Americans among any of the ethnic groups selected, indicating that ethnicity in and of itself does little to account for racial attitudes among new immigrants.[11]

Length of residence. Length of residence is measured by the response to the question asking respondent how long have they lived in the

Table 3 OLS regression models of African American stereotypes for immigrants—differentiation models

	All immigs.	Asian immigs.	Latino immigs.	White immigs.
Male	−.03**	−.03 +	−.01	−.01
	(.013)	(.016)	(.017)	(.047)
Age	.02	−.03	.09*	.07
	(.030)	(.036)	(.042)	(.119)
Republican	−.00	−.00	−.02	.02
	(.016)	(.019)	(.029)	(.062)
Ideology	−.04	−.02	−.030	−.06
	(.026)	(.033)	(.030)	(.087)
Education	−.05 +	−.08**	.01	.01
	(.027)	(.031)	(.045)	(.120)
Income	−.01	−.00	−.02	−.21*
	(.022)	(.025)	(.043)	(.096)
Working	−.02	−.04*	.00	.00
	(.014)	(.018)	(.017)	(.046)
Los Angeles	−.05*	.05	−.14	.01
	(.024)	(.062)	(.164)	(.068)
Race of interviewer	N/A	−.06	−.13***	−.01
		(.043)	(.020)	(.048)
Chinese	N/A	.03	N/A	N/A
		(.059)		
Japanese	N/A	.06	N/A	N/A
		(.063)		
Korean	N/A	.01	N/A	N/A
		(.061)		
Mexican	N/A	N/A	.03	N/A
			(.040)	
Salvadoran	N/A	N/A	.01	N/A
			(.043)	
Guatemalan	N/A	N/A	.03	N/A
			(.046)	
Puerto Rican	N/A	N/A	−.02	N/A
			(.088)	
English	N/A	N/A	N/A	.04
				(.216)
Eastern European	N/A	N/A	N/A	−.10
				(.107)
Yrs in U.S.	−.04	−.04	−.01	−.13
	(.027)	(.034)	(.034)	(.105)

Table 3 (*continued*)

	All immigs.	Asian immigs.	Latino immigs.	White immigs.
Skin color	.03 (.023)	−.02 (.033)	−.02 (.025)	.12 (.078)
English proficiency	.07* (.028)	.06 + (.037)	.04 (.035)	.18 (.126)
Neighborhood association	.00 (.021)	.01 (.031)	−.07* (.033)	−.02 (.075)
PTA	−.00 (.015)	−.00 (.019)	−.03 + (.018)	.02 (.048)
Political organization	.07* (.029)	−.01 (.046)	−.04 (.061)	.08 (.088)
Church organization	.01 (.013)	.01 (.017)	.00 (.019)	.09 + (.048)
Eth /cult organization	−.00 (.018)	.01 (.023)	.05 + (.030)	−.02 (.076)
White contact	.02 (.019)	.04 (.026)	.03 (.026)	−.05 (.060)
Latino	.02 (.026)	N/A	N/A	N/A
White	−.03 (.039)	N/A	N/A	N/A
Black	−.03 (.041)	N/A	N/A	N/A
Asian	−.10* (.044)	N/A	N/A	N/A
N	609	339	449	99
Constant	.475	.368	.509	.335
R^2	.224	.102	.143	.227
Adjusted R^2	.197	.043	.099	.024
Standard error	.14324	.12698	.15521	.17951

$^+ p < .10$ $^* p < .05$ $^{**} p < .01$ $^{***} p < .001$

Note: Figures listed are unstandardized regression coefficients and standard errors. All variables coded 0−1.

United States. It is measured from 0 to 1, where 0 indicates a new immigrant and 1 indicates a long-term immigrant. In line with the literature on sociopolitical incorporation, the more years an immigrant spends in the United States, the more likely that individual will reflect and internalize the norms, beliefs, and values of the dominant society, and these include norms, beliefs, and values regarding race and race relations (Barkan 1995, Alba and Nee 1997). Thus, we should expect that long-term immigrants are more likely to express negative stereotypes toward African Americans in line with the continued negative stereotyping by native-born whites (Schuman et al. 1997; see also Farley 1996, Kinder and Sanders 1996). However, across immigrant groups, length of residence was not a significant predictor of racial attitudes toward African Americans.

Skin color. Skin color is measured using a subjective assessment of the skin color of the respondent made by the interviewer, where 0 is a dark-skinned respondent and 1 is a light-skinned respondent. Kim and Forman (2003) have found that skin color, specifically lighter-skinned Asians relative to darker-skinned Asians, express more negative attitudes toward African Americans. This finding reflects the dominance of skin color hierarchies both here in the United States and abroad, as well as the tendency of lighter-skinned Asian, blacks, and Latinos to hold higher socioeconomic and political positions relative to their dark-skinned brethren (Rothman 2003; Menchaca 2001; Wagatsuma 1968).

The expectation is that among new immigrants, light-skinned respondents are more likely to express negative attitudes toward African Americans, while the darker-skinned respondents, who are more likely to be victims of the discrimination and prejudice experienced by African Americans, will express more positive attitudes toward African Americans. Table 3 tests the utility of skin color on immigrant racial attitudes. Here, skin color is not a significant predictor of racial attitudes toward African Americans across immigrant groups.

English proficiency. English proficiency is measured by self-identification on a scale that asks respondents how well they speak English, where 0 is cannot speak English at all and 1 is can speak English very well. Given that language skills are a proxy for educational attainment among new immigrant groups, the expectation is that higher levels of English proficiency will lead to opposition to negative stereotyping of African Americans among new immigrant groups. Among all immigrant groups, English proficiency is positively related to racial attitudes such that higher levels of proficiency lead to opposition to negative stereotyping of African Americans. English proficiency is a significant predictor of racial attitudes among all immigrants and Asian immigrants as seen in table 3.

Civic participation. Civic participation is measured by responses to items that tap whether the respondent has attended one or more meetings of the PTA, a block association, a political organization, a church group, or an ethnic/cultural organization in the past year. In line with the literature on sociopolitical incorporation, individuals who are more likely to participate in a civic organization are also more likely to reflect the norms, values, and beliefs of the dominant society, including the norms, values, and beliefs regarding race, race relations, and racial groups. Thus, individuals who are highly engaged with civic organizations are more likely to support negative stereotyping of African Americans in line with the continued negative stereotyping of African Americans by native whites.

As seen in table 3, among Latino immigrants, involvement in neighborhood associations, ethnic and cultural organizations, and the PTA are significant predictors of racial attitudes, as is involvement in church organizations among white immigrants. Interestingly, involvement in ethnic/cultural associations and church organizations, unlike involvement in neighborhood associations and the PTA, is positively related to racial attitudes for Latino and white immigrants respectively, indicating that not all forms of civic participation lead to the espousal of negative stereotypes regarding African Americans for Latino and white immigrants.

White contact. Contact with whites is measured using an index of six items that tap the level of contact with whites in the workplace and in the respondent's social network. New immigrants who have a high level of contact with whites are more likely to be exposed to and eventually internalize the norms, beliefs, and values of whites concerning issues such as race, according to the literature on sociopolitical theory (Barkan 1995, Alba and Nee 1997). Thus, it is likely that, with higher levels of contact with whites on the job and in social settings, new immigrants are more likely to support negative stereotyping of African Americans. As table 3 shows, among all immigrant groups, contact with whites is not a significant predictor of racial attitudes toward African Americans.

Discussion

This analysis examined three sets of research questions. First, are new immigrants engaging in differentiation from African Americans as indicated by their racial attitudes toward African Americans? Examining the racial attitudes of new immigrant groups, it is clear that new immigrant groups do indeed engage in negative stereotyping of African Americans. More important, when compared with the native born, new immigrants tend to express more negative attitudes toward African Americans, indicating that these groups are indeed engaging in one means of differentiation from African Americans, the expression of negative racial attitudes. However, this analysis only uncovers evidence of one aspect of differentiation. To fully determine if new immigrants are indeed differentiating from African Americans, future research must examine the behavior of these immigrant groups, particularly the incidence of violence between immigrant groups and African Americans, the active restriction of African Americans from economic industries dominated by immigrant groups, active residential segregation of African Americans by these groups, and political opposition to policies, candidates, and political parties that support African Americans by these groups.

It is also important to determine if these groups have the socio-economic and political power to engage in the strategy of differentiation. As noted above, European immigrants could successfully use the strategy of differentiation, because they in large part controlled the means by which differentiation and distancing could be accomplished. Do today's immigrant groups from Latin America and Asia hold similar powers over the urban bureaucracy, labor unions, and political parties that allow these groups to control the means by which differentiation can be accomplished? There is evidence that Latino and Asian immigrant groups are increasingly gaining a foothold in these areas as a result, in large part, of their numerical strength in various urban municipal institutions, unions, and political parties (Jones-Correa 2000, Defreitas 2003, Cain et al. 1989; Lien et al. 2001). Future research should focus on the increasing clout immigrant groups have in these institutions in order to fully account for the use of the strategy of differentiation among new immigrant groups.

The second set of questions examined in this analysis relate to whether existing theoretical models of white racial attitudes account for the racial attitudes of new immigrants. I hypothesized that contact, context, and group conflict, developed in large part to account for the attitudes of native-born whites toward African Americans, will explain the attitudes of native-born whites, but do not account for the attitudes of new immigrants. This analysis finds mixed support for my hypothesis. Among native-born whites, contact and group conflict are significant predictors of racial attitudes, but context is not. Among all immigrant groups, contact and context have no statistically significant effect on racial attitudes. However, among Latino immigrants, group conflict does have a significant impact on racial attitudes.

What accounts for the weak relationship between context and racial attitudes for both native-born whites and new immigrant groups? These results regarding context could reflect the small number of white respondents who live in African American neighborhoods. These results could also reflect the sea change in the composition of cities as immigrant groups, particularly Asian and Latino immigrants, have replaced native-born whites as the most likely groups to live in close proximity to African Americans. However, even though the majority of new immigrants live in America's urban areas, a small percentage of these new immigrants, primarily those with low levels of economic and social capital, live in predominately African American neighborhoods. This has led Douglas Massey and Nancy Denton to note that, "within a large, diverse, and highly mobile post-industrial society such as the United States, blacks living in the heart of the ghetto are among the most isolated people on earth" (1993, 77).

As a result, context could no longer be a significant predictor of either white racial attitudes toward African Americans, given high levels of "white flight" or the racial attitudes of new immigrants who live in closer proximity to African Americans relative to native-born but typically live in adjacent neighborhoods to African Americans. Future research should seek to enlarge the sample size of new immigrants and native-born whites living in African American neighborhoods to uncover the influence of context on racial attitudes toward African Americans.

In line with expectations, contact with African Americans is a significant predictor of positive racial attitudes among native-born whites. However, among new immigrants, contact is not a significant predictor, and contact leads to the expression of more negative assessments of African Americans among Latino and Asian immigrant groups. These results could reflect the distinct, contentious, and competitive experiences between African Americans and immigrant groups (relative to whites and African Americans) for employment opportunities, in the workplace, and in the political arena in America's urban centers. "As in the private sector and in the neighborhoods themselves, the competition between African Americans and Latinos for public jobs and political influence generates mutual resentment and negative stereotyping" (Morawska 2001a, 60). Thus, contact with African Americans among immigrant groups could be viewed as a combative experience, in large part, because of animosity expressed by both immigrant groups and African Americans in competition for scarce social, economic, and political resources in urban centers, leading to the bolstering and expression of negative stereotypes regarding African Americans. Future research should focus on the ways in which not only contact, but also the animosity directed at immigrants by African Americans, might affect the racial attitudes of new immigrants.

An unexpected finding of this study regards Latino immigrants and group conflict theory. For Latino immigrants, perceptions of group conflict are a significant predictor of racial attitudes toward African Americans. This is not entirely surprising, given the real conflict between African Americans and Latinos in urban centers for political power and employment (McClain and Karnig 1990, McClain 1993, Meier and Stewart 1991, Tate 1993). What is surprising is that Latino immigrants who perceive high levels of competition with African Americans also are more likely to espouse more positive racial attitudes toward African Americans relative to Latino immigrants who do not perceive a high level of competition. This finding could reflect the possible relationship between perceptions of competition and commonality among Latino immigrants in the arenas of education, income levels, racial segregation, racial discrimination, and crime. In short, although Latino respondents viewed African Americans as competition for jobs and political influence, the expression of negative racial attitudes might be stunted by the belief that the groups face the same socioeconomic barriers in urban areas. These barriers might better explain the status of African Americans relative to traditional stereotypes that supposedly account for this status. Again, further research is warranted to uncover the relationship between group conflict and racial attitudes among Latino immigrants, particularly in uncovering perceptions of commonality with African Americans.

The final set of research questions relate to whether immigrant-related factors account for the racial attitudes of new immigrants. This analysis indicates that there is a relationship between racial attitudes and measures of English proficiency and civic engagement among new immigrants. This suggests that attitudes toward race, and African Americans in particular, are part of the process of sociopolitical incorporation, but these measures operate in different ways, according to the immigrant group.

Among white immigrants, involvement in church organizations is an important predictor of racial attitudes, with immigrants who are involved in church organizations more likely to express more positive views of African Americans. Among Asian immigrants, higher levels of English proficiency lead to more positive expressions of attitudes toward African Americans. Among Latino immigrants, involvement with ethnic/cultural organizations leads to expression of more positive attitudes toward African Americans. These findings indicate that the strategy of differentiation in today's racial landscape does not mean the expression of negative racial attitudes toward African Americans, but that sociopolitical incorporation might be contingent on embracing racial attitudes that are in line with existing norms that stress racial equality and dismiss biological inferiority, innate differences, and continued racial stereotyping.

Conversely, among Latino immigrants, involvement in both neighborhood organizations and the PTA are significant predictors, but have a negative relationship with racial attitudes. Latino immigrants who are highly involved in these types of civic organizations are also more likely to express negative attitudes toward African Americans. These findings lend credence to the possibility that today's immigrant groups are involved in the process of differentiation through the expression of negative racial attitudes toward African Americans: *plus ça change, plus c'est la même chose.* At the same time, other measures of immigrant adaptation indicate that negative attitudes toward African Americans diminish across immigrant generations.

To uncover the true relationships that exist between incorporation and racial attitudes, future research must employ better measures of incorporation that include identification with national identity, level of homeland interests, level of residential integration, and immigrant generation. We also need better measures of English proficiency and civic engagement to uncover the processes whereby language skills and involvement in local organizations influence racial attitudes. More data collection efforts with an eye toward immigrant adaptation and racial differentiation will help us better assess the comparability of new immigrants and earlier waves of European immigrants with respect to questions such as: Where do negative racial attitudes come from? What motivation/justification do immigrants have for maintaining (or changing) these attitudes? How do new immigrants view the role of race in the process of becoming American, and are immigrant racial attitudes based on notions of biological inferiority or cultural differences? The answers to these questions will further our understanding of the processes of incorporation among America's new and old waves of immigration and the role of race in these various processes.

Appendix: Variable Coding Schemes

This appendix provides information regarding how each of the variables in question was measured in the essay.

Dependent Variable

The dependent variable is an index of three items that measure stereotypical attitudes toward African Americans in the MCSUI with regard to intelligence, welfare utilization, and involvement in drugs and gangs. Index scores range from −1 to 1, where −1 is holding negative racial stereotype regarding African Americans and 1 is holding positive stereotype regarding African Americans. Scale reliabilities (alpha) of this index were .42.

Independent Variables

All independent variables were coded on a 0 to 1 scale.

Male: Dummy variable where 0 is female and 1 is male.

Age: Continuous variable where 0 is eighteen years old and 1 is ninety-five years old.

Republican: Measured by self-identification on a seven-point scale and coded 0 to 1, where 0 is all other (Democrat, Independent, No preference) and 1 is Republican.

Ideology: Measured by self-identification on a seven-point scale and coded 0 to 1, where 0 is extremely conservative and 1 is extremely liberal.

Income: Continuous variable, where 0 is income bracket $0–20,000 and 1 is more than $80,000.

Education: Continuous variable, where 0 is no degree received and 1 is PhD or other professional degree.

Working: Dummy variable, where 0 is not working and 1 is working

Race of interviewer: Dummy variable, where 0 is all other races and 1 is the race of the interviewer.

Years in the U.S.: Continuous variable, where 0 is a new immigrant (immigrated in past ten years) and 1 is an old immigrant (immigrated over forty years ago).

Skin: Measured based on subjective perspective of interviewer. Continuous variable, where 0 is dark skin and 1 is light skin

English proficiency: Measured by self-identification on a five-point scale and coded 0 to 1, where 0 is cannot speak English at all and 1 is can speak English very well

Civic engagement: An index of five items that measure the level of civic engagement, with participation in Neighborhood or tenant's group or block association, PTA or school-related groups, political organizations, church-related groups, and ethnic or cultural organizations

White contact: An index of six items that measure contact with whites, relating to employment, social relationships, and neighborhood activities. Scale reliabilities (alpha) of this index were .90.

Registered to vote: Dummy variable where 0 is not registered to vote and 1 is registered to vote.

Citizen: Dummy variable where 0 is a noncitizen and 1 is a naturalized citizen.

Contact: An index of six items that measure contact with African Americans, relating to employment, social relationships, and neighborhood activities. Scale reliabilities (alpha) of this index were .90.

Group conflict: An index of two items that measure perceptions of group conflict and zero sum relations between races, relating to employment prospects and political influence. Scale reliabilities (alpha) of this index were .84.

African American neighborhood: An index derived from the MCSUI sampling strata within cities, where African American neighborhood was coded as >50 percent (Boston), high-density black (Detroit), black (non) Poverty (Atlanta & Los Angeles). 0 represents all other neighborhoods and 1 represents African American neighborhoods.

Notes

I would like to thank Jill Greenlee, Taeku Lee, Karthick Ramakrishnan, Ricardo Ramírez, Rachel Van-Sickle Ward, and Kevin Wallsten for their helpful comments and suggestions throughout the evolution of this paper.

1. It is important to note that although the strategy of differentiation is most clearly seen in the behaviors of immigrant groups toward African Americans, a necessary component of differentiation is support for negative racial attitudes toward African Americans that undergird the behavior of immigrants toward African Americans.

2. Clearly, this theory contradicts the findings of the power threat theory; yet as Wong and Oliver (2002) argue, the unit of analysis of power threat theory tends to be metropolitan areas rather than neighborhoods and workplaces.

3. Although these studies do not focus solely on immigrant attitudes, because of the large percentages of immigrants within these larger racial groups, they do provide a good starting point in analyses of the racial attitudes of Asian, black, Latino, and white immigrants. According to the Census Bureau, 40 percent of the 35.5 million Latinos in the United States are foreign born, 69 percent of the 10.2 million Asians, 6 percent of the 211 million whites, and 6 percent of the 34 million blacks.

4. Lee finds that almost all Asians (with the exception of Filipino Americans) are opposed to racial intermarriage with African Americans, 40% of Chinese and Filipino Americans had friendship ties outside their group, and Filipino, Koreans, and Vietnamese respondents were more likely to live in racially heterogeneous neighborhoods.

5. These variables are in line with the research on Latinos and Asians that have found that ethnicity, length of residence, and skin color are significant predictors of attitudes among these groups.

6. It is important to note here that not all survey questions were asked in all cities. As a result, respondents from Detroit were not included in this analysis because of the lack of response to questions involving African Americans.

7. In the survey (except in Los Angeles), Latinos were initially asked to select their race and then were asked a question regarding Spanish or Hispanic origin leading to a number of Latinos among blacks, whites, Asians, and Native American categories.

8. It is important to note that across the range of stereotype items, the mean score for most items is below 0, indicating the likelihood that respondents believe at least somewhat in the stereotype in question. This finding is in line with the literature on white racial attitudes that argues that whites maintain stereotypical views of African Americans in the post–civil rights movement era (Schuman et al. 1997; see also Farley 1996, Kinder and Sanders 1996).

9. Unfortunately, because of the small number of black immigrants (>25), they were not included in this analysis

10. Unfortunately, the MCSUI does not differentiate among East Asian respondents when asking about ethnicity. Thus, to see differences among Korean, Japanese, and Chinese respondents, I used this proxy for ethnicity.

11. Ethnic groups were selected based on theoretical considerations as well as sample size (>25).

The Political Assimilation of the Fourth Wave

Kathryn Pearson and Jack Citrin

As a nation of immigrants, the United States has always confronted the challenge of balancing unity and diversity. By bringing strangers into one's land, to use John Higham's evocative phrase (1985), large-scale immigration poses a potential threat to the sense of shared identity that is the foundation of nationhood. When America faced this challenge as a result of European immigration in the nineteenth and early twentieth centuries, intense political conflicts arose over how many and what sort of immigrants to allow into the country and how to absorb the cultural outsiders who had already arrived. By abolishing the racist national origins system and greatly increasing the level of immigration, the Immigration and Nationality Act of 1965 and subsequent legislation have transformed the ethnic composition of American society.

These demographic changes renewed the normative and empirical debates about the consequences of immigration, both for the American political system and for immigrants themselves. Will ongoing immigration result in cultural balkanization and the fragmentation of the national interest (Schlesinger 1991; Brimelow 1995; Huntington 2000, 2004a)? Will the Hispanic and Asian immigrants blend into the "melting pot" as their European predecessors ultimately did (Alba 1990)? Or will changes in the legal and political climate beginning in the 1960s facilitate the maintenance of native customs and values in a multiethnic society? And what are the processes that encourage the involvement of immigrants in political life through naturalization, voting, and participation in civic organizations (Jones-Correa 2002, Citrin and Highton 2002, Ramakrishnan 2005)?

As indicated by the editors' introduction to this volume, assimilation is a unifying theme in these questions about contemporary immigration. Assimilation as a scholarly concept and government policy emerged in the nineteenth century as one model for managing ethnic relations in the United States. *Webster's New World Dictionary of the American Language* defines "to assimilate" as "to make similar to." This definition leaves open the question of who is being made similar to whom with regard to what. Nonetheless, the phrase "to make" implies agency, and the following dictionary entry for the term "assimilationism" is "the policy of completely absorbing minority cultural groups into the main cultural body." It is this meaning of assimilation that evokes intense controversies in American politics. On a normative level, is assimilation a desirable process that creates a sense of community and national purpose in a diverse society or a coercive policy that tears people emotionally, socially, and intellectually from their cultural origins? And on an empirical level, are the new immigrants blending into the mainstream and is the process of assimilation the same across immigrant groups and in all regions of the country?

By any definition, assimilation refers to change over time. Ethnic differences erode as immigrants and their offspring are exposed to and absorb the dominant habits of their new country (Portes and Rumbaut 2001, Jones-Correa 2002). The standard "straight-line" hypothesis thus predicts that successive immigrant generations, whatever their national origins, increasingly will resemble each other, socially and culturally. On the assumption that native-born Americans of European origin are the carriers of these mainstream values, this would mean that third-generation Latinos should be more similar to native-born whites than are recent Latino immigrants. The same should be true for immigrants from Asia, Africa, Eastern Europe, and so forth. Both the melting as cleansing and melting as blending models of assimilation assume the gradual homogenization of ethnic groups through socioeconomic integration and acculturation.

But there are two alternative possibilities derived from an interpretation of American identity that rejects the notion of a single mainstream culture. According to multiculturalist thinkers (Lukes and Joppke 1999), the persistence of distinct ethnic subcultures imported by immigrants is what makes America unique. New immigrants gradually adopt the norms of the native-born members of their own ethnicity rather than an overarching national outlook. In other words, the "assimilation to what" question is answered differently, depending on one's ethnic origin. This hypothesis of several parallel assimilatory tracks would be consistent with the emergence of a distinctive pan-ethnic Asian-American viewpoint; the absorption of West Indian immigrants into the larger, native-born African American community (Rogers 2000a); and the integration of diverse Spanish-speaking groups into a common Latino collectivity (Abramson 1980).

Alejandro Portes and Ruben Rumbaut (2001) discount such fears of cultural separation, while emphasizing that the promise of economic mobility embedded in the idea of assimilation may not apply to today's immigrants who face a less-favorable labor market than their European predecessors did. For Latino and Asian immigrants asking the question "assimilation to what," Portes and Min Zhou (1993) present a segmented path with two destinations: the traditional mainstream culture of the white middle class and the oppositional culture of a minority underclass in which self-reliance and educational achievement are downplayed.

The melting pot model predicts that today's immigrants will follow their European predecessors and assimilate materially and psychologically. The idea of "segmented assimilation" holds that some, perhaps even a majority of Latino immigrants, will be pushed by economic failure or ideological choice to retain their ethnic identities and maintain strong ties to their home countries. Deciding which of these paradigms best approximates the actual experience of late-twentieth-century immigrants can only be answered when we have evidence about their children and grandchildren. This essay makes a modest start by analyzing California public opinion surveys that include information about the nativity and citizenship of immigrants from both Latin America and Asia. The analyses of patterns of political self-identification, political participation, attitudes toward government, and selected policy preferences assess the extent to which prevailing patterns in the political incorporation of immigrants fit this dominant, "straight-line" model of assimilation for American ethnic relations.

Dimensions of Assimilation: Structural, Cultural, and Political

Milton Gordon's seminal *Assimilation in American Life* (1964) outlines a multidimensional conception of assimilation. His primary distinction is between structural assimilation—involving the large-scale entry of native minorities and immigrants into the economic, social, and political institutions of the "host" society and ultimately leading to intermarriage—and cultural assimilation, involving the adoption of the dominant values and customs of American popular culture. In the political domain, cultural assimilation implied endorsing the national creed of democracy, equality, and individualism, and identifying oneself as an American (Gordon 1964, Salins 1997). Gordon believed that structural assimilation would inevitably lead to cultural unity. However, cultural assimilation is both easier and faster, because it can be achieved without the permission of the majority group. Moreover, cultural assimilation can occur even if ethnic groups retain, whether by choice or not, formal and informal ethnic associations and social institutions. In *Beyond the Melting Pot* (1993), Nathan Glazer and Daniel Moynihan pointed to the persistence of institutional rather than cultural pluralism among European ethnic groups, and this remains the circumstance for African Americans who to this day are structurally apart (Glazer 1997).

To what extent are the post-1965 immigrants assimilating into American society? This empirical study of immigrant assimilation concentrates on a particular aspect of the cultural dimension of the process: political attitudes and behavior. Because conflict and disagreement are defining features of political life, the question of "assimilation to what" may appear especially problematic in this domain. If homogeneity among groups differing in national origin is the end of the process, the idea of political assimilation seems to deny the legitimacy of political preferences founded on membership in cultural, linguistic, religious, or racial groups. Indeed, a maximal definition of political assimilation expresses the liberal (and Marxist) expectancy that, in modern states, affiliations based on social class supersede ethnic identifications (Glazer and Moynihan 1975). In our view, this is too stringent a requirement for the existence of political assimilation. The concept itself assumes the existence of group norms, or a dominant political culture, so we can adopt a more-restricted definition of political assimilation as adherence to just those values and behaviors that define the dominant conception of what it means to be an American (Citrin, Reingold, and Green 1990; Smith 1997; Gleason 1980).

Clearly, the contours of American national identity are contested (Smith 1997). Nevertheless, a number of the criteria we employ recur in virtually all the leading conceptions of assimilation (Salins 1997, Huntington 1983): a primary self-identification as an American rather than as a member of a particular ethnic group, patriotism, acceptance of the national creed of democracy and individualism, and belief in the importance of learning English. The image of the melting pot as an ideal is a more-contested norm, but we investigate the degree to which immigrants themselves embrace the value of cultural assimilation as part of a process of adopting a common identity as "nationals" as well as or rather than "ethnics."

We also treat political involvement as an indicator of assimilation. Rogers Smith (1997) has outlined a civic republican model of American identity in which membership in the national community is expressed through political interest and participation. Like patriotism, civic engagement can be considered a consensual ideal, if not a common practice. Many scholars use the term "incorporation" rather than assimilation when studying the political activities of immigrants. A broad definition of these activities would include not just naturalization, voting, and electoral activities, but also participation in voluntary organizations and appointment to political and administrative positions (Jones-Correa 2002).

While some of these activities, such as naturalization, registering to vote, or joining the League of Women Voters are, in principle, politically neutral, others, such as running for office or donating to a campaign, are, by nature, partisan, so the concepts of incorporation and assimilation are not identical. Civic engagement is an official virtue in the United States, but it also represents the process through which immigrants have achieved political representation, often using ethnic political mobilization as a means of gaining acceptance in mainstream institutions.

In turning to attitudes toward government and what it should do, we enter the domain of politics, where conflict rather than consensus prevails. When it comes to specific public policies, such as questions about government spending or abortion rights, divisions within as well as across ethnic groups are to be expected. This is where assimilation, in the sense of increased homogeneity among ethnic groups, implies the replacement of ethnic divisions over time by cleavages based on class, gender, generation, or other categories that cut across ethnic lines.

Assimilation is a process that takes time; whether today's Latino and Asian immigrants are assimilating is a question about the future. Absent longitudinal data about particular immigrants, our current, tentative inferences about assimilation therefore rest on comparisons of immigrant generations. The standard hypothesis is that assimilation occurs through exposure to American culture and institutions. Hence, Gordon's presumed link between structural and cultural assimilation means that the frequency and duration of contacts with the host country's institutions should result in exposure to and, derivatively, a greater acceptance of mainstream values and customs. The second generation should be more assimilated than the foreign born, the third generation more assimilated than the second, and so forth. Similarly, new immigrants should be more likely to assimilate the longer they live in the United States.

Among the factors that are hypothesized to facilitate political assimilation are the immigrant's *personal skills and resources,* such as speaking English and having a middle-class occupation; his or her opportunities to acculturate, the immigrant's *motivations,* such as the persistence of gratification based on engagement in homogeneous ethnic networks and associations; and the similarity between the individual's native culture, including the political culture and that of the United States (Glazer and Moynihan 1975, Jones-Correa 2002). One important question in the study of immigration today is whether there is a single immigrant experience or whether the extent and speed of assimilation, in all its varied aspects, depends on one's region or country of origin. The present research pays particular attention to comparing people of Latino and Asian background. The ability to do so allows us to refine and extend recent analyses of ethnic group relations in the more complex environment engendered by immigration patterns (Oliver and Wong 2003, Welch and Sigelman 2000, Hochschild and Rogers 2000).

Data and Method

The main source of data for this study comes from the series of statewide surveys conducted by the Public Policy Institute of California (PPIC) between 1998 and 2002. PPIC conducts six to eight surveys a year, so pooling the data from these numerous separate samples of 2000 or more respondents provides a very large initial pool of respondents. These surveys used a computer-generated sample of telephone numbers to ensure both listed and unlisted numbers were called. Telephone numbers in the survey sample were called up to ten times to increase the likelihood of reaching eligible households. Respondents were age eighteen or older and included both citizens and noncitizens. Those who identified themselves as Hispanic could choose the language of the interview: 17 percent of all respondents were interviewed in Spanish. All Asian, white, and black respondents, including immigrants, were interviewed in English, so it is important to acknowledge that some group differences may reflect variation in the initial level of assimilation as a result of the sampling.

Nevertheless, pooling the PPIC surveys makes it possible to obtain large enough numbers of respondents—in some cases more than

20,000—to systematically compare immigrant and native-born residents of Latino, Asian, and European background. Because some questions were asked repeatedly in PPIC surveys and others more episodically, the number of respondents fluctuates with the specific dependent variable considered. Nevertheless, these data are a rich resource for the study of contemporary immigration, given that California is the main destination for newcomers to the United States. We supplement these data by reporting relevant results from the *Washington Post/Kaiser Family Foundation/Harvard University Latino Survey* conducted in the summer of 1999, the Los Angeles County Social Surveys (LACSS) conducted by UCLA (Citrin et al. 2002, Pearson and Citrin 2002), and from the Pew Hispanic Center's National Latino Survey of 2002.

The statistical technique used in multivariate analyses to assess assimilation is simple. We analyze homogeneity across ethnic groups, with predicted outcomes for each group based on statistical models that control for various demographic factors. We divide each ethnic group by immigrant generation, distinguishing among foreign-born noncitizens, naturalized citizens, and native-born respondents. We briefly describe the frequency of selected attitudes and political behaviors among these groups and then employ multivariate analysis to estimate the effects of ethnicity, nativity, and citizenship status of these indicia of assimilation in the California surveys, including controls for gender, education, income, and age.

National Identification

In the United States, nationality and ethnicity are overlapping group identities. Whether and when they compete and which group membership is prioritized are empirical questions. Nationalists insist that when the chips are down, attachment to the nation should dominate all other affiliations, including those based on race, religion, or language. One stated reason for restricting immigration throughout American history is that newcomers would retain potentially subversive loyalties to their country of origin (Higham 1985). As Peter Salins (1997), Milton Gordon (1964), and other advocates of assimilation assert, becoming an American entails defining oneself first as an American, and only then as a member of a specific ethnic group, and developing strong feelings of patriotism.

Several recent studies of Latino and Asian Americans indicate that this process is occurring. The Los Angeles County Social Survey

(LACSS) asks respondents whether they view themselves mainly as "just an American" or as members of a particular ethnic group. Pooling the results for the 1994, 1995, and 1997 surveys, Jack Citrin and colleagues (2002) found that whites are virtually unanimous in choosing the overarching national self-identification, but also that more than two-thirds of African American, Latino, and Asian American respondents do so as well. When given a choice, however, the modal self-identification for ethnic minorities is a hyphenated identity: they prefer to designate themselves as "both an American and a member of an ethnic group." However, the longer one's tenure in the United States, the more likely one is to opt for the assimilated "just an American" self-categorization: 61 percent of third-generation Latino and Asian respondents in the LACSS do so, compared to just 20 percent of the naturalized citizens and only 4 percent of noncitizen immigrants (Citrin et al. 2002, 14).

These results are consistent with two other studies of Asian and Hispanic political self-identification. In the Pilot National Asian American Political Survey, a multiethnic, multilingual, and multicity study of 1,218 adults eighteen years or older residing in five major population centers, respondents were asked how they identified themselves, *in general,* and were given the choices of American, Asian American, Asian, ethnic (e.g., Chinese or Korean American), or just one's national origin. The authors of this study, Pei-te Lien, Margaret Conway, and Janelle Wong (2003), report that 61 percent of the sample chose some form of American identity: 12 percent of this sample chose the American identity, 15 percent opted for the pan-ethnic Asian American, 34 percent preferred a hyphenated national-origin American self-designation. Of the remainder, 30 percent chose the purely ethnic identity.

In keeping with the assimilation model, U.S.-born Asians were much more likely to identify simply as American (33 percent) than respondents born in Asia (5 percent), and among third-generation Asian immigrants, fully 43 percent made a purely American national identity their choice. Both structural and cultural integration fostered identification as an American. Asian respondents who mainly spoke English at home and at work, supported intermarriage, participated in Asian American events, were naturalized citizens, and had a longer family history in the United States were more likely to choose the "just American" self-categorization than those lacking these attributes. Also consistent with the assimilation model is the finding that participation in purely ethnic organizations, being educated outside the

United States, and the experience of racial discrimination led people to prefer a purely ethnic self-identification.

The 2002 Pew National Survey of Latinos reaches a similar conclusion. Native-born Hispanics are much more likely than foreign-born Hispanics to describe themselves as American (90 percent to 32 percent). Among the foreign born, the likelihood of describing oneself as American increases with income, education, and the tendency to speak English more than Spanish, along with arriving in this country at a young age (Brodie et al. 2002, 24). Structural and linguistic assimilation clearly enhances a sense of American national identity.

The LACSS data indicate that thinking of oneself as "just an American" boosts feelings of patriotism, as measured by questions about whether one feels proud to be an American, loves America, and is moved by the sight of the American flag (Citrin et al. 2002, 10). In fact, after controlling for political self-identification, Latinos are *more* likely to express pride in America than any other ethnic group, including whites. Predictably, the native-born and naturalized first-generation immigrants express more pride in America than more recent, noncitizen immigrants.

Several studies (Pearson and Citrin 2002; Citrin, Reingold, and Green 1990) have shown that white Americans overwhelmingly believe that speaking English is very important for making someone "a true American." In the 2000 national General Social Survey, Latinos were significantly less likely to express this belief, but this too varied by immigrant generation. Second-generation Latinos—native-born children of foreign-born parents—were more likely than those whose parents were also born in the United States to emphasize the importance of speaking English, a possible indication of their own experience in assimilating and gaining acceptance from other ethnic groups (Pearson and Citrin 2002, 15). The 2002 Pew National Latino Survey confirms the presence of a pragmatic consensus among Latinos that speaking English is important to succeed in the United States: 91 percent of foreign-born Latinos and 86 percent of the native-born Latinos express this opinion (Brodie et al. 2002, 44). While Latinos of all immigrant generations consistently are more likely to favor bilingual education programs and oppose English-only laws than whites (Pearson and Citrin 2002), the evidence is overwhelming that they, along with immigrants from all regions, accept the status of English as the nation's common language and see that their children and grandchildren learn it.

Cultural and Social Integration

Historically, the political debate over assimilation centered on whether immigrants had to shed their native customs. Recent studies of public opinion, however, indicate that ordinary Americans may not regard cultural assimilation and cultural pluralism as incompatible (Citrin, Sears, Muste, and Wong 2001). When asked whether racial and ethnic minorities should blend into the mainstream or retain their native cultures, a plurality chose the idea of the melting pot. Blacks, Latinos, and Asians are more likely to opt for the position of preserving one's ethnic heritage, but many respondents in every ethnic group find it difficult to choose, opting for a middle position or volunteering the answer "both."

In the surveys analyzed here, respondents again were asked whether they believe minority groups should change so they blend into the larger society as in the idea of a melting pot or maintain their distinct cultures. The results generally confirm that there is support both for the assimilation of immigrants and the retention of diverse cultural identities. The national survey asked two separate questions about whether it was important for Latinos (and minority ethnic groups) to assimilate or maintain their distinct cultures.[1] In fact, the correlation between the two questions was only .06, strong evidence for Peter Salins's (1997) claim that the prototype of assimilation in America combines the adoption of many American values and customs with the retention of elements of one's original ethnic heritage.

The PPIC surveys of Californians asked the more conventional question in which respondents had to choose between blending into the mainstream and maintaining one's original culture as the best policy for minorities. Overall, respondents preferred the melting pot option, with whites (72 percent) being more favorable to this position than blacks (64 percent), Latinos (63 percent), and Asians (53 percent). Differences by immigrant generation tend to be small, although in both the California and national surveys, *white* noncitizen immigrants are more reluctant to endorse the idea of the melting pot than others in this ethnic group.

The PPIC surveys also asked respondents how often they met people from other racial groups. First-generation immigrants, regardless of whether they were white, Latino, or Asian, were less likely to say they "often" met people from other racial groups, a finding consistent with the common observation that one's first home in a new country is likely to be an ethnic enclave. Not surprisingly, higher levels of education facilitated contact with other groups. In addition, among Latinos, those interviewed in Spanish were significantly less likely to report frequent contacts with members of other groups. Overall, then, to the extent that interethnic contacts are indicators of assimilation, the generational differences observed in these data suggest that the process is proceeding among the fourth wave.

To estimate more precisely how ethnicity and immigrant status influence the trajectory of assimilation, we conducted a multivariate analysis that included age, education, and income as controls. Table 1 reports the results of a logit regression for the dichotomous "melting pot" item and an ordinary least squares regression for the question asking respondents how often they met people from other racial and ethnic groups. Rather than presenting regression coefficients, which have little meaning by themselves, we calculated predicted probabilities for each independent variable holding age, education, and income at their sample means. The predicted probabilities and standard errors are calculated using Gary King's CLARIFY program for Stata (Tomz, Wittenberg, and King 1999), are expressed in percentage terms except for those cases where the outcomes have a range of values other than zero to one.

Table 1 reports the predicted values for the assimilationist outcomes of believing that different racial and ethnic groups should blend into the larger society and meeting members of other groups "very often." We compare respondents grouped by ethnicity, nativity, and citizenship, holding age, and education at the sample means, and the figures with asterisks in the table represent the predicted probabilities and estimated values that differ significantly at p < .05 from the estimate for the baseline group of native-born whites. The results indicate that native-born Asians and naturalized first-generation Latino immigrants are significantly more in favor of ethnic groups maintaining their own culture than are native-born whites, a finding contrary to the prediction of the straight-line assimilation model. Noncitizen white, Latino, and Asian immigrants, however, are as likely to endorse the melting pot idea as native-born whites, suggesting that whatever the level of support for multiculturalist ideology among ethnic minorities in the United States, there is little evidence today's immigrants, wherever they come from, reject the value of cultural adaptation. Finally, the frequency of contact with member of other ethnic groups does reflect a pattern of greater social assimilation over time:

Table 1 Predicting beliefs about assimilation and social contacts of ethnic and immigrant groups

	Melting pot (% in agreement)	Meet people of other races (1 = min, 4 = max)
Whites		
Native-born	70 (04)	3.85 (.06)
Naturalized citizens	79 (08)	3.70 (.10)
Noncitizens	62 (15)	3.62 (.15)
Native-born blacks	62 (06)	3.74 (.18)
Latinos		
Native-born	68 (04)	3.81 (.09)
Naturalized citizens	59* (07)	3.50* (.10)
Noncitizens	63 (07)	2.83 (.09)
Asians		
Native-born	53* (10)	3.91 (.13)
Naturalized citizens	56 (08)	3.47* (.11)
Noncitizens	66 (13)	3.45* (.17)
Constant	47	3.57
-2*Log-likelihood	2,019	
χ^2	39.76	30.88
Pseudo R^2	.02	
Adjusted R^2		.19
N	1619	1718

*$p < .05$

Note: Table entries in column one are logit predicted probabilities calculated, using Clarify, and entries in column two are expected values computed, using Clarify. Dependent variables are described in essay appendix. Estimated standard errors are in parentheses. White native-born citizens is the excluded group. Controls include income, age, and education (held at their mean) and sex. Data come from Public Policy Institute of California survey.

immigrant Latinos and Asians are significantly less likely to report meeting people of other races than native-born members of these ethnic groups.

Political Participation

Political participation is an important way for immigrants to learn about American politics and society. Participation in civic life not only brings immigrants into contact with other groups but also provides opportunities for focusing official attention on their distinctive needs and problems. Because only citizens are eligible to vote, naturalization is a necessary first step for immigrants to undertake this kind of political activity. But noncitizens are able to participate in other ways, such as writing letters to public officials or attending meetings and rallies. Nevertheless, lower socioeconomic status, a lack of fluency in English, and other cultural barriers deriving from socialization experiences in undemocratic societies that discourage political activity may depress participation by immigrant groups (Ramakrishnan and Espenshade 2001, Citrin and Highton 2002). Lower voter turnout rates among Latinos and Asians in the United States are partly the result of the large number of foreign-born citizens in these ethnic groups and partly the result of the distribution of personal resources and civic attitudes that predispose one to vote.

The PPIC surveys asked about additional forms of civic engagement beyond voting, including interest in politics, writing letters to public officials, and involvement in election campaigns. The familiar ethnic differences in political participation emerge: native-born whites are more likely to be politically interested and active than Latinos and Asians. Whatever their ethnic origin, first generation immigrants—particularly noncitizens—are predictably less politically interested or engaged than the native born. For example, of the native-born Latinos, 59 percent say they are very interested in politics, compared to 41 percent of the noncitizens immigrants. Among Asian respondents, the equivalent figures are 59 percent for the native born and 47 percent for noncitizen immigrants.

Table 2 reports the predicted probabilities and expected values for the various ethnic groups broken down by nativity and citizenship, with the other demographic predictors held at the sample means. Regardless of ethnicity, being foreign born or a noncitizen significantly lowers the probability of active engagement in election campaigns, as measured by a three-item Participation Index.[2] Asian and Latino

Table 2 Predicting the civic engagement of ethnic and immigrant groups

	Participation index (0 = min, 1 = max)	Write representative (%)	Interest in politics (0 = min, 4 = max)
Whites			
Native-born	.69 (.03)	31 (02)	2.94 (.01)
Naturalized citizens	.56* (.06)	33 (04)	2.94 (.03)
Noncitizens	.33* (.12)	28 (07)	2.76* (.04)
Native-born blacks	.71 (.06)	24* (03)	2.93 (.02)
Latinos			
Native-born	.61* (.04)	25* (03)	2.91* (.02)
Naturalized citizens	.57* (.05)	27 (04)	2.94 (.02)
Noncitizens	.49* (.05)	08* (03)	2.90* (.02)
Asians			
Native-born	.67 (.08)	24 (04)	2.79* (.03)
Naturalized citizens	.44* (.07)	20* (03)	2.72* (.03)
Noncitizens	.30* (.13)	10* (05)	2.63* (.04)
Constant	−.10	−300	2.15
Adjusted R^2	.12		.09
−2*LLR		5526	
Pseudo R^2		.11	
χ^2		690.92	
N	5,217	5,207	36,623

*$p < .05$
Note: Column one and three table entries are expected values; column two entries are predicted probabilities computed using Clarify, as explained in the text. Estimated standard errors are in parentheses. Dependent variables are described in essay appendix. White native-born citizens is the excluded group. Controls include income, age, and education (held at their mean) and sex. Data come from the Public Policy Institute of California 1998–2002.

immigrants also are significantly less likely than the baseline group of native-born whites to have written a letter to an elected representative or to have a high level of interest in politics. However, table 2 also confirms the "Asian anomaly" of lower political interest among the native born among this ethnic group than their socioeconomic resources would predict (Ramakrishnan and Espenshade 2001, Citrin and Highton 2002).

The Kaiser/Harvard/*Washington Post* national survey asked Latino respondents about their participation in Latino organizations and activities directed at helping Latino political candidates, including volunteering and making campaign contributions. We combined these three items into a summed index, with scores ranging from 0 to 3, of participation in Latino politics. Multivariate analysis found that first-generation immigrants were significantly less likely to report involvement in Latino electoral politics than third-generation Latinos were. In addition, fluency in and use of English were negatively related to involvement in Latino politics specifically. Spanish-dominant Latinos were more likely, all else equal, to participate in Latino politics. For reasons of space, we do not report the findings here. To apply Portes and Rumbaut's phrase in another context, this hints at a segmented path of political incorporation in which more complete assimilation to the cultural mainstream, at least linguistically, directs political activities away from a purely ethnic context. However, given that English-language use increases dramatically after the first immigrant generation, the overall support for the straight-line assimilation model still stands. Additional analysis of the PPIC data for Latino respondents confirms that knowing English (as measured here by language of interview) boosts one's interest and participation in politics.

Attitudes toward Government and Policy Preferences

Americans historically have combined intense patriotism with suspicion of governmental power (Huntington 1983). Adult immigrants are not necessarily exposed to this mix of values in their political socialization. On the one hand, they often come from traditional societies whose dominant cultural outlook is more deferential to authority in general, but, on the other hand, they are also a self-selected population with the sufficient degree of self-reliance and determination to settle in another country. How these outlooks interact with objective economic circumstances in shaping their expectations of governmental assistance is an open question. We investigate how ethnicity and nativity interact to influence trust in government, preferences about the size of government, and ideological self-identification as either a liberal or conservative. An obvious point is that these attitudes are central to the enduring division between Republicans and Democrats, so it is misleading to posit any position as part of a common cultural identity that functions as a standard of assimilation. The guiding question here is whether immigrants diverge from the native-born members of their own ethnicity.

The data reveal significant ethnic differences in political trust, as measured by the standard American National Election Studies question, "How often do you trust the government in Washington to do what is right?" Because responses to this item are strongly influenced by feelings about the incumbent president and his policies (Citrin and Green 1986), the data are presented separately for the pooled 1998–2000 surveys, when President Bill Clinton was in office, and the 2001–2002 studies, which captures the George W. Bush presidency and the shift in opinion after the events of 9/11. During both administrations, Latinos expressed more trust in government than the other ethnic groups. For example, the PPIC 1998–2000 data show that 41 percent of Latino respondents said they trusted the national government to do what is right always or most of the time, compared to 37 percent of the Asian respondents, 29 percent of the African Americans, and 27 percent of the whites. With the exception of blacks, all ethnic groups expressed more trust after 9/11, but Latinos remained the most trusting group. Moreover, Latino and Asian immigrants were more trusting than the native-born members of their ethnic groups. Indeed, fully 23 percent of Latino noncitizen immigrants surveyed by PPIC in 2001–2002 said they trust the government to do what was right "just about always." Only 6 percent of the native-born whites gave this response.

As revealed in table 3, these ethnic group differences remain statistically significant after the imposition of controls for social background. For example, during the Clinton era, the expected value for noncitizen Latinos on the four-point trust in government item was 2.76, compared to only 2.29 for native-born whites and 2.33 for native-born blacks. Similarly, regardless of nativity and citizenship status, Asian respondents were more trusting than either whites or blacks between 1998 and 2000. After the election of George W. Bush, however, this pattern holds only for Latinos, an interesting result, suggesting that partisanship plays a lesser role in determining beliefs in the trustworthiness of government among Latinos than the other groups.

Table 3 Predicting the political trust and political ideology of ethnic and immigrant groups

	Trust in government (Clinton era) (1 = min, 3 = max)	Trust in government (Bush era) (1 = min, 3 = max)	Support larger government (%)	Conservative ideology (1 = min, 5 = max)
Whites				
Native-born	2.29 (.02)	2.37 (.03)	17 (03)	3.26 (.02)
Naturalized citizens	2.27 (.05)	2.45 (.06)	22 (06)	3.22 (.04)
Noncitizens	2.37 (.08)	2.33 (.09)	29 (11)	3.03* (.06)
Native-born blacks	2.33 (.04)	2.17* (.05)	36* (06)	3.11* (.04)
Latinos				
Native-born	2.43* (.03)	2.49* (.04)	24* (04)	3.15* (.02)
Naturalized citizens	2.70* (.04)	2.74* (.05)	43* (08)	3.29 (.03)
Noncitizens	2.76* (.04)	2.88* (.05)	68* (08)	3.44* (.03)
Asians				
Native-born	2.39* (.06)	2.42 (.06)	29 (09)	3.16* (.04)
Naturalized citizens	2.51* (.05)	2.46 (.06)	30* (07)	3.24 (.04)
Noncitizens	2.63* (.10)	2.42 (.09)	37 (15)	3.15* (.05)
Constant	2.38	2.52	−57	3.30
Adjusted R^2	.06	.06		.03
−2*LLR			2000.78	
Pseudo R^2			.11	
χ^2			251.67	
N	7,010	5,142	1,652	39,284

*$p < .05$

Note: Entries in columns one through three are expected values; entries in column four are predicted probabilities computed using Clarify, as explained in the text. Estimated standard errors are in parentheses. Dependent variables are described in essay appendix. White native-born citizens is the excluded group. Controls include income, age, and education (held at their mean) and sex. Data come from the Public Policy Institute of California 1998–2002.

Along with the results of the 1999 Kaiser/Harvard/*Washington Post* survey showing that trust in government among Latinos declines from one generation to the next, these data do indicate that recent Latino (and to a lesser extent Asian) immigrants express more trust in government than does the native-born population (Baldassare 2003). This may reflect a more generalized disposition to defer to authority among immigrants or a belief that to express trust in government is a form of indicating loyalty to one's new country, or, perhaps, just a cautious tendency of immigrants to "keep one's head down." Assimilation to American culture, it seems, makes one more cynical about government, a conclusion reinforced by the finding in PPIC data that English-language ability among Latino respondents is significantly related to less trust in government.

The patterns of ideological self-identification and preferences for a larger government providing more services rather than a smaller government that costs less are more nuanced. As the expected values reported in table 3 show, first-generation Latino and Asian immigrants are more likely to favor a "larger government" than either native-born members of their own ethnic group or whites, even after one controls for the social background variables that may capture the need for more public services. This preference does not, however, extend to white immigrants, who do not differ significantly from native-born whites. In addition, a preference for the liberal position on the size of government among first-generation Latino immigrants is not reflected when it comes to their overall ideological identification. Here, noncitizen Latinos are significantly more likely to call themselves *conservative* (3.44) than native-born Latinos (3.15) or native-born whites (3.26). Interestingly, noncitizen white immigrants (3.03) are significantly more likely to call themselves liberal.

Synthesizing these findings with those regarding the development of a sense of national identity yields an image of assimilation with two faces. Over time, the attitudes of today's immigrants come to resemble those of the modal American. This is a critical citizen who combines patriotism with cynicism toward politicians and government officials. The traditional deference to authority—political as well as familial—seems to erode with exposure to life in America. At the same time, the preferences of immigrants regarding what government should do in the way of providing services conforms to the pattern of ethnic differences prevailing in the public as a whole.

The disappearance of ethnic differences in issue positions is too strict a test for successful political assimilation, because ethnicity can function as a marker for distinctive group interests, as when government policy allocates benefits to favor members of a particular race or religion. Some issues may cue ethnic identifications that unite people across immigrant generations and ideological outlook, whereas other issues are governed by broader partisan and philosophical predispositions. As an example, proposals to restrict immigration and foreign policy decisions with consequences for one's country of origin may engage ethnic identifications in a way that environmental and budget issues do not.

In investigating the connections between ethnicity, immigrant status and policy preferences among PPIC respondents, we considered issues that vary substantially in how directly they engage group identities and interests. These range from approval of restricting legal immigration and Proposition 227, a statewide ballot measure that severely limited the scope of bilingual education California, at one end of the continuum, to beliefs about abortion rights at the other.

The results confirm previous studies (Citrin et al. 2001), showing that whites (58 percent) more strongly favor reducing the current level of immigration into the United States than either blacks (50 percent), Asians (34 percent), or Latinos (31 percent). However, first-generation immigrants, particularly the noncitizens who tend to be the most recent arrivals, are the strongest proponents of maintaining or increasing the current, high levels of immigration, a pattern of support that reflects both validation of a group identity and a tangible interest in the potential immigration of other family members. Recent Latino immigrants (43 percent) also were less supportive of Proposition 227 than any other group in the sample, including Asian noncitizens (71 percent) and white noncitizens (88 percent).

Table 4 presents the expected values and predicted probabilities for the issue positions of ethnic and immigrant subgroups after the usual adjustment for social background. Regardless of ethnicity, immigrants are more approving of a liberal immigration policy than native-born whites are, as are native-born Asians and Latinos. The predicted probabilities of support for Proposition 227 among native-born (62 percent), naturalized (57 percent), and noncitizen Latinos (47 percent) are significantly lower than among native-born whites (81 percent).[3] However, Asians, regardless of nativity, did not significantly differ from whites in their level of approval for the antibilingual education initiative.

Not surprisingly, affirmative action tapped ethnic differences before differences in immigrant generation. Blacks, Latinos, and Asians, with

Table 4 Predicting policy preferences of ethnic and immigrant groups

	Support increasing immigration (1 = min, 3 = max)	Support for Prop. 227 (%)	Support for affirmative action (1 = min, 3 = max)	Opposition to abortion (1 = min, 3 = max)
Whites				
Native-born	1.53 (.05)	.81 (.02)	1.73 (.06)	1.38 (.05)
Naturalized citizens	1.54 (.11)	.78 (.05)	1.66 (.14)	1.46 (.11)
Noncitizens	2.20* (.20)	.87 (.07)	1.87 (.22)	1.14 (.19)
Native-born blacks	1.67 (.09)	.78 (.03)	2.45* (.10)	1.40 (.08)
Latinos				
Native-born	1.79* (.07)	.62* (.04)	2.30* (.07)	1.59* (.07)
Naturalized citizens	2.0* (.09)	.57* (.05)	2.33* (.10)	1.79* (.08)
Noncitizens	2.16* (.08)	.47* (.05)	2.09* (.11)	1.89* (.09)
Asians				
Native-born	1.77* (.14)	.77 (.06)	2.03* (.14)	1.26 (.13)
Naturalized citizens	1.89* (.11)	.74 (.05)	2.05* (.13)	1.53 (.12)
Noncitizens	1.82* (.14)	.83 (.06)	2.00 (.22)	1.86* (.15)
Constant	1.70	1.07	1.93	1.52
Adjusted R^2	.11		.15	.07
Pseudo R^2		.06		
−2*LRR		3726		
χ^2		234.66		
N	1,685	3,403	1,690	1,772

*$p < .05$

Note: Table entries in columns one, three, and four are expected values; table entries in column two are predicted probabilities; standard errors are in parentheses. Dependent variables are described in essay appendix. White native-born citizens is the excluded group. Age, education, and income are included as controls, held at their mean. Controls include income, age, and education (held at their mean) and sex. Education is excluded from models two and three. Data come from the Public Policy Institute of California 1998–2002.

the exception of noncitizen Asian immigrants, expressed significantly higher levels of support for affirmative action than all groups of whites. Blacks were the strongest supporters of affirmative action. All Latinos expressed much higher levels of support than whites, but support for affirmative action among naturalized and native-born citizens was higher than among noncitizens. Among Asians, citizenship status increased support for affirmative action.

Latinos in general, perhaps because they are predominantly Catholic, were significantly more likely to oppose the idea of leaving abortion as a choice for a woman and her doctor to make in all circumstances. However, this tendency was strongest among the most recent, noncitizen immigrant Latinos. Noncitizen Asians were also significantly more likely to adopt an antiabortion position than whites, blacks, or native-born Asians. On both this ostensibly nonethnic issue and the issue of support for stricter environmental protection, we find more evidence of increasing ethnic homogeneity as immigrant streams are exposed to American political controversies. Overall, support for abortion rights is weaker among Latinos and Asians than whites. But this difference is predominantly a function of the more conservative views of first generation immigrants. Indicators of structural assimilation—more years of formal education and a higher income—are predictors of support for broad abortion rights, the dominant position among white elites. This suggests that ethnic differences in policy preferences are more likely to persist—or even grow—on issues, like affirmative action, immigration, or language policy, that have a clearer salience to distinctive group interests and identities. In other domains, assimilation is more rapid and intragroup differences reflect a similar pattern in most ethnic groups.

Conclusion

Advocates of assimilation emphasize the utility of a shared culture for national solidarity and the achievement of collective purposes. Those who question this goal point to its psychological and social costs. Our focus here is empirical. We asked whether recent Latino and Asian immigrants to the United States are assimilating in the political domain. Any analysis of assimilation requires deciding how to answer the "assimilation to what" and "assimilation to whom" questions. Here we isolated four sets of dependent variables—national identity and support for a common culture, civic engagement, general attitudes about government, and selected policy preferences.

Although most of the survey data we report are confined to California, the available national surveys generally are consistent with our results. When it comes to developing a strong sense of national attachment and belief in the value of a common culture, we provide some evidence that Latino and Asian immigrants are assimilating. As tenure in the United States increases, so does self-identification as "just an American" rather than as a member of a particular ethnic group, patriotism, belief in linguistic assimilation, and acceptance of the melting pot as an appropriate model of cultural development. Whatever the level of support for multiculturalist ideology among ethnic minorities in the United States, there is little evidence that immigrants, wherever they come from, reject cultural adaptation. Moreover, there is substantial evidence that there is an emergent consensus among all ethnic groups that immigrants and minority groups should preserve elements of their ethnic heritage while adopting core "American" values and political principles.

Assimilation is occurring in the realm of civic engagement—quickly, as assessed by some indicators. Naturalized Latinos in California are as likely to express an interest in politics and write their representative as native-born whites, all else equal. Conversely, some ethnic group differences persist—and even develop. Third-generation California Latinos are less likely to express an interest in and participate in politics than native-born whites and naturalized Latinos. From the national data, we find that native-born Latinos are much more likely to participate in politics that specifically support Latino candidates or issues, but this depends in part on their retaining an ability to speak and use Spanish. The Asian anomaly of lower levels of political engagement than their level of socioeconomic resources would predict recurs in this study's consideration of other aspects of civic engagement. The political incorporation of this immigrant group is somewhat less complete than that of Latinos, despite their higher level of socioeconomic resources (Baldassare and Ramakrishnan 2004).

Even as their tenure in the United States increases and the party affiliation of the president changes, there is a higher level of political trust among Latinos than other ethnic groups. More generally, first-generation immigrants express a more trusting attitude toward political authority, and here assimilation apparently means movement to the more cynical view characteristic of American political culture.

In the ideological realm, however, the pattern of change among newcomers differs with their ethnic origin. Naturalization and nativity makes Latinos, and to a less extent Asians, more liberal, while whites become more conservative with greater tenure in the United States. If we frame this attitude change as assimilation, the movement is toward an ethnic group norm rather than the modal viewpoint of the "dominant" or majority group. The policy domain is characterized by conflict, and we find that assimilation "to what" varies with how clearly an issue taps one's ethnic identity and interests. As tenure in the United States increases, Latinos become less homogeneous on policy issues that do not tap ethnicity, such as abortion rights. By the second generation, differences between Latinos and native-born whites on this issue have largely disappeared. When it comes to immigration policy and affirmative action however, opposition to restriction remains high among Latinos and Asians regardless of whether they were born in the United States or abroad.

We have concentrated on assimilation in terms of generation and ethnic group differences, but the concept has a broader meaning. The mechanisms by which structural assimilation occurs—English-language facility, education, income, and residential integration—are critically important. The present analysis was confined to just a few of these potential process of assimilation, but we did consistently find strong effects for the influence of linguistic assimilation. Initial differences in the presence of factors that facilitate assimilation probably helps account for the seemingly more rapid pace of political incorporation of white immigrants revealed in the PPIC data, but this needs to be investigated further, as do the potential differences in the outcomes for Asian and Latino immigrants related to their country of origin or region of residence.

Our results found support for both the standard, "straight-line assimilation" hypothesis and for the persistence of ethnic subcultures. In some political domains, ethnic differences erode over time as immigrants absorb American culture, yet in other domains, new immigrants gradually adopt the distinctive political norms of the native members of their own ethnicity. Another outcome, particularly evident in the realm of popular culture, is the incorporation of immigrant habits, customs, and vocabulary into the mainstream. Two-way assimilation occurs as karaoke and sushi, dim sum and tai chi, piñatas and salsa join the hora and chutzpah as ingredients in our evolving cultural mix.

Samuel Huntington (2004a) has raised the specter of a movement for a Hispanic version of Quebec emerging in the American Southwest as a result of the massive and ongoing influx of immigrants from Mexico who speak a common language and retain strong ties with their native country. Predictions about the future are notoriously risky, but the evidence presented here, along with other studies of structural assimilation (Alba and Nee 2003) are generally hostile to Huntington's thesis. There is little reason to doubt that the overall pattern of political assimilation of the fourth great wave of immigrants to the United States resembles that of their European predecessors when it comes to core beliefs about national identity, patriotism, and language.

Nonetheless, questions remain. As America's ethnic groups become increasingly diverse, does the economic and political trajectory of different immigrant groups become more variegated, depending on their personal skills, economic resources, and cultural norms? And does the path taken depend on relations not just with the white majority but also with African Americans, the "exceptional" minority of involuntary immigrants who are culturally assimilated yet who remain structurally isolated? The pattern of ethnic group relations in the United States is increasingly complex, varying with the ethnic composition, economic development, and political setting of a region or locality. How immigrant groups influence the pace and character of their integration into national life will depend on the scope of their political participation, civic engagement, and coalitions with other groups. On this point, our results indicate both progressive increases in participation from one immigrant generation and a large residual gap between the involvement of native-born whites and minority ethnic groups.

Appendix: Question Wording from Public Policy Institute of California Surveys, 1998–2002

Assimilation

Melting pot: "Which of these views about racial and ethnic groups in your region today is closest to your opinion? (a) It is better if different racial and ethnic groups change so that they blend into the larger society as in the idea of a melting pot. (b) It is better if different racial and ethnic groups maintain their distinct cultures."

Meet other groups: "In your own daily life, how often do you come into contact with people from racial groups different from your own—very often, fairly often, once in a while, or hardly ever?"

Civic Engagement

Political interest: Generally speaking, how much interest would you say you have in politics—a great deal, a fair amount, only a little, or none?

Participation index: The index sums responses to the following three questions: "The next set of questions is about activities in the last year. For each one, please tell me if you have or have not done any of the following in the past twelve months:

1) Signed a petition such as the signatures gathered for local or state initiative?

2) Worked for a political party, candidate, or initiative campaign?

3) Given money to a political party, candidate, or initiative campaign?

4) Written or e-mailed a local, state, or federal elected official?"

Political Attitudes and Opinions

Ideology: 'Would you consider yourself to be politically: Very Liberal, Somewhat Liberal, middle of the road, Somewhat Conservative, Very Conservative?"

Trust: "People have different ideas about the government in Washington. These ideas don't refer to Democrats or Republicans in particular, but just to government in general. We want to see how you feel about these ideas. How much of the time do you think you can trust the government in Washington to do what is right—just about always, most of the time, or only some of the time?"

Size of government: "On another topic, people have different ideas about the government in Washington. These ideas don't refer to Democrats or Republicans in particular, but just to government in general. Would you say you favor smaller government with fewer services, or larger government with many services?"

Policy Issues

Immigration: "In your view, should legal immigration into the United States be kept at its present level, increased, or decreased?" (1 decreased—3 increased).

Anti-abortion: "Which of the following best represents your views about abortion—the choice on abortion should be left up to the woman and her doctor; abortion should be legal only in cases where pregnancy results from rape or incest or when the life of the mother is at risk; or abortion should be illegal in all circumstances?" (1–3)

Bilingual education/227: "Proposition 227, the "English for the Children" initiative on the June ballot, requires that all public school instruction be conducted in English. It provides short-term placement, usually for not more than one year, in English immersion programs for children not fluent in English. If the election were being held today, would you vote yes or no on Proposition 227?" 0 no, 1 yes.

Affirmative action: What should happen with affirmative action programs? "Ended now," "Phased out," or "Continued for the future."

Notes

An earlier version of this paper, coauthored with Jonathan Cohen, was presented at the 2003 Annual Meeting of the Midwest Political Science Association. The authors thank Jonathan Cohen, Jocelyn Kiley, and John Sides for their assistance. We also acknowledge the assistance of the Public Policy Institute of California and the Survey Research Center at UC Berkeley in obtaining the data for this paper.

1. That is, the survey asked four questions—two about Latinos and two about ethnic groups in general. There was a slightly greater degree of support for maintaining one's distinct culture when the focus was exclusively on Latinos.

2. The index sums responses to the following three questions: "The next set of questions is about activities in the last year. For each one, please tell me if you have or have not done any of the following in the past twelve months: Signed a petition such as the signatures gathered for local or state initiative?; Worked for a political party, candidate, or initiative campaign?; Given money to a political party, candidate, or initiative campaign?"

3. It should be noted that the question does not ask about how one voted for Proposition 227 but how one would vote if the election were held today. Most of the respondents were asked this after the passage of the initiative in 1998.

But Do They Bowl?
Race, Immigrant Incorporation, and Civic Voluntarism in the United States

S. Karthick Ramakrishnan

The relationships between race, immigrant incorporation, and voting participation in the United States are by now well established. Studies based on state- and national-level datasets have shown that first-generation immigrants are generally less likely to vote in elections than those in higher immigrant generations are. Furthermore, factors related to immigration such as length of stay in the United States, English-language ability, and country of origin characteristics all bear a significant relationship to voting participation (DeSipio 1996a, Cho 1999, Ramakrishnan and Espenshade 2001, Citrin and Highton 2002, Ramakrishnan 2005). More recently, a few studies have begun to consider the relationships between race, immigrant generation, and other forms of political participation such as attending local meetings, writing elected officials, and contributing money to politics (Ramakrishnan and Baldassare 2004, see Pearson and Citrin in this volume). So far, the findings indicate that inequalities in these forms of political participation generally mirror those found in the realm of voter turnout. With participation higher among whites and the native born, the analyses point to a worrisome pattern of compounding inequalities in participation, with activities such as campaign donations and writing to elected officials playing particularly significant roles in dividing those who are active in politics from those who do not participate.

While much is known about the relationship between race, immigration, and political participation in the United States, far less is known about the "other half" of civic engagement—those activities relating to volunteerism and civic association. The study of group differences in volunteerism and civic association (hereafter *civic voluntarism*) is important to the study of politics for several reasons. First, civic associations often serve as important conduits to more formal means of political participation, either through the acquisition of relevant political knowledge and skills (Verba, Schlozman, and Brady 1995), or through attempts by political actors to mobilize those who are already involved in the civic life of their communities (Rosenstone and Hansen 1993). Thus, while the group differences in writing elected officials and contributing money to politics may point to inequalities in political access in the contemporary period, group disparities in civic voluntarism may lead to continued inequalities in political participation over the long term.

Civic voluntarism has other, potentially important, relationships to matters of public policy. As Robert Putnam (1993) has suggested in his study of public administration in the various provinces of Italy, the speed and efficiency of government services is consistently related to the level of civic voluntarism in the region. Places with higher densities of civic association tend to reinforce norms of generalized interpersonal trust, which in turn allow for the provision of important public goods. While Putnam's study focused on the role of local governments in the provision of public goods and other services, policymakers in the United States have also seen civic engagement as a crucial component in the provision of public goods by nongovernmental actors. With state and local governments in various regions experiencing severe budget shortfalls, many expect civic associations, religious groups and charities to provide public goods in the absence of government spending (Marimow 2003).

Finally, the study of civic voluntarism also has potentially significant implications for the study of immigrant incorporation. Standard accounts of immigrant assimilation posit that socioeconomic outcomes increase among first-generation immigrants with time spent in the United States and proceed in a linear fashion from the first generation to each succeeding immigrant generation. Over the past decade, several studies have challenged the applicability of "straight-line" theories of immigrant adaptation to second-generation children of the post-1965 wave of immigrants (Gans 1992, Portes and Zhou 1993, Rumbaut 1997). These studies note that there is no universally linear increase in socioeconomic outcomes from the first generation to higher generations. Instead, they note that different group characteristics and modes of incorporation lead to diverse outcomes that even include second-generation decline. While considerable attention has been paid in the immigrant adaptation literature to outcomes such as educational attainment, occupational mobility, language use, and fertility, very little attention has been paid to civic voluntarism and its implications for the ongoing debate over the relevance of straight-line assimilationist theories to the contemporary wave of immigrants.

This essay provides a systematic analysis of differences in civic voluntarism across racial groups and immigrant generations in the United States, using recent data from the Current Population Survey. First, I address the question of whether members of certain groups are overrepresented or underrepresented in the share of the population that volunteers. The essay then takes up the issue of whether group differences remain significant after controlling for the effects of other demographic factors such as age, education, marital status, and homeownership. Next, it considers the effects of various aspects of immigrant incorporation on the likelihood of participation—including duration of stay in the United States, language use, and residential contexts of ethnic concentration. Finally, it addresses the implications of the findings for debates over the continued relevance of straight-line models of immigrant assimilation, and for the future of immigrant politics in the United States.

Data

The primary dataset used in this analysis is the September 2002 Volunteer Supplement of the Current Population Survey (CPS), which asks several detailed questions about engagement in civic voluntarism. The CPS is a good dataset for this study of voluntarism across racial groups and immigrant generations for several reasons. First, it is one of the few large datasets on civic voluntarism that contains information about the nativity of respondents and their parents. Other sources, such as the 2000 Social Capital Community Benchmark Survey, do not include measures of nativity or national origin, while others, such as the yearly General Social Survey and the 1990 Civic Participation Study, lack the sample sizes necessary to make reliable comparisons across racial groups and immigrant generations. The CPS, by contrast, contains 92,357 valid responses among adult residents of the United States to the question on volunteerism, including 71,448 whites, 8,288 blacks, 8,208 Latinos, and 3,426 Asians. Among first-generation immigrants alone, the CPS contains valid responses from 2,769 whites, 682 blacks, 4,293 Latinos, and 2,360 Asians. The CPS also has the advantage of being a nationally representative sample, with a methodology that is stable from year to year and that serves as the central source of information regarding labor force and demographic trends.

Finally, the Current Population Survey is not primarily a dataset about civic voluntarism or political participation. Consequently, sources of bias like respondents "overreporting" their participation or having active participants overrepresented among completed interviews is considerably less severe in the CPS than in other surveys geared primarily toward civic engagement and political participation.

Admittedly, there are limitations to the CPS data as well. First, it does not contain detailed information on the organizations in which individuals participate—including membership demographics and organization size and structure. The CPS also limits our ability to examine broader linkages between civic voluntarism, social norms, political attitudes and behavior. Finally, the CPS tends to underreport participation in two important respects: it focuses on participation in organizations, thus missing informal activities such as participation in kinship networks; it also underrepresents participation by allowing a household member to respond on behalf of another member of the same household (Verba, Schlozman, and Brady 1995). These are significant limitations, but other datasets that compensate for one shortfall face even more significant deficits of their own. Moreover, formal participation in organizations is important to study in its own right because of its implications for immigrant adaptation and political participation in the United States, and the biases in underreporting voluntarism do not appear to bear on group comparisons. On net, given the various strengths of the data, and ways to overcome some of its limitations, the 2002 CPS Volunteer Supplement is a valuable dataset with which to examine contemporary group differences in civic participation.

Results

Are members of some groups more likely to volunteer than others? Table 1 presents differences in participation by race and immigrant generation on three key measures of civic voluntarism: (1) overall rates of participation, (2) the average number of hours spent doing volunteer work, and (3) the average number of organizations for which people volunteered. These latter two measures are considered in two parts—the first, as the average value for volunteers only, and the other as the average among all respondents. Measuring activity per volunteer is important, because it gives a sense of the intensity of participation among those who engage in civic voluntarism. Thus, we can know not only whether members of certain groups are more likely to volunteer, but also whether such volunteers engage in more time-intensive activities than others. The average measure of hours and organizations per respondent is also important because it gives some sense of the bias in the participating memberships of civic organizations. For instance, if the average number of organizations among all white respondents is greater than the average number for members of other racial groups, then we can surmise that whites are overrepresented in the participating memberships of civic organizations. Thus, we have several ways to measure differences in civic voluntarism across racial groups, citizenship status and immigrant generations.

When we consider the most basic metric of volunteerism—whether or not the respondent had done any volunteer work in the previous twelve months—whites have the highest levels of participation. Nearly one third of white respondents report having volunteered, while less than a fifth of blacks, Latinos, and Asian Americans report doing the same. It should be noted that nearly all racial differences in the rates of volunteerism are statistically significant at the 95 percent level or greater. The only exceptions are differences between Latinos and Asian Americans, which are significant at the 90 percent level, and black-Asian differences, which are not statistically significant.

When we measure civic voluntarism as hours spent doing volunteer work, blacks report the highest intensity of activity among those who volunteered in the previous twelve months, followed next by Asian Americans, whites, and Latinos. However, this higher intensity of participation among black volunteers is not sufficient to bridge the gap in overall levels of volunteerism with whites. As table 1 indicates, the average number of hours volunteered among all respondents is still considerably higher among whites than blacks. Still, the higher intensity of participation among blacks is sufficient to bring the overall hours volunteered closer to the white average, and above the average reported by Asian Americans. The intensity of participation among Asian American volunteers is similar to those among whites, and so, differences in the average time spent volunteering are largely reflective of differences in the proportion of respondents who volunteer. Finally, the lower intensity of participation among Latino volunteers, when combined with the fact that Latinos have lowest rates of participation, leads to the lowest number of hours volunteered among all respondents.

Next, we turn to the average number of organizations in which respondents of different racial groups participated. The results indicate that volunteers who are white participate, on average, in more organizations than volunteers who are black, Latino, or Asian American.

Table 1   Differences in civic voluntarism by race, ethnicity, and immigrant generation

	Race/Ethnicity			
	White	Black	Latino	Asian
Volunteered	31%	19%	15%	18%
Hours volunteered per capita				
All participants	144	157	132	146
All respondents	43	29	19	24
Organizations per capita				
All participants	1.53	1.38	1.28	1.29
All respondents	0.48	0.27	0.20	0.23

The mean number of organizations among white volunteers is 10 percent greater than the number among black volunteers, and is nearly 20 percent greater than the number for Latino and Asian volunteers. This disparity, when combined with initial disparities in the overall rates of volunteerism, produces a situation where whites make up a disproportionately large share of the participating memberships of civic organizations. The average number of organizations in which whites participate is two-thirds greater than the similar number among blacks, and more than twice as high as the number among Asian Americans and Latinos. All metrics used to gauge racial disparities in participation thus point to an overrepresentation of whites among the civically engaged.

Next, we consider differences in the rates and intensity of volunteerism by citizenship status and across immigrant generations. As indicated earlier, theories of straight-line assimilation would predict higher levels of participation among naturalized citizens than among noncitizens, and progressively higher levels of participation from the first generation to higher immigrant generations. Results from table 1 support these expectations with regard to the proportion of respondents who reported volunteering in the previous twelve months. The highest rates of participation are among those respondents in the third immigrant generation and higher, while the lowest rates of participation are found among first-generation immigrants who are not citizens of the United States. Interestingly enough, among those who report to have volunteered, the total number of hours volunteered is considerably higher for naturalized citizens than for any other group, including third-generation immigrants.

Just as in the case of blacks, however, this higher intensity of par-

Immigrant generation			
1st gen. nonctzn.	1st gen. U.S. ctzn.	2nd gen.	3rd gen.
11%	17%	27%	30%
110	168	151	144
12	27	40	41
1.18	1.28	1.50	1.52
0.13	0.22	0.41	0.45

ticipation among naturalized citizens is not sufficient to bridge the gap in participation with those in higher immigrant generations, although it does serve to widen the gap associated with U.S. citizenship. Finally, differences in the organizations per capita among volunteers also conform to the predictions of a straight-line theory of immigrant assimilation, with participation lowest among noncitizens, and highest among those in the third generation and higher.

So far, we have examined tabulated differences in civic voluntarism across racial groups and immigrant generations. These bivariate differences identify the bias in participation among members of particular racial groups or immigrant generations. To explain these disparities, however, we need to analyze the effects of race and immigrant generation in a multivariate context that controls for other factors such as age, education, gender, marital status, homeownership, and the presence of children under eighteen. Furthermore, we need to consider the joint influence of race and immigrant generation by interacting the two variables. A more detailed listing of the regressions coefficients can be found in the appendix table 3, which indicates that age, education, homeownership, and having children at home are all associated with greater participation among respondents of different immigrant generations. Here, however, we focus attention on differences in the rates of participation across racial groups and immigrant generations after controlling for these various other factors. Figure 1 presents racial differences in participation within each immigrant generation, with predicted values from multivariate regressions for each generational subsample.

There are several interesting results to note from the multivariate results. First, differences in participation are stronger across citizenship

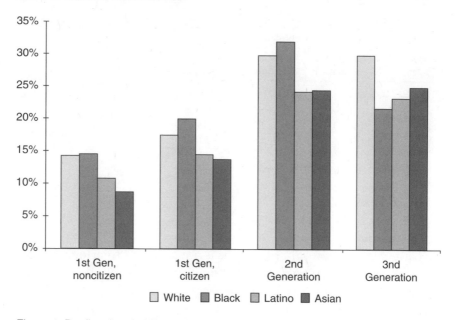

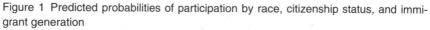

Figure 1 Predicted probabilities of participation by race, citizenship status, and immigrant generation
Note: The predicted values vary from the group means presented in Table 1 because all other variables (such as age, education, homeownership, etc.) are held at the same value—the mean for the overall adult population.

status and immigrant generation than across racial groups. For instance, when comparing the participation of second-generation immigrants with first-generation U.S. citizens, the strongest differences are found not across racial lines within each group but between the two generational groups. At the same time, it should be noted that racial differences remain statistically significant within each immigrant generation and even among immigrant noncitizens. Similar results—of stronger generational differences than racial differences in volunteerism—hold in all other group comparisons. The only exception is for comparisons between second-generation respondents and those in the third generation and higher, where racial differences are more prominent than generational differences. This exception aside, however, citizenship status and immigrant generation play a more prominent role than race in differentiating between those who volunteer and those who do not.

Another significant finding from the results in figure 1 is that the straight-line pattern of immigrant assimilation applies across immigrant generations for whites, Latinos, and Asian Americans. For all three groups, participation increases in the first generation between noncitizens and citizens. The likelihood of volunteering increases even more between the first and second generations, before reaching a plateau by the third generation. For black respondents, by contrast, intergenerational differences in participation follow an inverse U-shape pattern, with the highest level of participation among second-generation immigrants. This drop in participation after the second generation leads to a black-white gap in participation in the third generation that is not found among second-generation respondents.

There may be several explanations as to why civic voluntarism among blacks decreases after the second generation, some of which center on the fact that blacks characterized as "third generation and higher" are overwhelmingly the descendants of slaves in the United States. With a gulf many generations wide between second-generation black immigrants and those in the third generation and higher, we may expect social institutions, customs, and practices to vary considerably between the two groups. Still, this finding is surprising, given that evidence from studies of voting participation show third-generation and higher African Americans to consistently display the highest levels of political participation (Ramakrishnan and Espenshade 2001). The CPS lacks sufficient measures on social norms, attitudes, and practices to get to the heart of this result. We can, however, claim with statistical certainty that these patterns are not the result of differences in factors such as age, education, marital status, or homeownership.

There are other aspects of immigrant incorporation that we need to consider in our analysis of group differences in participation, including duration of stay in the United States, language use, and residential contexts of ethnic concentration. As previous studies of political participation among immigrants have shown, those who live longer in the United States are more likely to be informed of domestic politics, develop stronger party attachments, vote in elections, and gain experience in dealing with government agencies (Cain, Kiewiet, and Uhlaner 1991; Wong 2000b; Ramakrishnan and Espenshade 2001). We may expect a similar dynamic to be operative in the realm of civic voluntarism, with immigrants learning more about their communities, gaining more information about opportunities, and feeling a greater sense of efficacy regarding their attempts to serve in a voluntary capacity. Results from the CPS indicate that those immigrants who have been in the United States for a long time (twenty years or more) are more likely to have volunteered than those who have lived in the country for the short to medium terms (table 2). Indeed, the predicted probability of participation more than doubles between those living in the United

Table 2   Predicted probabilities of participation among first-generation immigrants, by length of stay in the United States

	All respondents	Citizens	Noncitizens
0–10 years	8.2%	8.8%	8.0%
10–20 years	13.0%	13.6%	12.5%
20+ years	17.2%	17.6%	16.2%

Note: All differences are statistically significant at the .01 level.

States for less than ten years and those who are long-term residents of the country. It is also important to note that these increases remain statistically significant even after controlling for citizenship status. While the results in table 2 are presented for all foreign-born respondents, similar results hold true when the model is applied to each racial group separately. In results not reported here, the positive relationship between length of residence and volunteerism holds true not only for Latinos and Asian Americans, but also for white and black immigrants.

Even when we subdivide first-generation immigrants by national origin, length of stay in the United States is generally associated with a higher likelihood of civic voluntarism. Among Latinos, the increasing likelihood of participation with longer stay in the United States holds true for immigrants from Mexico, Cuba, Central America, and South America. Among Asian immigrants, length of stay bears a strong relationship to civic participation among South Asians and Filipinos, but not for Chinese and Korean immigrants. This divergence among Asian groups may result from the fact that English proficiency is lower among long-term Chinese and Korean immigrants than among long-term South Asians and Filipinos. There may also be other aspects of immigrant acculturation that may account for these national-origin differences, such as rates of intermarriage in the United States, residential segregation, experience with volunteerism, and political participation in the homeland. Whatever the reason, it is important to note that the case of Chinese and Korean immigrants is an exception to the more general rule—that volunteerism increases with exposure to the social and political institutions of the United States.

Another important aspect of immigrant incorporation that may be related to civic voluntarism is language use and English proficiency. The ability of immigrants to communicate effectively in English is often a prerequisite to participate in civic and political life in the United States. English proficiency among first-generation immigrants is a function of many factors, including the age at which people entered the United States and the number of years they have lived in the country (Espenshade and Fu 1997). Indeed, the fact that English proficiency increases over time is one of the reasons why political knowledge and participation among immigrants increases with time spent in the United States. At the same time, English proficiency is not synonymous with duration of stay in the United States, with other factors such as national origin, residential segregation, and sociopolitical attitudes also playing important roles.

While English proficiency may be an important determinant of participation in mainstream politics for first-generation immigrants, it is not clear whether it plays a similarly important role in civic voluntarism. As Milton Gordon (1964) noted several decades ago, immigrants can create and participate in their own social and cultural institutions long before they gain acceptance and incorporation into mainstream institutions. Thus, immigrants can engage in civic voluntarism through organizations such as churches, athletic clubs, and national-origin, hometown and home-region associations without needing to have significant proficiency in English. While the CPS lacks detailed questions about English proficiency, we can still examine the suggestive evidence offered by a related measure—language of interview. The CPS is conducted primarily in English but is conducted in Spanish for Spanish-dominant households. Language of interview in the CPS is not an unreasonable proxy for English proficiency as far as participation is concerned. Other surveys such as the *Washington Post*/Kaiser/Harvard University Survey of Latinos (1999) show a strong correlation (0.80) between English proficiency and language of interview. The relationship is likely to be stronger in the Current Population Survey, because respondents have less latitude in choosing their language of interview.[1] Still, there are sufficient concerns regarding the differences between language proficiency and language of interview among native-born Latinos that the analysis merits replication in future surveys that include measures of language proficiency (Lee 2001b).

The results from the CPS indicate that English-language interviewees display greater levels of civic voluntarism for all immigrant generations, even after controlling for factors such as age, education, gender, and homeownership. In the case of first-generation immigrants, adding controls for citizenship status and duration of stay in the United States does not nullify the effects associated with language of interview. First-generation Latino immigrants who interview in En-

glish are 28 percent more likely to participate than their Spanish interview counterparts. While the effects among second-generation immigrants are not statistically significant, they are particularly strong
among those in the third generation and higher, with nearly a dou-
bling in the rate of civic voluntarism. The surprisingly strong results
among third-generation Latinos suggest that there may be other factors that lead both to lower English-language use and to lower civic
participation.

In particular, the enclaves in Texas, New Mexico, and elsewhere in
which third- and higher-generation Latinos can continue to rely on
Spanish may also be areas with high levels of poverty. Thus, the negative relationship between Spanish-language use and volunteerism
may be less a reflection of the ability of immigrants to participate in
the civic voluntarism than of the lack of community infrastructures
and resources necessary to sustain such activities. We can test for this
possibility by controlling for the level of poverty in the county, and
also creating an interaction variable of county-level poverty and individual language use. Doing so causes the pure effects of language of
interview to disappear, indicating that the negative effects associated
with Spanish-language use is indeed largely related to the level of residential poverty in the county. Still, the interaction of the two factors is
negative and statistically significant, suggesting that Spanish-language
interviewees in poor areas are still less likely than English-language interviewees to participate in civic organizations.

Finally, language use and language proficiency are also related to
another aspect of immigrant incorporation that may bear significantly
on civic voluntarism—the extent to which people live in areas with
high concentrations of coethnics. Living in areas with high concentrations of coethnics may serve as a spur to greater participation for several reasons. First, respondents may feel a greater stake in their communities that prompt them to initiate or sustain their volunteerism
efforts. They may also have the strength of numbers to create ethnic-
specific civic associations. Finally, mainstream civic organizations
may engage in more recruitment efforts in communities that represent
a large share of the local population. Studies of political participation
among immigrants generally show that higher levels of ethnic concentration usually do not lead to higher voter turnout (DeSipio 1996a,
Ramakrishnan and Espenshade 2001, Ramakrishnan 2002).

Some suggest that this is because political organizations refrain
from mobilizing in areas with high proportions of immigrant ethnics,
because such areas also tend to have higher levels of residential pov-

erty and noncitizenship. While noncitizenship is less of a barrier for participation in civic voluntarism than for voting, contexts of high poverty may still serve to nullify the positive effects of ethnic concentration on volunteerism among the foreign born.

While the CPS does not contain information on the racial and ethnic composition of neighborhoods, we can still use measures of ethnic concentration at the county and metropolitan statistical area (MSA) levels to see if these have any effects on the likelihood of civic voluntarism among immigrants. In most cases, ethnic concentration does not bear a significant relationship to the likelihood of participation among members of different racial groups and immigrant generations. There are, however, two important exceptions. Among first-generation Latinos, those living in areas with high proportions of coethnics have a greater likelihood of engaging in civic voluntarism. Furthermore, the positive effects associated with higher ethnic concentration remain significant even after controlling for the level of poverty in the area. Finally, for first-generation Asian immigrants, living in ethnic enclaves is associated with lower levels of civic voluntarism. However, once controls for residential poverty are introduced, the coefficient for ethnic concentration becomes positive and statistically significant. So, the results indicate that, while the lack of English proficiency may hinder civic voluntarism among immigrants, living in areas with high proportions of coethnics does lead to greater participation among first-generation immigrants.

So far, we have seen that patterns of volunteerism are largely in keeping with the expectations of straight-line theories of immigrant assimilation, with English-language use, duration of stay in the United States, and higher immigrant generations all associated with a higher likelihood of civic participation. There are, however, two important qualifications to the story: first, that racial differences in participation remain significant even among second- and third-generation immigrants; second, that ethnic enclaves seem to aid civic voluntarism among first-generation Asian and Latino immigrants. Questions still remain, however, as to the sociological processes that underlie these differences across immigrant generations.

Several reasons why first-generation immigrants may be less likely to volunteer than those in higher immigrant generations are conceivable. First, they may face greater demands on their time as they seek to secure an economic foothold in the United States. Or, they may lack sufficient information regarding opportunities and organizations through which to volunteer. Immigrants may also be less likely to be part of social networks that serve as venues for recruitment into civic organizations. The CPS data allow us to test for these various possibilities through basic questions regarding the contexts in which people first became volunteers, as well as factors that would encourage non-participants to volunteer.

First, we can address the issue of whether lower participation among immigrants is a question of free time. The survey asked the following open-ended question of respondents: "There are many good reasons why people don't volunteer. What would encourage (you/name of respondent) to volunteer?" More time was the most common answer given by respondents, followed by "nothing," "health," and "better information about volunteering opportunities."[2] If free time were scarcer among first-generation immigrants, then we would expect the foreign born to be the ones most likely to mention this barrier. However, as analyses of the CPS data indicate, first-generation immigrants are not more likely than others to mention "more time" as a solution to greater participation.[3]

Indeed, after controlling for factors such as age and education, foreign-born whites, Latinos, and Asians are actually less likely to mention the issue of time than third-generation whites. Even for Latinos who choose to interview in English, the importance of free time is less salient than it is for third-generation whites. Another barrier to voluntarism given by many respondents is their health, with about 13 percent of nonparticipants mentioning concerns about the issue. However, health is less of a concern among first-generation immigrants, even after controlling for the fact that first-generation respondents have a younger age distribution than those in higher immigrant generations.

One issue that does receive a higher response among first-generation immigrants is the need for better information regarding volunteering opportunities. First-generation Latinos, blacks, and Asians are all significantly more likely than native-born whites and blacks to mention the need for better information.[4] Interestingly enough, the same need is not felt as strongly among first-generation whites. This disparity between foreign-born whites and immigrants of color may point to differences in the social incorporation of first-generation immigrants into networks that provide information about opportunities for civic voluntarism. Indeed, when volunteers are asked how they first became involved, first-generation blacks and Asians are less likely than native-born whites and blacks to say that they were recruited into participation. The same does not hold true for white immigrant volunteers, who are just as likely to be asked to participate as their native-born counterparts. This finding provides some further evidence of processes of segmented assimilation operating within the first generation.

Conclusions

This essay offers several findings regarding the relationship between race, immigrant incorporation, and civic voluntarism in the United States. In general, the results are in line with the expectations of assimilationist theories that predict straight-line patterns in immigrant adaptation. The likelihood of engaging in civic voluntarism increases among first-generation immigrants with duration of stay in the United States, and with the acquisition of U.S. citizenship. Furthermore, participation increases from the first generation to higher immigrant generations and is higher among those immigrants who are proficient in English. There is, however, some limited support for theories of segmented assimilation. Immigrant whites are more likely than Latinos, blacks, and Asians to receive information about volunteering opportunities and are more likely to have joined organizations through the process of recruitment. Furthermore, ethnic enclaves have a modest effect of raising the level of participation among first-generation Latinos and Asian Americans. Finally, there is no convergence in participation across racial groups, even by the third immigrant generation.

What are the implications of these results for politics and policy? First, they indicate that, barring any changes in contemporary policies and behavior, it will take many decades for immigrants to reach parity in participation with their native-born coethnics. Gaps in civic voluntarism will likely mean a continuation of racial gaps in participation for activities such as writing letters to elected officials, working on political campaigns, and serving on boards and commissions. There are, however, areas for optimism and fruitful intervention. Volunteerism in immigrant communities will increase the longer immigrants live in the United States and the older the immigrant second generation grows. Recruitment and outreach may also have a strong impact among first-generation immigrants, who are most likely to lack information about volunteering opportunities and fall outside of recruitment networks for civic associations. Thus, mainstream and ethnic nonprofits can work to overcome these problems by tapping into immigrant social networks and providing information on volunteering opportunities in various languages. These recruitment efforts, in addition to the political mobilization efforts by unions, ethnic organizations, and political campaigns, can therefore lay a solid foundation on which future increases in political participation may rest.

Appendix

Table A.1   Civic voluntarism, by immigrant generation, adult respondents

	1st generation		2nd generation		3rd generation	
	β	S.E.	β	S.E.	β	S.E.
Black	0.111	0.116	0.112	0.200	−0.427***	0.032
Latino	−0.289***	0.081	−0.276***	0.086	−0.336***	0.051
Asian	−0.396***	0.079	−0.280**	0.114	−0.238***	0.097
Age	0.037***	0.012	0.048***	0.010	0.018***	0.003
Age-squared	0.000***	0.000	0.000***	0.000	0.000***	0.000
High school grad	0.469***	0.087	0.667***	0.097	0.850***	0.035
Some college	0.960***	0.131	0.735***	0.136	1.206***	0.043
College and beyond	1.209***	0.092	1.391***	0.105	1.737***	0.037
Female	0.382***	0.060	0.425***	0.056	0.422***	0.017
Married	0.009	0.073	0.117*	0.064	0.293***	0.020
Owns house	0.301***	0.064	0.299***	0.072	0.290***	0.022
Children	0.409***	0.071	0.651***	0.076	0.541***	0.020
Constant	−3.551***	0.273	−3.447***	0.247	−3.061***	0.075
N	10,135		7,346		74,876	
Pseudo-R^2	0.060		0.076		0.085	

*$p < .10$ **$p < .05$ ***$p < .01$
Source: Current Population Survey, September 2002 Volunteerism Supplement.

Survey Questions

Select questions from the September 2002 Volunteer Supplement survey instrument (original emphasis):

This month, we are interested in volunteer activities, that is activities for which people are not paid, except perhaps expenses. We only want you to include volunteer activities that you did through or for an organization, even if you only did them once in a while.

1. Since September 1st of last year, (have you/has NAME) done any volunteer activities through or for an organization?

2. Sometimes people don't think of activities they do infrequently or activities they do for children's schools or youth organizations as volunteer activities. Since September 1st of last year, (have you/has NAME) done any of these types of volunteer activities?

3. How many different organizations (have you/has NAME) volunteered through or for in the last year, that is, since September 1, 2001?

12. There are many good reasons why people do not volunteer. What would encourage (you/NAME) to volunteer?
DO NOT READ TO RESPONDENT. MARK ALL THAT APPLY. ENTER <N> FOR NO MORE.

<1> Better information about opportunities
<2> Child care
<3> Employer has a program that promotes volunteering
<4> Good match between skills/interests and volunteer activity
<5> Health
<6> More time
<7> Paid expenses, like meals
<8> Transportation
<9> Nothing/not interested
<10> Other/specify

Notes

1. This is because the decision to interview in Spanish is based on whether the household is Spanish dominant—so that if there is anyone in the household who is proficient in English, an English-language interview would be used to report for the household. Also, given the long battery of detailed questions in the CPS regarding individual and household characteristics, those answering the CPS questionnaire are likely to do so in the language in which they are most proficient.

2. Respondents could name one factor or several factors, each of which would get coded by the interviewer. The appendix contains a list of the various coded responses to this question.

3. The only exception is for comparisons between first-generation blacks and blacks in the third generation and higher, where the former are more likely to mention "more time" than the latter.

4. The lack of relevant information is not related to language use, with Spanish-interview respondents actually less likely to mention the need for better information than English-interview respondents. These results indicate that the barrier to participation among Spanish-speaking immigrants does not result from the lack of knowledge or information regarding volunteering opportunities, but perhaps from other factors such as a lower sense of internal or external efficacy regarding volunteerism.

Conclusions

Taeku Lee, S. Karthick Ramakrishnan, and Ricardo Ramírez

This volume starts with a simple observation. The study of immigrant adaptation has, until now, been dominated more by questions of economic, social, and cultural adjustment than of civic and political incorporation. This volume aims to bring us closer to an understanding of the political life of Latinos, Asian Americans, and other new immigrants to the United States. Its contributors have examined the shifting boundaries of ethnoracial classification and citizenship status; questioned the links from collective identity to group politics; analyzed the multiple dimensions of dual citizenship and transnational politics; brought new data, methods, and frameworks to bear on the adaptation of immigrants, the role of civic and political institutions, and the partisan and nonpartisan mobilization of immigrants; and taken stock of how the current dynamics of immigrant political incorporation are likely to evolve in the coming years.

That said, scholarship in the social sciences ebbs and flows with the shifting tides of current events and scholarly paradigms, and it is no different in the case of immigrant adaptation. Thus, research on immigrants constituted some of the earliest and most foundational works in American sociology, such as the pioneering works of the "Chicago school," Robert Park's *Race and Culture* (1950) and W. I. Thomas and Florian Znaniecki's *The Polish Peasant in Europe and America* (1928). By the 1960s, however, the discipline had all but turned its academic gaze away, in no small part because the Immigration Act of 1924 and other restrictionist immigration policies had pulled the reins on large-scale migration to the United States. In addition, the assimilationist views of Milton Gordon (1964) and others had become sufficiently dominant in sociology that the focus on immigration per se gave way to focus acutely on race and ethnicity, especially with the ascendance of the civil rights movement in the 1950s (see Pedraza 2000, Portes 1978).

Inch closer to the present day and we see yet another turn with the renewed interest in immigration by the 1970s. This rebirth was sown out of the post–civil rights political and intellectual Zeitgeist. In the political arena, this "fourth wave" of immigration (Muller and Espenshade 1985, Pedraza and Rumbaut 1996) was punctuated by the 1965 Hart-Cellar amendments to the Immigration and Nationality Act of 1952. Significantly, however, this single legislative moment arose out of a broader historical context wrought by the Second World War, the subsequent role of the United States as a globally engaged superpower in the cold war, and a civil rights movement at home that was closely conjoined ideologically and economically with the cold war struggle over democracy, liberty, and equal citizenship. In the intellectual arena, scholars began to pull apart the seams of assimilation theory (see, e.g., Glazer and Moynihan 1963, Gans 1979, Portes and Zhou 1993). Israel Zangwill's vision of an Anglo-conformist "melting pot" seemed not to materialize. Nor did Milton Gordon's (1964) painstakingly elaborated slog through seven stages of assimilation—cultural, structural, marital, identificational, attitude receptional, behavioral receptional, and civic.

Today, we are seemingly at the crest of yet another sea change in immigration and immigrant incorporation. The warm afterglow of a post–civil rights era open-door policy is slowly shifting to a palpably chillier climate of restrictions on immigrant services and benefits, fueled in part by economic recessions, the hollowing out of the manufacturing sector, and the gradual but systematic dismantling of affirmative action programs, racial redistricting, and other hard-won successes of the Great Society. Most recently, the real and perceived threats to the security of the nation and the safety of its people after the terrorist attacks of 9/11 have led to a curtailing of immigrants' political rights, the absorption of the Immigration and Naturalization Services under the administrative aegis of the new Department of Homeland Security, and a generally pervasive jingoistic milieu—witness the emergence of the vigilante Minuteman Project in the U.S. Southwest border with Mexico and congressional legislation pushing states to link drivers licenses with proof of legal status in the United States.

At the same time, the closing of America's borders (both literal and figurative) is by no means inevitable. As the various essays in this volume demonstrate, changes in the rules and the players of the political game are occurring at the same time as these other changes in the politics of immigration in America. Immigrants continue to act as vital agents of their own destiny (and that of their coethnics), echoing Oscar Handlin's enduring and incisive observation some three decade ago that "Once I thought to write a history of the immigrants in America. Then I discovered that the immigrants *were* American history" (1973 [emphasis in original]). Many immigrants and their advocacy groups have responded in kind to the current environment of anti-immigrant sentiments and policies by naturalizing as citizens, registering as voters, organizing as activists, and ultimately, moving up the rank and file of parties and other institutions into elite positions of power within the political system. Yet, as the essays in this volume attest, immigrants are far from having an equal voice in the politics and policies of the United States.

The political incorporation of immigrants today therefore proceeds in a paradoxical context, where immigration is allowed and processes of acculturation and political socialization are ongoing, but immigrants are warily received and accorded partial rights and access to social benefits. Given this context, the essays in this volume engage with six distinct aspects of immigrant politics in the United States: racial categorization, citizenship, partisanship, mobilization, participation, and incorporation. Our goal here is not to recap the findings in each essay but to situate them in the context of the ongoing changes and identify avenues for future inquiry.

First among these ongoing changes is the growing complexity of race and ethnicity as concepts and as social categories. Even the tasks of "seeing like a state"—of making changes in society legible to the modern administrative state—have become increasing complex (Scott 1998). With the marked changes to our systems of ethnoracial classification over the last few decennial censuses, for instance, come new questions about the collection of government data, the administration and enforcement of race-sensitive and immigration-specific policies, and the resulting access of emerging immigration-based communities to group-based rights and social benefits. Which rights and benefits should immigrants be eligible for, and should these vary according to legal status and visa category? Also, should multiracial/multiethnic persons benefit from race-sensitive policies, and should first- and second-generation immigrants be treated differently from Native Americans and descendants of American slaves?

Continued immigration also underscores the fact that citizenship is not a universal, unchanging concept. It brings into the fore questions of who is eligible for citizenship and what are the legitimate avenues toward its attainment. The explicit barter of service is again seen as a legitimate means to citizenship. Enlistment and active duty in the military is one such form of service, but questions still remain as to why other types of activity fall below the mark—for example, participating in parent-teacher associations, working in public-sector jobs, or volunteering for a religious charity. Even beyond the question of service is the more general matter of vestment in and contribution to American society, such as living in a community, raising children, contributing to Social Security, Medicare, and varied other forms of taxation without representation.

Increased complexity, furthermore, is not confined to issues of racial categorization or citizenship. The labels we use to define ourselves politically—"Democrat," "Republican," "liberal," "conservative"— are both less familiar to new Americans and more open to redefinition. Not only are Latinos and Asian Americans more inclined to reject partisanship (as either a Democrat or a Republican) as the sole marker for political self-identification, but they are also more inclined to build their relationship with the two-party system on something other than a liberal-conservative ideology or the partisan habits of their parents. Thus questions remain as to how Asians and Latinos will balance their economic well-being, foreign policy preferences, home country politics, civic morality, and the like as the basis for their political interests. Also, this relationship is built concurrently with others—based on neighborhood, country of origin, pan-ethnic race, multiracial ties, gender, sexual orientation, religious faith, professional life, civic voluntarism, and so on—with both uncertainty and potential for what will result.

Similarly, the influx of new immigrants changes, and is likely to continue to change, the political calculus of partisan and nonpartisan elites. In strategizing over whom to mobilize, certain segments of the electorate are targeted, while others are neglected. Moreover, as Don Green and his colleagues (and Ramirez and Wong in this volume) show, the effectiveness of Get Out the Vote efforts is contingent on the quality of contact and the selection of mobilization targets. This selection, in turn, is dependent on immigrants' shares of relevant electorates, their vote histories, and the perceived competitiveness of elections. Hence, certain segments of the immigrant population are trapped in a vicious cycle of nonparticipation and nonmobilization, while others are selectively and strategically targeted for mobilization, sometimes based on stereotypes about immigrants, sometimes based on election-specific opportunities.

This is a status quo that Republican and Democratic party elites have an incentive to perpetuate, but not without challenges from nonpartisan elites struggling to pry open the political process to more fully include and incorporate immigrants. It remains to be seen whether parties will pay attention to such nonpartisan mobilization efforts—for instance, with efforts by organized labor in Los Angeles to elect progressive candidates to state and local office. Finally, perceptions of social or political threat activate individual immigrants to seek political recourse through naturalization, registration, and voting even in the absence of elite efforts (Pantoja, Ramírez, and Segura 2001; Ramakrishnan 2005; Barreto, Ramírez, and Woods 2005).

Conceptions of what constitutes politically relevant participation have also changed because of immigration. Existing studies of volunteerism among immigrants and their connection to political participation, for instance, do not adequately capture the experiences of immigrants today, including transnational activities, extended kinship networks, and varying conceptions of what constitutes public and private goods, charity, and volunteering. Future studies in immigrant political participation also need to consider how the pathways to political participation from civic volunteerism may differ according to factors such as nativity, immigrant legal status, and ethnic residential concentration.

More generally, most political science research on political participation focuses principally on voting in national elections—with a residual focus on "nonvoting" as a general class of political action (for example, working on campaigns, exhibiting a button or bumper sticker, writing to elected officials and newspaper editors, attending a rally) and an even more peripheral glance at informal, voluntary, civic spheres of engagement. It is increasingly evident, however, that the concepts of "nation" and "state" impose arbitrary boundaries on what constitutes participation. Specifically, as a burgeoning literature shows, immigrants retain, sustain, and even rediscover their ties to their home country through multiple modes of transnational activism—sometimes in ways that divorce their loyalties between nations, but at other times enabling flexible forms of citizenship and the engagement of activism without borders (see, e.g., Jones-Correa 1998, Ong 1999, Levitt and Waters 2002).

Contemporary transnational political activities may not be as pervasive or intense as they were during the pre–World War One period, where Germans and others became heavily involved to attempt to shape U.S. foreign policy toward Europe and its entry into war (Portes and Rumbaut 1996; Guarnizo, Portes, and Haller 2003). However, the forms of transnational participation today are more regularized and the technologies for maintaining transnational ties more vast. As a result, we need to rethink and retool our studies of political involvement, influence, and the potential for political incorporation (Morawska 2003, Guarnizo 2001, Levitt and Glick Schiller 2004).

As the contributions to this volume suggest, we need to explicitly address multiple dimensions of political incorporation, largely as ongoing and contingent processes rather than fixed, linear goals to be achieved. By shifting away from the view of incorporation as a linear process, we also need to move away from the assumption that immigrant incorporation in one aspect of politics necessarily implies parallel incorporations in other aspects of politics and in outside political life. Processes of incorporation are also likely to vary based on particular local contexts and historical moments. The future research agenda on immigrant participation and political incorporation therefore needs to include local-level studies in addition to national ones, attention to particular immigrant nationalities in addition to pan-ethnic groups, and a shift in attention away from a narrow set of political outcomes toward an interrelated set of processes.

Beyond these potential avenues for future research on the role of immigrants in transforming our understanding of politics, more attention needs to be applied to the social changes they are bringing about, particularly within existing sociological frameworks of immigrant adaptation. As many essays note, the "straight-line" assimilation model—based largely on the experiences of European immigrants in the early twentieth century—is still potent as an empirical account of the convergence in civic and political outcomes across national origin groups. For instance, there are sharper differences in volunteerism across immigrant generations than across racial and ethnic groups—with participation increasing sharply between the first generation and those in later immigrant generations.

Similarly, patterns of political socialization and party identification proceed in a different manner for immigrant residents, naturalized citizens, and native-born citizens. Ethnopolitical identities also tend to shift according to the predictions of an assimilationist model, with beliefs regarding the desirability of linguistic and cultural assimilation increasing from the first generation to higher immigrant generations.

Finally, participation in transnational politics is highest among first-generation immigrants and declines as immigrants spend a greater proportion of their lives in the United States.

Still, there are significant limitations to the straight-line assimilation model of immigrant adaptation. Most obviously, there is little in this volume to sustain the antiquated belief that "assimilation" implies Anglo-conformity or absorption into whiteness and Judeo-Christian values. Race and ethnicity remain—over and beyond immigrant status markers—significant determinants of the political beliefs, institutional attachments, and participatory behavior of Latinos and Asian Americans. In addition, the standard, unrehabilitated assimilation model of immigrant adaptation fails to take account of the critical role of civic and political institutions in shaping the political trajectories of immigrants over time.

Several essays in this volume indicate that state policies and other institutional practices play a selective but significant role in shaping which groups have political voice and access to power. For instance, the ability to contact first-generation immigrants is comparable to those in higher immigrant generations. And yet, political parties and campaigns are less likely to reach out to naturalized citizens than to the native born. Similarly, the inequalities in voting behavior are situated in bureaucratic policies and rules regarding citizenship, visa classifications, immigrant status, and service to the U.S. military.

These limitations to the straight-line assimilation model point to the need for new theoretical frameworks that bridge new developments and insights in sociology with the traditional concerns of political science in areas such as citizenship, political attitudes, mobilization, and participation. Rogers Brubaker formulates the challenge as a needed shift from the question of "how much assimilation?" to the question of "assimilation in what respect, over what period of time, and to what reference population?" (2001, 544). For instance, there is a growing body of literature (Portes and Zhou 1993, Zhou and Bankston 1998, Portes and Rumbaut 2001, Espiritu and Wolf 2001) that suggests that immigrants today are undergoing a process of *segmented assimilation,* where intergenerational outcomes vary across groups and residential contexts.

Significantly, the segmented assimilation literature underscores the fact that the life chances of immigrant communities often depend not on assimilation, but on retaining dense ties and networks within decided unassimilated ethnic enclaves. These studies point to the importance of examining not only the experiences and skills that immigrants bring upon their entry into the United States but also the social and political contexts they encounter after their arrival. Thus, government policies and the attitudes and behavior of coethnics, native-born, and other foreign-born residents can play a significant role in shaping outcomes such as educational attainment, occupational mobility, ethnic identification, and the like.

In a similar vein, future research of immigrant politics needs to give a more thorough consideration to the effects of social and political contexts on subsequent participation. A growing number of studies examine the effects of demographic concentration, mobilization, and party competition on political participation. And yet, these contextual factors have been examined mostly with respect to particular elections and issues, with less attention being paid to longer-term effects on the political socialization of immigrants. Finally, future studies of immigrant politics need not only to consider different contexts of reception—beyond the present sociological focus on labor markets and social stratification—but also different modes of entry into the United States. Factors such as visa status (family based, employer based, refugee, undocumented) and age of entry into the United States influence not only the socioeconomic adaptation of immigrants, but also their political and civic incorporation.

Finally, just as the essays in this volume provide ample fodder for future theorizing and new research in the field of immigrant political incorporation, they also bear upon day-to-day practices and policies. One major implication derives from the marginalized position of first-generation immigrants, who are less likely to be mobilized by political parties and campaigns and less likely to belong to civic organizations. These disparities, combined with barriers to citizenship for many long-term residents, means that first-generation immigrants are shut out of the political process more often than their numbers would suggest. Some may argue that bridging these gaps will have no significant political consequences, because they are unlikely to change electoral outcomes (Citrin, Schickler, and Sides 2003). Yet, studies of local elections (cf. the previous focus on national elections) find that turnout gaps do, in fact, have the potential to change electoral outcomes (Hajnal, Gerber, and Louch 2005). Turnout gaps more generally perpetuate the cycle of exclusion in which political parties and campaigns refrain from contacting voters who have not previously participated in elections. Finally, when the analysis is extended beyond voting, studies show that political participation (writing letters to elected officials, contributing money to campaigns, and engaging in political party work) shapes one's policy preferences and political orientations (Verba, Schlozman, and Brady 1995).

Even beyond efforts to narrow the immigrant gap in political participation, significant challenges remain. E. E. Schattschneider (1960) famously claimed that the choir of the great American pluralist heaven sang with a distinctly upper-class accent. So too it may sing with a distinctly native-born accent. That is, elected officials may give differential weight to participation depending on who is participating. This disparity in citizen influence may result from gaps in voter turnout, but it may also result from prevailing stereotypes and institutional biases that are part of the long history of racial discrimination and nativism in the United States. Even within the same racial and ethnic group, there is evidence suggesting that elected officials are more responsive to the native born, even when first generation naturalized citizens vote more often (Barreto 2005). It is unsurprising, then, that striking and durable disparities remain in the representation of Latino, Asian, and black immigrants among the ranks of elected and appointed officials, from the national level down to the state and local levels. The consequences here may vary by jurisdiction vis-à-vis policy-making and policy enforcement, but they are likely to perpetuate the "mobilization of bias" in favor of native-born constituencies.

What, then, can be done to address these disparities in political incorporation? Many immigrant advocacy groups are already engaged in protests, letter-writing campaigns, and mobilization drives to bridge gaps in participation across racial groups and immigrant generations. But these are not enough. As many essays in this volume suggest, there also need to be changes in institutional practices, including: reforming the naturalization process to reduce delays and expand the qualifications for citizenship based on service, reducing linguistic barriers to civic and political participation through the consistent provision of translated documents and interpreters, increasing party contact with those wrongly deemed to be unreachable or incapable of being mobilized, prodding elected officials to pay more attention to immigrant religious and transnational organizations, and encouraging mainstream civic organizations to do more active outreach in immigrant-heavy areas so that first- and second-generation immigrants also benefit from having access to City Hall, the state capitol, and Washington, D.C.

Moreover, as other essays in this volume suggest, there also need to be changes in the enduring stereotypes and ideologies that sustain and reinscribe the prevailing inequalities in participation and representation between immigrant America and native-born America, including underlying beliefs about who constitutes the body politic; what bounds the political sphere; which groups and identities organize our social, economic, and political life; and whether political participation legitimates or challenges the status quo. If the past is prologue, such changes will not take place without coordination and contestation— from partisan and nonpartisan elites, civic and political institutions, and the ordinary citizens and noncitizens themselves. Until and unless that story unfolds, the promises and perils of immigrant political incorporation remain a story half-told.

References

Abramson, Harold. 1980. "Assimilation and Pluralis." In *Harvard Encyclopedia of American Ethnic Groups,* edited by S. Thernstrom, 150–60. Cambridge, MA: Harvard University Press.

Alba, Richard. 1990. *Ethnic Identity: The Transformation of White America.* New Haven: Yale University Press.

Alba, Richard, and Victor Nee. 1997. "Rethinking Assimilation Theory for a New Era of Immigration." *International Migration Review* 31, no. 4:826.

———. 2003. *Remaking the American Mainstream: Assimilation and Contemporary Immigration.* Cambridge, MA: Harvard University Press.

Aldrich, John, and Forrest Nelson. 1984. *Linear Probability, Logit, and Probit Models.* Newbury Park, CA: Sage Publications.

Aleinikoff, T. Alexander, and Douglas Klusmeyer. 2001. "Plural Nationality: Facing the Future in a Migratory World." In *Citizenship Today Global Perspectives and Practices,* edited by T. Alexander Aleinikoff and Douglas Klusmeyer, 63–88. Washington, DC: Carnegie Endowment for International Peace.

Allport, Gordon. 1954. *The Nature of Prejudice.* Garden City, NY: Doubleday Anchor.

Allsop, Dee, and Herbert F. Weisberg. 1988. "Measuring Change in Party Identification in an Election Campaign." *American Journal of Political Science* 32, no. 4:996-1017.

Alvarez, Robert R. 1987. "A Profile of the Citizenship Process among Hispanics in the United States." *International Migration Review* 21, no. 2 (Summer): 327–51.

Alvarez, R. Michael, and Lisa García Bedolla. 2003. "The Foundations of Latino Voter Partisanship: Evidence from the 2000 Election." *Journal of Politics* 65, no. 1 (February): 31–49.

Andersen, Kristi. 1979. *The Creation of a Democratic Majority, 1828–1936.* Chicago: University of Chicago Press.

Anderson, Margo J. 1988. *The American Census: A Social History.* New Haven, CT: Yale University Press.

Arellano, Anselmo. 2000. "The People's Movement: Las Gorras Blancas." In *The Contested Homeland: A Chicano History of New Mexico*, edited by Erlinda Gonzalez-Berry and David R. Maciel, 59–82. Albuquerque, NM: University of New Mexico Press.

Arnold, Michael S. 1993. "Getting Out the Vote among Hispanics: Takoma Park Pamphlet Reflects Liberal Rules." *Washington Post*. 30 September.

Avila, Joaquín. 2003. "Political Apartheid in California: Consequences of Excluding a Growing Noncitizen Population." *Latino Policy and Issues Brief*. Los Angeles: UCLA Chicano Studies Research Center.

Aylsworth, Leon E. 1931. "The Passing of Alien Suffrage." *American Political Science Review* 25:114–16.

Baldassare, Mark. 2003. *The California State of Mind*. Berkeley: University of California Press.

Baldassare, Mark, and S. Karthick Ramakrsihnan. 2004. *The Ties That Bind: Changing Demographics and Civic Engagement in CA*. San Francisco: Public Policy Institute of California.

Ball T. 1976. From paradigms to research programs: toward a post-Kuhnian political science. *American Journal of Political Science* 20:151–77.

Barkan, E. 1995. "Race, Religion, and Nationality in American Society: A Model of Ethnicity from Contact to Assimilation." *Journal of American Ethnic History* 14:38–101.

Barkan, Elliot R., and N. Khokolov. 1980. "Socioeconomic Data as Indices of Naturalization Patterns in the United States: A Theory Revisited." *Ethnicity* 7:159–90.

Barreto, Matt. 2004. "Latino Immigrants at the Polls: Foreign-born Voter Turnout in the 2002 Election." *Political Research Quarterly* 57 (December).

———. 2005. "Latino Immigrants at the Polls: Foreign-born Voter Turnout in the 2002 Election." *Political Research Quarterly* 58:79–86.

Barreto, Matt, Rodolfo Espino, Adrian Pantoja, and Ricardo Ramírez. 2003. "Selective Recruitment or Empowered Communities." Revised version of a paper presented at the 2003 Annual Meeting of the American Political Science Association, Philadelphia, Pennsylvania.

Barreto, Matt, Ricardo Ramírez, and Nathan Woods. 2005. "Are Naturalized Voters Driving the California Latino Electorate? Measuring the Impact of IRCA Citizens on Latino Voting." *Social Science Quarterly* 86 (December).

Barreto, Matt A., Gary M. Segura, and Nathan Woods. 2004. "The Mobilizing Effect of Majority-Minority Districts on Latino Turnout," *American Political Science Review* 98, no. 1:65–75.

Barreto, Matt, and Nathan Woods. 2005. "Latino Voting Behavior in an Anti-Latino Political Context." In *Diversity in Democracy: Minority Representation in the United States*, edited by Gary Segura and Shawn Bowler, 148–69. Charlottesville: University of Virginia Press.

Bartels, Larry M. 2000. "Partisanship and Voting Behavior, 1952–1996." *American Journal of Political Science* 44:35–50.

Bean, Frank, and Gillian Stevens. 2003. *America's Newcomers and the Dynamics of Diversity.* New York: Russell Sage.

Beck, Paul Allen, and M. Kent Jennings. 1991. "Family Traditions, Political Periods, and the Development of Partisan Orientations." *Journal of Politics* 53, no. 3 (August): 742–63.

Beltran, Christina. 2003. "A Nation in Your Heart: Latino Political Identity and the Quest for Unity." Ph.D. dissertation. New Brunswick, NJ: Rutgers University.

Benhabib, Seyla. 1996. "Toward a Deliberative Model of Democratic Legitimacy." In *Democracy and Difference,* edited by Seyla Benhabib, 67–94. Princeton, NJ: Princeton University Press.

———. 2002. *The Claims of Culture: Equality and Diversity in the Global Era.* Princeton, NJ: Princeton University Press.

Benn Michaels, Walter. 1995. *Our America.* Durham, NC: Duke University Press.

Berns, Walter. *Making Patriots.* 2001. Chicago: University of Chicago Press.

Blais, André. 2000. *To Vote or Not to Vote: The Merits and Limits of Rational Choice Theory.* Pittsburgh, PA: University of Pittsburgh Press.

Bledsoe, Timothy et al. 1995. "Residential Context and Racial Solidarity among African Americans." *American Journal of Political Science.* 39: 434–58.

Bloemraad, Irene. 2003. "Who Claims Dual Citizenship? The Limits of Postnationalism, the Possibilities of Transnationalism, and the Persistence of Traditional Citizenship." *International Migration Review* 37, no. 2:389–426.

Blumer, H. 1958. "Race Prejudice as a Sense of Group Position." *Pacific Sociological Review* 1:3–7.

Bobo, Lawrence. 1999. "Prejudice as Group Position: Micro-Foundations of a Sociological Approach to Racism and Race Relations." *Journal of Social Issues* 55, no. 3:445–72.

———. 2000. "Race and Beliefs about Affirmative Action: Assessing the Effects of Interests, Group Threat, Ideology, and Racism." In *Racialized Politics: The Debate about Racism in America,* edited by D. O. Sears, J. Sidanius, L. Bobo, 137–64. Chicago: Univ. Chicago Press.

———. 2001. Racial Attitudes and Relations at the Close of the Twentieth Century. In *America Becoming: Racial Trends and Their Implications,* edited by N. Smelser, W. J. Wilson, F. Mitchell. Washington, DC: National Academy Press.

Bobo, Lawrence, and Franklin D. Gilliam Jr. 1990. "Race, Socio-Political Participation, and Black Empowerment." *American Political Science Review* 84:377–93.

Bobo, Lawrence, Melvin Oliver, James Johnson, and Abel Valenzuela, eds. 2000. *Prismatic Metropolis: Inequality in Los Angeles.* New York: Russell Sage Foundation.

Bosniak, Linda. 2001. "Denationalizing Citizenship." In *Citizenship Today:*

Global Perspectives and Practices, edited by T. Alexander Aleinikoff and Douglas Klusmeyer, 237–52. Washington, DC: Carnegie Endowment for International Peace.

Brimelow, Peter. 1995. *Alien Nation.* New York: Harper Perennial.

Brodie, Mollyann. 1995. *The Four Americas: Government and Social Policy through the Eyes of America's Multi-Racial and Multi-Ethnic Society: A Report of the* Washington Post/*Kaiser Family Foundation/Harvard Survey Project.* Menlo Park, CA: Kaiser Family Foundation.

Brodie, Mollyann, Annie Steffenson, Jaime Valdez, Rebecca Levin, and Roberto Suro. 2002. *2002 National Survey of Latinos.* Washington DC: Pew Hispanic Center/Kaiser Family Foundation.

Browning, Rufus P., Dale Rogers Marshall, and David H. Tabb. 1984. *Protest Is Not Enough: The Struggle of Blacks and Hispanics for Equality in Urban Politics.* Berkeley: University of California Press.

———. 2003. *Racial Politics in American Cities.* New York: Longman.

Brubaker, Rogers. 1992. *Citizenship and Nationhood in France and Germany.* Cambridge, MA: Harvard University Press.

———. 2001. "The Return of Assimilation? Changing Perspectives on Immigration and Its Sequels in France, Germany, and the United States." *Ethnic and Racial Studies* 24, no. 4:531–48.

Buckley, Gail. 2001. *American Patriots: The Story of Blacks in the Military from the Revolution to Desert Storm.* New York: Random House.

Burns, Nancy, Kay Lehman Schlozman, and Sidney Verba. 2001. *The Private Roots of Public Action: Gender, Equality, and Political Participation.* Cambridge, MA: Harvard University Press.

Bustos, Sergio. 2003. "Bill Would Ease Foreign-Born Soldiers' Path to Citizenship." *Gannett News Service,* 10 April. http://content.gannettonline.com/gns/iraq/20030410–20641.shtml

Cain, Bruce E., Roderick D. Kiewiet, and Carole J. Uhlaner. 1989. "The Acquisition of Partisanship by Latinos and Asian Americans." *American Journal of Political Science* 35, no. 2:390–422.

Calvo, Hernando, and Katlijn Declercq. 2000. *The Cuban Exile Movement: Dissidents or Mercenaries?* Hoboken, NJ: Ocean Press.

Campbell, Angus, Philip E. Converse, Warren E. Miller, and Donald E. Stokes. 1960. *The American Voter.* Chicago: University of Chicago Press.

Carens, Joseph H. 2000. *Culture, Citizenship and Community: A Contextual Exploration of Justice as Evenhandedness.* New York: Oxford University Press.

Ceaser, James. 1978. "Political Parties and Presidential Ambition." *Journal of Politics* 40:708–39.

Chambers, John Whiteclay, II. 1987. *To Raise an Army: The Draft Comes to Modern America.* New York: The Free Press.

Chan, Sucheng. 1991. *Asian Americans: An Interpretive History.* Boston: Twayne.

Chen, David W., and Somini Sengupta. 2001. "Not Yet Citizens but Eager to Fight for the U.S." *New York Times,* 26 October.

Cho, Wendy K. Tam. 1999. "Naturalization, Socialization, Participation: Immigrants and Non-Voting," *Journal of Politics* 61, no. 4:1140–55.

Chong, Dennis, and Reuel Rogers. 2002. "Reviving Group Consciousness." Paper presented at "The Politics of Democratic Inclusion" Conference, Notre Dame University. South Bend, IN.

Citrin, Jack, and Donald. P. Green. 1986. "Presidential Leadership and the Resurgence of Political Trust." *British Journal of Political Science* 16: 431–53.

Citrin, Jack, and Ben Highton. 2002. *How Race, Ethnicity and Immigration Are Changing the California Electorate.* San Francisco: Public Policy Institute of California.

Citrin, Jack, Kathryn Pearson, John Sides, and David O. Sears. 2002. "National and Ethnic Identities: Competing or Complementary." Paper prepared for presentation at the 2002 Annual Meeting of the Midwest Political Science Association, Chicago, Illinois.

Citrin, Jack, Beth Reingold, and Donald P. Green. 1990. "American Identity and the Politics of Ethnic Change." *Journal of Politics* 52:1124–54.

Citrin, Jack, Eric Schickler, and John Sides. 2003. "What if Everyone Voted: Simulating the Impact of Increased Turnout." *American Journal of Political Science* 47:75–90.

Citrin, Jack, David O. Sears, Christopher Muste, and Cara Wong. 2001. "Multiculturalism in American Public Opinion," *British Journal of Political Science* 31:2.

Claggett, William. 1981. "Partisan Acquisition versus Partisan Intensity." *American Journal of Political Science* 25:193–214.

Cohen, Joshua. 1997. "Deliberation and Democratic Legitimacy." In *Deliberative Democracy: Essays on Reason and Politics,* edited by J. Bohman and W. Rehg, 67–91. Cambridge, MA: MIT Press.

Cohen, Patricia Cline. 1982. *A Calculating People: The Spread of Numeracy in Early America.* Chicago: University of Chicago Press. Republished by Routledge, 1999.

Connell, Rich, and Nora Zamichow. 2003. "Fighting for Their Citizenship." *Los Angeles Times,* 1 April.

Craig, Jon. 2004. "High Court Seeks Extra Pay for Jurors." *Columbus Dispatch,* 25 February.

Crotty, William J. 1983. *Party Reform.* New York, Longman.

Croucher, Sheila. 1997. *Imagining Miami: Ethnic Politics in a Postmodern World.* Charlottesville, VA: University Press of Virginia.

Danigelis, Nicholas L. 1978. "Black Political Participation in the United States: Some Recent Evidence." *American Sociological Review* 43:756–71.

———. 1982. "Race, Class, and Political Involvement in the U.S." *Social Forces* 61:532–50.

Dawson, Michael C. 1994. *Behind the Mule.* Princeton, NJ: Princeton University Press.

———. 2000. "Slowly Coming to Grips with the Effects of the American Racial Order on American Policy Preferences." In *Racialized Politics: The Debate about Racism in America,* edited by David O. Sears, Jim Sidanius, and Lawrence Bobo. Chicago: University of Chicago Press.

———. 2001. *Black Visions: The Roots of Contemporary African-American Ideologies.* Chicago: University of Chicago Press.

Dawson, Michael C., Ronald E. Brown, and Richard L. Allen. 1990. "Racial Belief Systems, Religious Guidance, and African-American Political Participation." *National Political Science Review* 2:22–44.

"Defenders Deserve Citizenship." 2003. *San Diego Union-Tribune,* 15 April.

Defreitas, Gregory. 1993. "Unionization among Racial and Ethnic Minorities." *Industrial Labor Relations Review* 46, no. 2:284–301.

de la Garza, Rodolfo. 1995. "The Effect of Ethnicity on Political Culture." In *Classifying By Race,* edited by Paul E. Peterson, 333–53. Princeton, NJ: Princeton University Press.

———. 2004. "Latino Politics." *Annual Review of Political Science* 7:91–123.

de la Garza, Rodolfo O., and Louis DeSipio. 1992. *From Rhetoric to Reality: Latino Politics in the 1998 Elections.* Boulder, CO: Westview Press.

———. 1993. "Save the Baby, Change the Bathwater, and Scrub the Tub: Latino Electoral Participation after Seventeen Years of Voting Rights Act Coverage." *Texas Law Review* 71, no. 7:1479–1539.

———. 1997. "Same the Baby, Change the Bathwater, and Scrub the Tub: Latino Electoral Participation after Twenty Years of Voting Rights Act Coverage." In *Pursuing Power: Latinos and the Political System,* edited by F. Chris Garcia, 72–126. Notre Dame, IN: University of Notre Dame Press.

———. 1999. *Awash in the Mainstream: Latino Politics in the 1996 Election.* New York: Westview Press.

de la Garza, Rodolfo O., Louis DeSipio, F. Chris Garcia, John Garcia, and Angelo Falcon. 1992. *Latino Voices: Mexican, Puerto Rican, and Cuban Perspectives on American Politics.* Boulder, CO: Westview Press.

de la Garza, Rodolfo O., and Brian Lindsay Lowell, eds. 2002. *Sending Money Home: Hispanic Remittances and Community Development.* Lanham, MD: Rowman and Littlefield.

de la Garza, Rodolfo O., with Fujia Lu. 1999. "Explorations into Latino Voluntarism." In *Nuevos Senderos: Reflections on Hispanics and Philanthropy,* edited by Diana Campoamor, William A. Díaz, and Henry A. J. Ramos, eds., 55–78. Houston, TX: Arte Público Press.

de la Garza, Rodolfo, Martha Menchaca, and Louis DeSipio. 1994. *Barrio Ballots: Latino Politics in the 1990 Elections.* Boulder, CO: Westview Press.

de la Garza, Rodolfo O., and Harry P. Pachon, eds. 2000. *Latinos and U.S. Foreign Policy: Representing the "Homeland?"* Lanham, MD: Rowman and Littlefield.

de la Garza, Rodolfo O., and Jesús Velasco, eds. 1997. *Bridging the Bor-*

der: Transforming U.S.-Mexico Relations. Lanham, MD: Rowman and Littlefield.

Demeo, Marisa J., and Steven A. Ochoa. 2003. *Diminished Voting Power in the Latino Community: The Impact of Felony Disenfranchisement Laws in Ten Targeted States*. Los Angeles: The Fund.

Dennis, Jack. 1992. "Political Independence in America: In Search of Closet Partisan." *Political Behavior* 14, no. 3:261–93.

DeSipio, Louis. 1996a. "After Proposition 187 the Deluge: Reforming Naturalization Administration while Making Good Citizens." *Harvard Journal of Hispanic Policy* 9:7–24.

———. 1996b. *Counting on the Latino Vote: Latinos as a New Electorate*. Charlottesville, VA: University Press of Virginia.

———. 2002. *Immigrant Organizing, Civic Outcomes: Civic Engagement Political Activity, National Attachment, and Identity in Latino Immigrant Communities*. University of California Irvine, Center for the Study of Democracy. Working Paper 02–08. http://repositories.cdlib.org/csd/02–08. Accessed January 20, 2003.

DeSipio, Louis, and Harry Pachon. 1992. "Making Americans: Administrative Discretion and Americanization." *Chicano-Latino Law Review* 12:52–60.

———. 2002. "Are Naturalized Citizens Leading Latinos to Electoral Empowerment? Voting among Naturalized Latinos Registered to Vote in the 2000 Election." Paper prepared for presentation at the Annual Meeting of the American Political Science Association, Boston. http://apsaproceedings.cup.org/Site/papers/032/032004DeSipioLou.pdf. Accessed 26 August 2002.

DeSipio, Louis, with Harry Pachon, Rodolfo O. de la Garza, and Jongho Lee. 2003. *Immigrant Politics at Home and Abroad: How Latino Immigrants Engage the Politics of Their Home Communities and the United States*. Claremont, CA: The Tomás Rivera Policy Institute.

DeSipio, Louis, Harry Pachon, Rosalind Gold, and Arturo Vargas. 1998. *America's Newest Voices: Colombians, Dominicans, Guatemalans, and Salvadorans in the United States Examine Their Public Policy Needs*. Los Angeles and Claremont, CA: NALEO Educational Fund and Tomás Rivera Policy Institute.

DeSipio, Louis, Harry P. Pachon, and W. Andrew Moellmer. 2001. *Reinventing the Naturalization Process at INS: For Better or Worse?* Claremont, CA: The Thomás Rivera Policy Institute.

DeSipio, Louis, and Adrian Pantoja. 2004. "Puerto Rican Exceptionalism? A Comparative Analysis of Puerto Rican, Mexican, Salvadoran, and Dominican Transnational Civic and Political Ties." Paper presented at Latino Politics: The State of the Discipline Conference, Texas A&M University, College Station, April 30-May 1.

DeWind, J, and Kasinitz, P. 1997. "Everything Old Is New Again? Processes and Theories of Immigrant Incorporation." *International Migration Review* 31, no. 4:1096–1111.

Diamond, Larry. 2001. "What Civil Society Can Do to Reform, Deepen and

Improve Democracy." Paper presented to the Workshop on Civil Society, Social Capital, and Civic Engagement in Japan and the United States, June 12–13. Tokyo, Japan.

Dinnerstein, Leonard, and David M. Reimers. 1999. *Ethnic Americans: A History of Immigration,* 4th ed. New York: Columbia University Press.

Dionne, E. J., Jr., Kayla Meltzer Drogosz, and Robert E. Litan, eds. 2003. *United We Serve: National Service and the Future of Citizenship.* Washington, DC: Brookings Institution Press.

Downs, Anthony. 1957. *An Economic Theory of Democracy.* New York: Harper and Row.

Dryzek, John. 2001. *Deliberative Democracy and Beyond: Liberals, Critics, Contestations.* New York: Oxford University Press.

Dyer, James et al. 1989. "Social Distance among Racial and Ethnic Groups in Texas: Some Geographic Correlates." *Social Science Quarterly* 70: 607–16.

Edmonston, Barry, Sharon M. Lee, and Jeffrey S. Passel. 2002. "Recent Trends in Intermarriage and Immigration and Their Effects on the Future Racial Composition of the U.S. Population." In *The New Race Question,* edited by Joel Perlmann and Mary C. Waters, 227–55. New York: Russell Sage Foundation.

Ellison, Christopher G., and David A. Gay. 1989. "Black Political Participation Revisited: A Test of Compensatory, Ethnic Community, and Public Arena Models." *Social Science Quarterly* 70:101–19.

Ellison, Christopher, and Daniel Powers. 1994. "The Contact Hypothesis and Racial Attitudes among Black Americans." *Social Science Quarterly* 75: 385–400.

Epstein, A. L. 1978. *Ethos and Identity: Three Studies in Ethnicity.* Chicago: Aldine.

Erie, Steven P. 1988. *Rainbow's End: Irish-Americans, and the Dilemmas of Urban Machine Politics, 1840–1985.* Berkeley: University of California Press.

Espenshade, Thomas J., and Haishan Fu. 1997. "An Analysis of English-Language Proficiency among U.S. Immigrants." *American Sociological Review* 62, no. 2:288–305.

Espiritu, Yen Le. 1992. *Asian American Panethnicity.* Philadelphia: Temple University Press.

Espiritu, Yen Le, and Diane L. Wolf. 2001. "The Paradox of Assimilation: Children of Filipino Immigrants in San Diego." In *Ethnicities: Children of Immigrants in America,* edited by Ruben G. Rumbaut and Alejandro Portes, 157–86. Berkeley: University of California Press.

Etzioni, Amitai. 1993. *The Spirit of Community.* New York: Crown.

Faulks, Keith. 2000. *Citizenship.* London: Routledge.

Farley, Reynolds. 1996. *The New American Reality: Who We Are, How We Got There, Where We Are Going.* New York: Russell Sage Foundation.

Feaver, Peter D., and Richard H. Kohn, eds. 2001. *Soldiers and Civilians: The Civil-Military Gap and American National Security.* Cambridge, MA: MIT Press.

"Federal Measures of Race and Ethnicity and the Implications for the 2000 Census." 1998. Hearings before the Subcommittee on Government Management, Information, and Technology, April 23, May 22, and July 25, 1997. Serial No. 105–57. Washington DC: U.S. Government Printing Office.

Federal Register. 1997. Volume 62 (210). 30 October.

Finifter, Ada W., and Bernard M. Finifter. 1989. "Party Identification and Political Adaptation of American Migrants in Australia." *The Journal of Politics* 51 (August): 599–630.

Fleming, Thomas. 1997. *Liberty!: The American Revolution.* New York: Viking.

Fouron, Georges E., and Nina Glick Schiller. 2001. "The Generation of Identity: Redefining the Second Generation Within a Transnational Social Field." In *Migration, Transnationalization, and Race in a Changing New York,* edited by Héctor R. Cordero-Guzmán, Robert C, Smith, and Ramón Grosfoguel, 58–86. Philadelphia: Temple University Press.

Fraga, Luis R. and Ricardo Ramírez. 2003. "Latino Political Incorporation in California, 1990–2000." In David López and Andrés Jiménez, eds., *Latinos and Public Policy in California: An Agenda for Opportunity.* Berkeley: University of California Press.

Franklin, Charles H. 1992. "Measurement and the Dynamics of Party Identification." *Political Behavior* 14:297–309.

Franklin, Charles H., and John E. Jackson. 1983. "The Dynamics of Party Identification." *American Political Science Review* 77:957–73.

Franklin, John Hope. 1998. *One America in the 21st Century, Forging a New Future, The President's Initiative on Race. The Advisory Board's Report to the President.* http://clinton2.nara.gov/Initiatives/OneAmerica/PIR.pdf

Frymer, Paul. 1999. *Uneasy Alliances: Race and Party Competition in America.* Princeton, NJ: Princeton University Press.

Fung, Archon, and Erik Olin Wright. 2003. *Deepening Democracy: Institutional Innovations in Empowered Participatory Governance.* London: Verso Press.

Gamm, Gerald. 1989. *The Making of New Deal Democrats: Voting Behavior and Realignment in Boston. 1920–1940.* Chicago: University Of Chicago Press.

Gans, Herbert. 1979. "Symbolic Ethnicity: The Future of Ethnic Groups and Cultures in America." *Ethnic and Racial Studies* 2:1–20.

———. 1992. "Second-Generation Decline: Scenarios for the Economic and Ethnic Futures of the Post-1965 American Immigrants." *Ethnic and Racial Studies* 15, no. 2:173–92.

Garcia, F. Chris, ed. 1997. *Pursuing Power: Latinos and the Political System.* Notre Dame, IN: University of Notre Dame Press.

García, John A. 1981. "Political Integration of Mexican Immigrants: Explorations into the Naturalization Process." *International Migration Review* 15, no. 4:608–25.

García, María Cristina. 1996. *Havana USA: Cuban Exiles and Cuban Americans in South Florida, 1959–1994.* Berkeley: University of California Press.

García Bedolla, Lisa. 2003. "The Identity Paradox: Latino Language, Politics and Selective Dissociation." *Latino Studies* 1:264–83.

———. 2005. *Fluid Borders: Latino Power, Identity, and Politics in Los Angeles.* Berkeley: University of California Press.

Gavit, John Palmer. 1922. *Americans by Choice.* New York: Harper Brothers.

Gerber, Alan S., and Donald P. Green. 2000. "The Effects of Canvassing, Direct Mail, and Telephone Contact on Voter Turnout: A Field Experiment." *American Political Science Review* 94:653–63.

———. 2001. "Do Phone Calls Increase Voter Turnout? A Field Experiment." *Public Opinion Quarterly* 65:75–85.

Gerstle, Gary, and John Mollenkopf, eds. 2001. *E Pluribus Unum? Contemporary and Historical Perspectives on Immigrant Political Incorporation.* New York: Russell Sage Foundation Press.

Gershtenson, Joseph. 2002. "Mobilization Strategies of the Democrats and Republicans, 1956–2000." Presented at the Annual Meeting of the American Political Science Association, San Francisco, California.

Gibson, C. J., and E. Lennon. 1999. "Historical Census Statistics on the Foreign-Born Population of the United States: 1850–1990." *Population Division Working Paper* 29. Washington, DC: U.S. Census Bureau.

Gilens, Martin. 1996. "'Race Coding' and White Opposition to Welfare." *American Political Science Review* 90:593–604.

Gimpel, James G., and Karen Kaufmann. 2001. "Impossible Dream or Distant Reality? Republican Efforts to Attract Latino Voters." *Backgrounder* 9, no. 1. Washington, DC: Center for Immigration Studies.

Glaser, James. 1994. "Back to the Black Belt: Racial Environment and White Racial Attitudes in the South." *Journal of Politics* 56:21–41.

Glazer, Nathan, and Daniel Moynihan. 1963. *Beyond the Melting Pot.* Cambridge, MA: MIT Press and Harvard University Press.

Glazer, Nathan, and Daniel Moynihan, eds. 1975. *Ethnicity: Theory and Experience.* Cambridge, MA: Harvard University Press.

Gleason, Phillip. 1980. "Americanization." In *Harvard Encyclopedia of American Ethnic Groups.* edited by S. Thernstrom, 31–58. Cambridge, MA: Harvard University Press.

Glick Schiller, Nina, Linda Basch, and Cristina Blanc-Szanton. 1992. *Toward a Transnational Perspective on Migration: Race, Class, Ethnicity, and Nationalism Reconsidered.* New York: New York Academy of Sciences.

González, Gilbert G., and Raúl Fernández. 2002. "Empire and the Origins of Twentieth-Century Migration from Mexico to the United States." *Pacific Historical Review* 71:19–57.

———. 2003. *A Century of Chicano History: Empires, Nations and Migration.* New York: Routledge.

González-Gutiérrez, Carlos. 1999. "Fostering Identities: Mexico's Relations with its Diaspora." *The Journal of American History* (September): 545–67.

Gordon, Milton. 1964. *Assimilation in American Life: The Role of Race, Religion, and National Origins.* New York: Oxford University Press.

Goring, Darlene C. 2000. "In Service to America: Naturalization of Undocumented Alien Veterans." *Seton Hall Law Review* 31:400–78.

Green, Donald P. 1998. "On the Dimensionality of Public Sentiment toward Partisan and Ideological Groups." *American Journal of Political Science* 32, no. 3 (August): 758–80.

Green, Donald P., and Alan S. Gerber. 2004. *Get Out the Vote! How to Increase Voter Turnout.* Washington DC: Brookings Institution Press.

Green, Donald P., and Bradley L. Palmquist. 1990. "Of Artifacts and Partisan Instability." *American Journal of Political Science* 34, no. 3:872–902.

Green, Donald P., Bradley Palmquist, and Eric Schickler. 2002. *Partisan Hearts and Minds: Political Parties and the Social Identity of Voters.* New Haven, CT: Yale University Press.

Grieco, Elizabeth M., and Rachel C. Cassidy. 2001. "Overview of Race and Hispanic Origin." *Census 2000 Brief, C2KBR/01–1.* Washington, DC: U.S. Census Bureau.

Guarnizo, Luis Eduardo. 1997b. "'Los Dominicanyorks:' The Making of a Binational Society." *Annals of the American Academy of Political and Social Science* 533:70–86.

———. 2001. "On the Political Participation of Transnational Migrants: Old Practices and New Trends." In *E Pluribus Unum? Contemporary and Historical Perspectives on Immigrant Political Incorporation,* edited by Gary Gerstle and John Mollenkopf, 213–63. New York: Russell Sage.

Guarnizo, Luis E., Alejandro Portes, and William Haller. 2003. "Assimilation and Transnationalism: Determinants of Transnational Political Action among Contemporary Migrants." *American Journal of Sociology* 108, no. 6:1211–1248.

Guglielmo, Thomas. 2003. *White on Arrival: Italians, Race, Color, and Power in Chicago, 1890–1945.* Oxford, UK: Oxford University Press.

Guterbock, Thomas M., and Bruce London. 1983. "Race, Political Orientation, and Participation: An Empirical Test of Four Competing Theories." *American Sociological Review* 48:439–53.

Gutiérrez, David G. 1995. *Walls and Mirrors: Mexican Americans, Mexican Immigrants, and the Politics of Ethnicity.* Berkeley: University of California Press.

Gutmann, Amy. 2003. *Identity in Democracy.* Princeton, NJ: Princeton University Press.

Gutmann, Amy, and Dennis Thompson. 1996. *Democracy and Disagreement.* Cambridge, MA: Belknap Press.

Habermas, Jürgen. 1998. *Between Facts and Norms: Contributions to a Discourse Theory of Law and Democracy,* trans. by William Rehg. Cambridge, MA: MIT Press.

Hacker, Andrew. 1992. *Two Nations: Black and White, Separate, Hostile, Unequal*. New York: Charles Scribner's Sons.

Hajnal, Zoltan L., Elisabeth Gerber, and Hugh Louch. 2005. "Tyranny of the Majority? Racial and Ethnic Minorities in Direct Democracy." In *Diversity in Democracy: Minority Representation in the United States*, edited by Gary M. Segura and Shaun Bowler, 123–47. Charlottesville: University of Virginia Press.

Hammar, Tomas. 1985. "Dual Citizenship and Political Integration." *International Migration Review* 19, no. 3.

Handlin, Oscar. 1973. *The Uprooted*. Boston: Little, Brown.

Haney Lopez, Ian. 1996. *White by Law: The Legal Construction of Race*. New York: New York University Press.

———. 2005. "Hispanics and the Shrinking White Majority." *Daedalus* (Winter): 42–52.

Hansen, J. Mark. 1985. "The Political Economy of Group Membership." *American Political Science Review* 79:79–96.

Hardy-Fanta, Carol. 1993. *Latina Politics, Latino Politics: Gender, Culture, and Political Participation in Boston*. Philadelphia: Temple University Press.

Harper-Ho, Virginia. 2000. "Noncitizen Voting Rights: The History, the Law and Current Prospects for Change." *Law and Inequality* 18:271–322.

Harris, Fredrick C. 1994. "Something Within: Religion as a Mobilizer of African-American Political Activism." *Journal of Politics* 56:42–68.

Harrison, Roderick J. 2002. "Inadequacies of Multiple-Response Race Data in the Federal Statistical System." In *The New Race Question*, edited by Joel Perlmann and Mary C. Waters, 137–60. New York: Russell Sage Foundation.

Hayduk Ronald. 2002. "Noncitizen Voting Rights: Shifts in Immigrant Political Status during the Progressive Era." Paper presented at the Annual Meeting of the American Political Science Association, Boston.

Heater, Derek. 1999. *What Is Citizenship?* Cambridge, UK: Polity Press.

Hero, Rodney. 2003. "Social Capital and Racial Inequality in America." *Perspectives on Politics* 1:113–22.

Hess, Stephen. 2003. "Military Service and the Middle Class: A Letter to My Sons." In *United We Serve: National Service and the Future of Citizenship*, edited by E. J. Dionne Jr., Kayla Meltzer Drogosz, and Robert E. Litan, 144–48. Washington, DC: Brookings Institution Press.

Higham, John. 1985. *Strangers in the Land*. Baltimore: Johns Hopkins University Press.

Highton, Ben, and Arthur Burris. 2001. "New Perspectives on Latino Voter Turnout in the United States." *American Politics Research* 30, no. 3: 285–306.

Hing, Bill Ong. 1993. *Making and Remaking Asian America through Immigration Policy, 1850–1990*. Palo Alto, CA: Stanford University Press.

Hochschild, Jennifer. 2002. "Multiple Racial Identifiers in the 2000 Census, and Then What?" In *The New Race Question,* edited by Joel Perlmann and Mary C. Waters, 340–53. New York: Russell Sage Foundation.

———. 2003a. "From Nominal to Ordinal to Interval: Reconceiving Racial and Ethnic Hierarchy in the United States." Arthur Allen Leff Lecture, Yale Law School, 10 March. New Haven, Connecticut.

———. 2003b. "Pluralism, Identity Politics and Coalitions: Toward Madisonian Constitutionalism." In *The Future of American Democratic Politics,* edited by Gerald Pomper and Marc Weiner, 11–28. New Brunswick, NJ: Rutgers University Press.

Hochschild, Jennifer L., and Reuel R. Rogers. 2000. "Race Relations in a Diversifying Nation." In *New Directions: African Americans in a Diversifying Nation.* Edited by James S. Jackson, 45–85. Washington, DC: National Policy Association.

Hollinger, David. 1995. *Postethnic America: Beyond Multiculturalism.* New York: Basic Books.

Holmes, Steven A. 2003. "For Jobs and Country: Is This Really an All-Volunteer Army?" *New York Times,* 6 April.

Honig, Bonnie. 2001. *Democracy and the Foreigner.* Princeton, NJ: Princeton University Press.

Huckfeldt, Robert, and John Sprague. 1995. *Citizens, Politics, and Social Communication: Information and Influence in an Election Campaign.* New York: Cambridge University Press.

Huddy, Leonie. 2001. "From Social to Political Identity: A Critical Examination of Social Identity Theory." *Political Psychology* 22, no. 1:127–56.

Hum, Tarry, and Zonata, Michela. 2000. "Residential Patterns of Asian Pacific Americans." In *The State of Asian Pacific America: Transforming Race Relations,* edited by Paul M. Ong, 191–242. Los Angeles: LEAP Asian Pacific American Policy Institute and UCLA Asian American Studies Center.

Huntington, Samuel. 1983. *American Politics: The Promise of Disharmony.* Cambridge, MA: Harvard University Press.

———. 1993. "If Not Civilizations, What?" *Foreign Affairs* 72 (November/December): 22–28.

———. 2000. "The Special Case of Mexican Immigration: Why Mexico Is a Problem." *American Enterprise* (December).

———. 2004a. "The Hispanic Challenge." *Foreign Policy* (March/April): 30–45.

———. 2004b. *Who Are We?: The Challenges to America's Identity.* New York: Simon and Schuster.

Ibarguen, Diego. 2003. "Bush Visits Injured Troops." *Knight Ridder Washington Bureau,* 12 April.

Ignatiev, Noel. 1995. *How the Irish Became White.* New York: Routledge.

Jackman, Mary R. 1994. *The Velvet Glove: Paternalism and Conflict in Gender, Class, and Race.* Berkeley: University of California Press.

Jackman, M. R., and M. J. Muha. 1984. "Education and Intergroup Attitudes: Moral Enlightment, Superficial Democratic Commitment, or Ideological Refinement?" *American Sociological Review* 49:751–69.

Jacobs, James B., and Leslie Anne Hayes. 1981. "Aliens in the U.S. Armed Forces." *Armed Forces and Society* 7:187–208.

Jacobson, Matthew Frye. 1998. *Whiteness of a Different Color: European Immigrants and the Alchemy of Race.* Cambridge, MA: Harvard University Press.

Jacobson, Michael. 2001. "From the 'Back' to the 'Front': The Changing Character of Punishment in New York City." In *Rethinking the Urban Agenda: Reinvigorating the Liberal Tradition in New York City and Urban America,* edited by John Mollenkopf and Ken Emerson, 171–86. New York: Twentieth Century Foundation.

Jacobson, Robin. 2003. "Characterizing Consent: Race, Citizenship and the New Restrictionists." Paper presented at the Annual Meeting of the American Political Science Association. Philadelphia, Pennsylvania.

Jamieson, Amie, Hyon B. Shin, and Jennifer Day. 2002. *Voting and Registration in the Election of November 2000.* Current Population Reports P20-542. Washington, DC: U.S. Department of Commerce, Bureau of the Census.

Janoski, Thomas. 1998. *Citizenship and Civil Society.* Cambridge, UK: Cambridge University Press.

Janowitz, Morris. 1983. *The Reconstruction of Patriotism.* Chicago: University of Chicago Press.

Jasso, Guillermina, and Mark R. Rosenzweig. 1990. *The New Chosen People: Immigrants in the United States.* New York: Russell Sage Foundation.

Johnson, Hans P., Belinda I. Reyes, Laura Marneesh, and Elisa Barbour. 1999. *Taking the Oath: An Analysis of Naturalization in California and the United States.* San Francisco, CA: Public Policy Institute of California.

Jones-Correa, Michael. 1998. *Between Two Nations: The Political Predicament of Latinos in New York City.* Ithaca, NY: Cornell University Press.

———. 2000. "Immigrants, Blacks and Cities." In *Black and Multiracial Politics in America,* edited by Yvette Marie Alex-Assensoh and Lawrence J. Hanks, 133–64. New York: New York University Press. 133–64.

———. 2001a. "Institutional and Contextual Factors in Immigrant Naturalization and Voting." *Citizenship Studies* 5, no. 1:41–56.

———. 2001b. "Under Two Flags: Dual Nationality in Latin America and Its Consequences for Naturalization in the United States." *International Migration Review* 35, no. 4:997–1029.

———. 2002. "Bringing Outsiders In: Questions of Immigrant Incorporation." Paper prepared for presentation at the Conference on the Politics of Democratic Inclusion. University of Notre Dame, Indiana.

Jones-Correa, Michael, and David L. Leal. 1996. "Becoming 'Hispanic': Secondary Panethnic Identification among Latin American-Origin Populations in the United States." *Hispanic Journal of Behavioral Sciences* 18:214–53.

Jung, Courtney. 2000. *Then I Was Black: South African Political Identities in Transition.* New Haven, CT: Yale University Press.

Junn, Jane. 1999. "Participation in Liberal Democracy: The Political Assimilation of Immigrants and Ethnic Minorities in the United States." *American Behavioral Scientist* 42 (9 June/July): 1417–38.

Kaiman, Beth, and Lynne K. Varner. 1992. "Immigrant Voting Advances in Takoma Park." *Washington Post,* 30 January.

Kasinitz, Phil. 1992. *Caribbean New York: Black Immigrants and the Politics of Race.* Ithaca NY: Cornell University Press.

Keith, Bruce, et al. 1992. *The Myth of the Independent Voter.* Berkeley: University of California Press.

Kerber, Linda K. 1997. "The Meanings of Citizenship." *Journal of American History* 84:833–54.

Kestnbaum, Meyer. 2000. "Citizenship and Compulsory Military Service: The Revolutionary Origins of Conscription in the United States." *Armed Forces and Society* 27:7–36.

Kettner, James H. 1978. The Development of American Citizenship, 1608–1870. Chapel Hill: University of North Carolina Press.

Key, V. O. 1949. *Southern Politics in State and Nation.* New York: Knopf.

Keyssar, Alexander. 2000. *The Right to Vote: The Contested History of Democracy in the United States.* New York: Basic Books.

Kim, Nadia, and Tyrone Forman. 2003. "Beyond Black and White: Asian Americans' Attitudes toward Blacks and Latinos. Unpublished paper.

Kinder, Douglas, and Lynn Sanders. 1996. *Divided by Color: Racial Politics and Democratic Ideals.* Chicago: University of Chicago Press.

Kondo, Atsushi, ed. 2001. *Citizenship in a Global World: Comparing Citizenship Rights for Aliens.* New York: Palgrave.

Krikorian, Mark. 2003. "Green-Card Soldiers." *National Review Online.* 22 April. www.nationalreview.com/nr_comment/nr_comment042203.asp

Kymlicka, Will. 2001. *Politics in the Vernacular: Nationalism, Multiculturalism and Citizenship.* New York: Oxford University Press.

Kymlicka, Will, and Wayne Norman, eds. 2000. *Citizenship in Diverse Societies.* New York: Oxford University Press.

Lai, Eric, and Dennis Arguelles, eds. 2003. The New Face of Asian Pacific America: Numbers, Diversity and Change in the 21st Century. San Francisco, CA: *AsianWeek* and the Asian American Studies Press.

Latif, Angie. 2003. "The New Arab Profilers." *Arab American Business Magazine* (February 3). http://www.arabamericanbusiness.com

Lee, Jennifer, and Frank Bean. 2004. "America's Changing Color Lines: Immigration, Race/Ethnicity, and Multiracial Identification." *Annual Review of Sociology* 30:221–42.

Lee, Sharon, and M. Fernandez. 1998. "Patterns in Asian American Racial/Ethnic Intermarriage." *Sociological Perspectives* 41:323–42.

Lee, Taeku. 2000a. "The Backdoor and the Backlash: Campaign Finance and the Politicization of Chinese Americans." *Asian American Policy Review* 9: 30–55.

———. 2000b. "Racial Attitudes and the Color Line(s) at the Close of the Twentieth Century." In *The State of Asian Pacific Americans: Race Relations,* edited by P. Ong, 103–58. Los Angeles: LEAP.

———. 2001a. "Language-of-Interview Effects, Ethnic Identity, and Polling the Opinions of Latinos." Paper presented at the Annual Meeting of the Midwest Political Science Association, April 19–22, Chicago, Illinois.

———. 2001b. "Language-of-Interview Effects and Latino Mass Opinion." Faculty Research Working Paper #01–041, John F. Kennedy School of Government.

Lee, Taeku, and Zoltan Hajnal. 2004. *Exit, Voice, and Identity: Race, Immigration, and the Rise of Political Independents in America.* Unpublished manuscript.

Leighley, Jan E. 2001. *Strength in Numbers? The Political Mobilization of Racial and Ethnic Minorities.* Princeton, NJ: Princeton University Press.

Leighley, Jan E., and Arnold Vedlitz. 1999. "Race, Ethnicity, and Political Participation: Competing Models and Contrasting Explanations." *The Journal of Politics* 61, no. 4:1092–1114.

Levitt, Peggy. 2001. *The Transnational Villagers.* Berkeley: University of California Press.

Levitt, Peggy, and Nina Glick Schiller. 2004. "Conceptualizing Simultaneity: Theorizing Society from a Transnational Social Field Perspective." *International Migration Review.*

Levitt, Peggy, and Mary Waters, eds. 2002. *The Changing Face of Home: The Transnational Lives of the Second Generation.* New York: Russell Sage Publications.

Lien, Pei-te. 1994. "Ethnicity and Political Participation: A Comparison between Asian and Mexican Americans." *Political Behavior* 16, no. 2:237–64.

———. 1997. *The Political Participation of Asian Americans.* New York: Garland.

———. 2000. "Who Votes in Multiracial America? An Analysis of Voting and Registration by Race and Ethnicity, 1990–96." In *Black and Multiracial Politics in America,* edited by Yvette Alex-Assensoh and Lawrence Hanks,199–224. New York: New York University Press.

———. 2001. *The Making of Asian America through Political Participation.* Philadelphia: Temple University Press.

Lien, Pei-te, Christian Collet, Janelle Wong, and S. Karthick Ramakrishnan. 2001. "Asian Pacific American Public Opinion and Political Participation," *PS: Political Science and Politics* 34:3.

Lien, Pei-te, M. Margaret Conway, and Janelle Wong. 2003. "The Contours and Sources of Ethic Identity Choices among Asian Americans." *Social Science Quarterly* 84, no. 2 (June): 461–81.

———. 2004. *The Politics of Asian Americans: Diversity and Community*. New York: Routledge.

Locke, John. 1988. *Two Treatises of Government*. Peter Laslett, ed. Cambridge, UK: Cambridge University Press.

Logan, John, and John Mollenkopf. 2003. "People and Politics in Urban America." Report to the Drum Major Institute, May, New York.

Lukes, Steven, and Christian Joppke, eds. 1999. *Multicultural Questions*. Oxford, UK: Oxford University Press.

Marimow, Ann E. 2003. "Davis Urges Volunteers to Help Ease Budget Cuts." San Jose *Mercury News,* 5 January.

Marquez, Benjamin. 2000. "Standing for the Whole: The Southwest Industrial Areas Foundation on Identity and Mexican-American Politics." *Social Service Review* 7:453–73.

Marwell, Nicole. 2004. "Ethnic and Post-Ethnic Politics: The Dominican Second Generation in New York City." In *Becoming New Yorkers: The Second Generation Comes of Age*, edited by Philip Kasinitz, John Mollenkopf, and Mary Waters, 227–56. New York: Russell Sage Foundation.

Marx, Anthony. 1998. *Making Race and Nation: A Comparison of the United States, South Africa, and Brazil*. New York: Cambridge University Press.

Massey, Douglas. 2000. "The Residential Segregation of Blacks, Hispanics, and Asians: 1970–1990." In *Immigration and Race,* edited by Gerald Jaynes, 44–73. New Haven, CT: Yale University Press.

Massey, Douglas, and Nancy Denton. 1993. *American Apartheid: Segregation and the Making of the Underclass*. Cambridge, MA: Harvard University Press.

Mayhew, David. 1986. *Placing Parties in American Politics: Organization, Electoral Setting, and Government Activity in the 20th Century*. Princeton, NJ: Princeton University Press.

McClain, Paula. 1993. "The Changing Dynamics of Urban Politics: Black and Hispanic Municipal Employment—Is There Competition?" *Journal of Politics* 55:399–414.

McClain, Paula, and Karnig, Albert. 1990. "Black and Hispanic Socioeconomic and Political Competition." *American Political Science Review* 84:535–45.

Meier, Kenneth, and Joseph Stewart. 1991. "Cooperation and Conflict in Multiracial School Districts." *Journal of Politics* 53:1123–33.

Menchaca, Martha. 2001. *Recovering History, Constructing Race: The Indian, Black, and White Roots of Mexican Americans*. Austin: University of Texas Press.

Merriam, Charles Edward. 1922. *The American Party System: An Introduction*. New York, Macmillan.

Mezey, Naomi. 2003. "Erasure and Recognition: The Census, Race and the National Imagination." *Northwestern University Law Review* 97, no. 4: 1701–68.

Miller, Arthur H., Patricia Gurin, Gerald Gurin, and Oksana Malanchuk. 1981. "Group Consciousness and Political Participation." *American Journal of Political Science* 25:494–511.

Miller, Arthur H., and Martin P. Wattenberg. 1983. "Measuring Party Identification: Independent or No Partisan Preference?" *American Journal of Political Science* 27, no. 1:106–21.

Minnite, Lorraine C., Jennifer Holdaway, and Ronald Hayduk. 2001. "The Political Participation of Immigrants in New York." In *In Defense of the Alien*, vol. 23, edited by Lydio F. Tomasi, 191–228. New York: Center for Migration Studies.

Mollenkopf, John. 2003. "New York: Still the Great Anomaly." In *Racial Politics in American Cities*, 3rd ed., edited by Rufus P. Browning, Dale Rogers Marshall, and David H. Tabb, 115–41. New York: Longman.

Mollenkopf, John, and Lorraine Minnite. 2001. "Between White and Black: Asian and Latino Political Participation in the 2000 Presidential Election in New York City." Paper presented to the Annual Meeting of the American Political Science Association, San Francisco.

Mollenkopf, John, David Olson, and Timothy Ross. 2001. "Immigrant Political Participation in New York and Los Angeles." In *Governing Urban America: Immigrants, Natives, and Urban Politics*, edited by Michael Jones-Correa, 17–70. New York: Russell Sage Foundation.

Montoya, Lisa. 1996. "Latino Gender Differences in Public Opinion: Results from the Latino National Political Survey." *Hispanic Journal of Behavioral Science* 18:255–76.

Morawska, Ewa. 2001a. "Immigrant-Black Dissensions in American Cities: An Argument for Multiple Explanations." In *Problem of the Century: Racial Stratification in the United States*, edited by Douglas Massey and Elijah Anderson, 47–96. New York: Russell Sage.

———. 2001b. "The New-Old Transmigrants, Their Transnational Lives, and Ethnicization: A Comparison of the 19th/20th and 20th/21st C. Situations." In *E Pluribus Unum? Contemporary and Historical Perspectives on Immigrant Political Incorporation*, edited by Gary Gerstle and John Mollenkopf, 175–214. New York: Russell Sage.

———. 2003. "Immigrant Transnationalism and Assimilation." In *Toward Assimilation and Citizenship*, edited by Christian Joppke and Ewa Morawska, 133–76. Hampshire, UK: Palgrave Macmillan.

Morrison, Toni. 1993. "On the Back of Blacks." *Time* (Special Issue, Fall), 57.

Moskos, Charles C., and John Sibley Butler. 1996. *All That We Can Be: Black Leadership and Racial Integration the Army Way*. New York: Basic Books.

Muller, Eric. 2001. *Free to Die for Their Country*. Chicago: University of Chicago Press.

Muller, Thomas, and Thomas Espenshade. 1985. *The Fourth Wave: California's Newest Immigrants*. Washington, DC: Urban Institute.

NALEO Educational Fund. 2004. "Four Million Latino Legal Permanent Residents Eligible for U.S. Citizenship as Exorbitant Fee Hike Takes Effect." Press Release, April 30. Los Angeles: NALEO Educational Fund.

Nalty, Bernard C. 1986. *Strength for the Fight: A History of Black Americans in the Military*. New York: Free Press.

Navarrette, Ruben. 2003. "Heroism Should Be Worth Citizenship." *Dallas Morning News*, 11 April.

Nelson, Alan C. 1991. "Undermining Democracy in Takoma Park." *Washington Post*, 8 December.

New California Media. 2002. *New California Media and University of Southern California Annenberg Institute for Justice and Journalism Post-9/11 Survey*. 5 September. http://www.ncmonline.com/media/pdf/911survey.pdf

Nicholson, Stephen, and Gary Segura. 2005. "Issue Agendas and the Politics of Latino Partisan Identification." In *Diversity and Democracy: Minority Representation in the United States*, edited by Shaun Bowler and Gary Segura, 51–71. Charlottesville, VA: University of Virginia Press.

Niemi, Richard G., and M. Kent Jennings. 1991. "Issues and Inheritance in the Formation of Party Identifications." *American Journal of Political Science* 35:970–88.

Nobles, Melissa. 2000. *Shades of Citizenship: Race and the Census in Modern Politics*. Stanford, CA: Stanford University Press.

Nussbaum, Martha. 1996. *For Love of Country: Debating the Limits of Patriotism*. Boston: Beacon.

O'Brien, Jeffrey R. 1999. "U.S. Dual Citizen Voting Rights: A Critical Examination of Aleinikoff's Solution." *Georgetown Immigration Law Journal* 13, no. 4.

Office of the Inspector General. 2003. "The September 11 Detaineers: A Review of the Treatment of Aliens Held on Immigration Charges in Connection with the Investigation of the September 11 Attacks." Washington, DC: Department of Justice. http://www.usdoj.gov/oig/special/03-06/index.htm

Office of Management and Budget. 1997. "Revisions to the Standards for the Classification of Federal Data on Race and Ethnicity." *Federal Register* Notice (October 30).

Oliver, Eric, and Janelle Wong. 2003. "Intergroup Prejudice in Multiethnic Settings." *American Journal of Political Science* 47, no. 4:567–82.

Olsen, Marvin. 1970. "Social and Political Participation of Blacks." *American Sociological Review* 35:682–97.

Olson, Mancur. 1965. *The Logic of Collective Action*. Cambridge, MA: Harvard University Press.

Omi, Michael, and Howard Winant. 1994. *Racial Formation in the United States*. New York: Routledge.

Ong, Aihwa. 1999. *Flexible Citizenship: The Cultural Logics of Transnationalism*. Durham, NC: Duke University Press.

Pachon, Harry, and Louis DeSipio. 1994. *New Americans by Choice: Political Perspectives of Latino Immigrants*. Boulder, CO: Westview Press.

Padilla, Felix M. 1984. *Latino Ethnic Consciousness: The Case of Mexican Americans and Puerto Ricans in Chicago.* Notre Dame, IN: University of Notre Dame Press.

Pantoja, Adrian, Ricardo Ramírez, and Gary M. Segura. 2001. "Citizens by Choice, Voters by Necessity: Patterns of Political Mobilization by Naturalized Latinos." *Political Research Quarterly* 54:729–50.

Pardo, Mary. 1998. *Mexican American Women Activists: Identity and Resistance in Two Los Angeles Communities.* Philadelphia, PA: Temple University Press.

Park, Robert. 1950. *Race and Culture.* Glencoe, IL: Free Press.

Passel, Jeffrey. 2005. *Estimates of the Size and Characteristics of the Undocumented Population.* Washington, DC: Pew Hispanic Center.

Pearson, Kathryn, and Jack Citrin. 2002. "Identity Choice and Language Politics in the United States." Paper presented at the 2002 Conference of the International Society for Political Psychology, Berlin, Germany.

Pedraza, Sylvia. 2000. "Beyond Black and White: Latinos and Social Science Research on Immigration, Race, and Ethnicity in America." *Social Science History* 24:697–726.

Pedraza, Sylvia, and Ruben G. Rumbaut, eds. 1996. *Origins and Destinies: Immigration, Race, and Ethnicity in America.* Belmont, CA: Wadsworth Press.

Perlmann, Joe, and Mary C. Waters. 2002. *The New Race Question: How the Census Counts Multiracial Individuals.* New York: Russell Sage Foundation.

Pickus, Noah M. J. 1998. "To Make Natural: Creating Citizens for the Twenty-First Century." In *Immigration and Citizenship in the Twenty-First Century,* edited by Noah M. J. Pickus, 107–40. Lanham, MD: Rowman & Littlefield Publishers, Inc.

Portes, Alejandro. 1978. "Immigrant Aspirations." *Sociology of Education* 51:241–60.

———, ed. 1996. *The New Second Generation.* New York: Russell Sage Foundation.

Portes, Alejandro, and John Curtis. 1987. "Changing Flags: Naturalization and Its Determinants among Mexican Immigrants." *International Migration Review* 21, no. 2:352–71.

Portes, Alejandro, and Rafael Mozo. 1985. "Naturalization, Registration, and Voting Patterns of Cubans and Other Ethnic Minorities: A Preliminary Analysis." In *Proceedings of the First National Conference on Citizenship and the Hispanic Community.* Washington, DC: The NALEO Educational Fund.

Portes, Alejandro, and Ruben Rumbaut. 1996. *Immigrant America: A Portrait.* Berkeley: University of California Press.

———. 2001. *Legacies: The Story of the Immigrant Second Generation.* Berkeley: University of California Press.

Portes, Alejandro, and Alex Stepik. 1993. *City on the Edge: The Transformation of Miami.* Berkeley: University of California Press.

Portes, Alejandro, and Min Zhou. 1993. "The New Second Generation: Segmented Assimilation and Its Variants." *Annals of the American Academy of Political and Social Science.* 530:74–96.

Portney, Kent E., and Jeffrey M. Berry. 1997. "Mobilizing Minority Communities: Social Capital and Participation in Urban Neighborhoods." *American Behavioral Scientist* 40, no. 5:632–44.

Prewitt, Kenneth. 2002. "Race in the 2000 Census: A Turning Point." In *The New Race Question,* edited by Joel Perlmann and Mary C. Waters, 354–62. New York: Russell Sage Foundation.

———. 2005. "Racial Classification in America: Where Do We Go from Here?" *Daedalus* (Winter): 5–17.

Putnam, Robert. 1993. *Making Democracy Work: Civic Traditions in Modern Italy.* Princeton, NJ: Princeton University Press.

———. 2000. *Bowling Alone: the Collapse and Revival of American Community.* New York: Simon & Schuster.

Ramakrishnan, S. Karthick. 2002. *Voters from Different Shores: Electoral Participation in Immigrant America.* Princeton, NJ: Princeton University.

———. 2004. "Second Generation Immigrants? The 2.5 Generation in the United States," *Social Science Quarterly* 85, no. 2:380–99.

———. 2005. *Democracy in Immigrant America: Changing Demographics and Political Participation.* Stanford, CA: Stanford University Press.

Ramakrishnan, S. Karthick, and Mark Baldassare. 2004. *The Ties that Bind: Demographic Diversity and Civic Engagement in California.* San Francisco: Public Policy Institute of California.

Ramakrishnan, S. Karthick, and Thomas Espenshade. 2001. "Immigrant Incorporation and Political Participation in the United States." *International Migration Review* 35:3.

Ramírez, Ricardo. 2002. "The Changing Landscape of California Politics, 1990–2000." Unpublished Dissertation. Palo Alto, CA: Stanford University Press.

———. 2005. "Giving Voice to Latino Voters," *Annals of the American Academy of Political and Social Science* 601:66–84.

Rangel, Charles. 2002. "Bring Back the Draft." *New York Times,* 31 December.

Raskin, Jamin B. 1993. "Legal Aliens, Local Citizens: The Historical, Constitutional and Theoretical Meanings of Alien Suffrage." *University of Pennsylvania Law Review* 141:1391–1470.

Rawls, John. 1993. *Political Liberalism.* New York: Columbia University Press.

Renshon, Stanley A. 2000. "Dual Citizens in America: An Issue of Vast Proportions and Significance." Brief in *Backgrounder* series: Washington, DC: Center for Immigration Studies.

———. 2001. "Dual Citizenship and American National Identity." Washington, D.C.: Center for Immigration Studies.

Riker, William H., and Peter C. Ordeshook. 1968. "A Theory of the Calculus of Voting." *The American Political Science Review* 62, no. 1:25–42.

Rodriguez, Clara. 2002. *Changing Race*. Philadelphia, PA: Temple University Press.

Roediger, David. 1991. *The Wages of Whiteness*. New York: Verso.

Rogers, Reuel. 2000a. "Afro-Caribbean Immigrants, African Americans, and the Politics of Group Identity." In *Black and Multiracial Politics in America*, edited by Yvette Marie Alex-Assensoh and Lawrence J. Hanks, 15–59. New York: New York University Press.

———. 2000b. "Between Race and Ethnicity: Afro Caribbean Immigrants, African-Americans, and the Politics of Incorporation." Doctoral Dissertation. Princeton, NJ: Princeton University.

———. 2001. "Black Like Who? Afro-Caribbean Immigrants, African-Americans, and the Politics of Group Identity," In Nancy Foner, ed., *Islands in the City: West Indian Migration to New York*, 162–92. Berkeley: University of California Press.

Rohrlich, Ted. 1998. "Noncitizens on Sidelines as Hernández Recall Sputters." *Los Angeles Times*, 2 February.

Rosberg, Gerald M. 1977. "Aliens and Equal Protection: Why Not the Right to Vote?" *Michigan Law Review* 75:1092–1136.

Rosenbaum, Marcus, et al. 2001. *National Survey on Civil Liberties*. Washington, DC. National Public Radio/Henry J. Kaiser Family Foundation/John F. Kennedy School of Government.

Rosenfeld, Michael. 2002. "Measures of Assimilation in the Marriage Market." *Journal of Marriage and the Family* 64:152–62.

Rosenstone, Steven J., and John Mark Hansen. 1993. *Mobilization, Participation, and Democracy in America*. New York: Macmillan Publishing Company.

Rothman, Joshua D. 2003. *Notorious in the Neighborhood : Sex and Families across the Color Line in Virginia, 1787–1861*. Chapel Hill: University of North Carolina Press.

Rumbaut, Ruben. 1997. "Assimilation and Its Discontents: Between Rhetoric and Reality." *International Migration Review* 31, no. 4:923–60.

Rumbaut, Ruben, and Kenji Ima. 1988. *The Adaptation of Southeast Asian Refugee Youth: A Comparative Study*. Washington, DC: U.S. Office of Refugee Resettlement.

Russell, John. 1991. Race and Reflexivity: The Black Other in Contemporary Japanese Mass Culture. *Cultural Anthropology.* 6, no. 1:3–25

Saito, Leland. 1998. *Race and Politics*. Bloomington: Indiana University Press.

Salins, Peter. 1997. *Assimilation, American Style*. New York: Basic Books.

Sanchez, Leonel. 2003. "Ready to Sacrifice." *San Diego Union-Tribune.* 11 April, B1.

Sánchez Korrol, Virginia E. 1994. *From Colonia to Community: The History of Puerto Ricans in New York City*. Berkeley: University of California Press.

Sandel, Michael J. 1984. "The Procedural Republic and the Unencumbered Self." *Political Theory* 12:81–96.

Santa Ana, Otto. 2002. *Brown Tide Rising*. Austin: University of Texas Press.

Schattschneider, E. E. 1960. *The Semi-Sovereign People*. New York: Holt, Rinehart, Winston.

Schlesinger, Joseph A. 1991. *Political Parties and the Winning of Office*. Ann Arbor: University of Michigan Press.

Schmidley, A. Dianne. 2001. "Profile of the Foreign-born Population in the United States: 2000." *Current Population Reports*, P23-306. Washington, DC, U.S. Census Bureau.

Schuck, Peter H., and Rogers M. Smith. 1985. *Citizenship without Consent: Illegal Aliens in the American Polity*. New Haven, CT: Yale University Press.

Schuman H., C. Steeh, L. Bobo, and M. Krysan. 1997. *Racial Attitudes in America: Trends and Interpretations*. Cambridge, MA: Harvard University Press. Revised edition.

Scott, James. 1998. *Seeing Like a State*. New Haven, CT: Yale University Press.

Segura, Gary M., Denis Falcon, and Harry Pachon. 1997. "Dynamics of Latino Partisanship in California: Immigration, Issue Salience, and their Implications." *Harvard Journal of Hispanic Politics* 10:62–80.

Shafir, Gershon. 1998. "Introduction: The Evolving Tradition of Citizenship." In *The Citizenship Debates: A Reader,* edited by Gershon Shafir, 1–31. Minneapolis, MN: University of Minneapolis Press.

Shapiro, Ian. 1999. *Democratic Justice*. New Haven: Yale University Press.

Shapiro, Ian, and Will Kymlicka, eds. 1997. *Ethnicity and Group Rights*. New York: New York University Press.

Shefter, Martin. 1994. *Political Parties and the State: The American Historical Experience*. Princeton, NJ: Princeton University Press.

Shingles, Richard D. 1981. "Black Consciousness and Political Participation: The Missing Link." *American Political Science Review* 75:76–91.

Shively, W. Phillips. 1979. "The Development of Party Identification among Adults." *American Political Science Review* 73, no. 4 (December): 1039–54.

Sidanius, Jim, and Felicia Pratto. 1999. *Social Dominance*. New York: Cambridge University Press.

Singer, Audrey, and Greta Gilbertson. 2000. "Naturalization in the Wake of Anti-Immigrant Legislation: Dominicans in New York City." Working Paper 10. Washington, DC: Carnegie Endowment.

Skerry, Peter. 2002. "Multiracialism and the Administrative State." In *The New Race Question,* edited by Joel Perlmann and Mary C. Waters, 327–39. New York: Russell Sage Foundation.

Skocpol, Theda. 1999. "Advocates without Members: The Recent Transformation of American Civic Life." In *Civic Engagement in American Democracy,* edited by Theda Skocpol and Morris P. Fiorina, 461–510. Washington, D.C., New York: Brookings Institution Press, Russell Sage Foundation.

———. 2003. *Diminished Democracy: From Membership to Management in American Civic Life*. Norman: University of Oklahoma Press.

Skrentny, John. 2002. *The Minority Rights Revolution.* Cambridge, MA: Belknap/Harvard.

Smith, Michael Peter, and Luis Guarnizo, eds. 1998. *Transnationalism from Below.* Somerset, NJ: Transaction Publishers.

Smith, Rogers. 1997. *Civic Ideals: Conflicting Visions of Citizenship in U.S. History.* New Haven, CT: Yale University Press.

Snipp, C. Matthew. 2003. "Racial Measurement in the American Census: Past Practices and Implications for the Future." *Annual Review of Sociology* 29: 563–88.

Soysal, Yasemin Nuhoglu. 1994. *Limits of Citizenship: Migrants and Postnational Membership in Europe.* Chicago: University of Chicago Press.

Spiro, Peter J. 1997. "Dual Nationality and the Meaning of Citizenship." *Emory Law Journal* 46, no. 4: 1411–85.

———. 1999. "Embracing Dual Nationality." Washington, DC: Carnegie Endowment for International Peace.

St. John de Crèvecoeur, J. Hector. 1981 (orig. pub. 1782). *Letters from an American Farmer.* New York: Penguin.

Sterne, Evelyn Savidge. 2001. "Beyond the Boss: Immigration and American Political Culture From 1880 to 1946." In *E Pluribus Unum? Contemporary and Historical Perspectives on Immigrant Political Incorporation,* edited by Gary Gerstle and John Mollenkopf, 33–66. New York: Russell Sage Foundation.

Tam, Wendy. 1995. "Asians—A Monolithic Voting Bloc?" *Political Behavior* 17: 223–49.

Tate, Katherine. 1993. *From Protest to Politics.* Cambridge, MA: Harvard University Press.

Taylor, Marylee. 1998. "Local Racial/Ethnic Proportions and White Attitudes: Numbers Count." *American Sociological Review* 63: 512–35.

Thomas, W. I., and Florian Znaniecki. 1928. *The Polish Peasant in Europe and America.* New York: Knopf.

Tiao, Paul. 1993. "Non-Citizen Suffrage: An Argument Based on the Voting Rights Act and Related Law." *Columbia Human Rights Law Review* 25: 71–218.

Tichenor, Daniel. 2002. *Dividing Lines: The Politics of Immigration Control in America.* Princeton, NJ: Princeton University Press.

Tilly, Charles. 1998. *Durable Inequality.* Berkeley: University of California Press.

Tomz, Michael, Jason Wittenberg, and Gary King. 1999. CLARIFY: Software for Interpreting and Presenting Statistical Results. Version 1.2.1, 1 June. Cambridge, MA: Harvard University.

Torres, María de los Angeles. 1999. *In the Land of Mirrors: Cuban Exile Politics in the United States.* Ann Arbor: University of Michigan Press.

Truman, David. 1971. *The Governmental Process: Political Interests and Public Opinion.* New York: Knopf.

Uggen, Christopher, and Jeff Manza. 2002. "Democratic Contraction? The

Political Consequences of Felon Disenfranchisement in the United States." *American Sociological Review* 67:777–803.

Uhlaner, Carole J., Bruce E. Cain, and D. Roderick Kiewiet. 1989. "Political Participation of Ethnic Minorities in the 1980s." *Political Behavior* 11, no. 3:195–231.

Uhlaner, Carole and F. Chris Garcia. 2001. "Learning Which Party Fits: Experience, Ethnic Identity, and the Demographic Foundations of Latino Party Identification." Paper presented at the Minority Representation: Institutions, Behavior, and Identity Conference, Claremont Graduate University, Claremont, California.

———. 2002. "Latino Public Opinion." In *Understanding Public Opinion,* edited by Barbara Norrander and Clyde Wilcox, 77–104. Washington, DC: Congressional Quarterly Press.

U.S. Bureau of Census. 2001. *United States Census 2000.* http://www.census .gov/popest/estimates.php

———. 2002a. *Current Population Survey: Monthly Demographic File.* March. Washington, DC: U.S. Bureau of Census.

———. 2002b. "Voting and Registration in the Election of November 2002." Series P-20 #542. Detailed tables. http://www.census.gov/population/www/ socdemo/voting/p20-542.html. Accessed 20 August 2002.

U.S. Commission on Civil Rights. 1974. "Counting the Forgotten: The 1970 Census Count of Persons of Spanish Speaking Background in the United States." Washington DC: Government Printing Office.

U.S. Department of Homeland Security. 2004. *Yearbook of Immigration Statistics, 2003.* U.S. Government Printing Office: Washington, DC.

U.S. Immigration and Naturalization Services. 2002. *2000 INS Statistical Yearbook.* Washington, DC: USGPO.

———. 2003. *2001 Statistical Yearbook of the Immigration and Naturalization Service.* Springfield, VA: National Technical Information Service.

Vagts, Alfred 1946. "The Foreigner as Soldier in the Second World War, I." *Journal of Politics* 8: 174–200.

Verba, Sidney. 2003. "Would the Dream of Political Equality Turn out to Be a Nightmare?" *Perspectives on Politics.* 1:663–79.

Verba, Sidney, Kay Lehman Schlozman, and Henry E. Brady. 1995. *Voice and Equality: Civic Voluntarism in American Politics.* Cambridge, MA: Harvard University Press.

Verba, Sidney, Kay Lehman Schlozman, Henry Brady, and Norman H. Nie. 1993. "Race Ethnicity and Political Resources: Participation in the United States." *British Journal of Political Science,* 23:453–97.

Verba, Sidney and Norman H. Nie. 1972. *Participation in America.* New York: Little Brown.

Wagatsuma, Hiroshi. 1968. "The Social Perception of Skin Color in Japan." In *Color and Race,* edited by John Hope Franklin, 129–65. Boston: Houghton Mifflin.

Waldinger, Roger, ed. 2001. *Strangers at the Gates*. Berkeley: University of California Press.

Wallman, Katherine K. 1998. "Data on Race and Ethnicity: Revising the Federal Standard." *The American Statistician* 52, no. 1 (February): 31–33.

Walzer, Michael. 1970. *Obligations: Essays on Disobedience, War, and Citizenship*. Cambridge, MA: Harvard University Press.

"*Washington Post*/Kaiser Family Foundation/Harvard University Latino Survey." 1999. ICR Survey Research Group. Roper Center for Public Opinion Research.

Waters, Mary. 1990. *Ethnic Options: Choosing Identities in America*. Berkeley: University of California Press.

———. 1999. *Black Identities: West Indian Immigrant Dreams and American Realities*. Cambridge, MA: Harvard University Press.

Waters, Mary, Philip Kasinitz, and John Mollenkopf. 2002. "Becoming American/Becoming New Yorkers: Immigrant Incorporation in a Majority Minority City." *International Migration Review* 36, no. 4 (Winter): 1020–36.

Wattenberg, Martin P. 1990. *The Decline of American Political Parties, 1952–1988*. Cambridge, MA: Harvard University Press.

———. 1994. *The Decline Of American Political Parties, 1952–1992*. Cambridge, MA: Harvard University Press.

Wei, William. 1993. *The Asian American Movement*. Philadelphia: Temple University Press.

Weil, Patrick. 2001. "Access to Citizenship: A Comparison of Twenty-Five Nationality Laws." In *Citizenship Today: Global Perspectives and Practices*, edited by T. Alexander Aleinikoff and Douglas Klusmeyer, 63–88. Washington, DC: Carnegie Endowment for International Peace.

Weiner, Tim. 2003. "A Nation at War: Immigrant Marines." *New York Times*. 4 April, B10.

Welch, Susan, and Lee Sigelman. 2000. "Getting to Know You? Latino-Anglo Social Contact." *Social Science Quarterly* 81, 1:67–83.

Wilkie, Dana. 2003. "Issa Wants Survivors of Fallen Noncitizens to Benefit." 11 April. www.signonsandiego.com/news/world/iraq/homefront/20030411–9999_1m11issa.html

Wills, Gary. 2003. *Negro President: Jefferson and the Slave Power*. New York: Houghton Mifflin.

Wilson, James Q. 1973. *Political Organizations*. New York: Basic Books.

Wolfinger, Raymond E. and Steven J. Rosenstone. 1980. *Who Votes?* New Haven, CT: Yale University Press.

Wong, Janelle. 2000a. "The Effects of Age and Political Exposure on the Development of Party Identification among Asian American and Latino Immigrants in the U.S." *Political Behavior* 22, no. 4:341–71.

———. 2000b. "Institutional Context and Political Mobilization Among Mexican and Chinese Immigrants in New York and Los Angeles." Paper presented at the CUNY Graduate Center Conference on Immigrant Political Participation, New York.

———. 2001. "The New Dynamics of Immigrants' Political Incorporation: A Multi-Method Study of Political Participation and Mobilization among Asian and Latino Immigrants in the United States." Unpublished dissertation manuscript. Department of Political Science, Yale University, New Haven, Connecticut.

———. 2002. "Gender and Political Participation among Asian Americans." In *Asian American Politics: Law, Participation, and Policy,* edited by James Lai and Don Nakanishi, 211–30. Boulder, CO: Rowman and Littlefield Publishers.

———. 2004. *Immigrants and Politics: The Political Mobilization of Asian Americans and Latinos.* Unpublished Manuscript.

———. 2005 *Democracy's Promise: Immigrants and American Civic Institutions.* Ann Arbor: University of Michigan Press.

Worth, Robert F. 2002. "Noncitizens Should Get Vote Too, Mayor Says." *Washington Post.* 1 October.

———. 2004. "Push Is On to Give Legal Immigrants Vote in New York." *New York Times,* 8 April.

Yang, Phillip Q. 1994. "Explaining Immigrant Naturalization." *International Migration Review* 28, no. 3:449–477.

Young, Iris Marion. 2000. *Inclusion and Democracy.* New York: Oxford University Press.

Zhou, M., and Bankston, C. L. 1998. *Growing Up American: How Vietnamese Children Adapt to Life in the United States.* New York: Russell Sage Foundation.

Ziff, Larzer, ed. 1959. *Benjamin Franklin's Selected Writings.* New York: Holt, Rinehart, and Winston.

Zolberg, Aristide. 2005. *A Nation by Design.* Cambridge, MA: Harvard University Press.

Contributors

Bruce Cain is Robson Professor of Political Science, Director of the Institute of Governmental Studies at the University of California, Berkeley, and Director of the University of California Washington Center, Washington, D.C.

Grace Cho is a doctoral candidate in political science at the University of Michigan.

Jack Citrin is Professor of Political Science and Associate Director of the Institute of Governmental Studies at the University of California, Berkeley.

Louis DeSipio is Associate Professor of Political Science and Chicano/Latino Studies in the School of Social Sciences at the University of California, Irvine.

Brendan Doherty is a doctoral candidate in political science at the University of California, Berkeley.

Lisa García Bedolla is Assistant Professor of Political Science and Chicano/Latino Studies in the School of Social Sciences at the University of California, Irvine.

Zoltan Hajnal is Assistant Professor of Political Science at the University of California, San Diego.

Jennifer Holdaway is Program Officer for the International Migration Program at the Social Science Research Council in New York City.

Jane Junn is Associate Professor of Political Science at Rutgers University.

Philip Kasinitz is Professor of Sociology at Hunter College and the City University of New York Graduate Center and Executive Officer of the CUNY Graduate Center's Program in Sociology.

Taeku Lee is Associate Professor of Political Science at the University of California, Berkeley.

John Mollenkopf is Distinguished Professor of Political Science and Sociology at the City University of New York Graduate Center and Director of its Center for Urban Research.

Tatishe M. Nteta is a doctoral candidate in political science at the University of California, Berkeley.

Kathryn Pearson is Assistant Professor of Political Science at the University of Minnesota.

Kenneth Prewitt is Carnegie Professor of Public Affairs, School of International and Public Affairs at Columbia University and formerly Director of the U.S. Census Bureau.

S. Karthick Ramakrishnan is Assistant Professor of Political Science at the University of California, Riverside.

Ricardo Ramírez is Assistant Professor in the Department of Political Science and the Program in American Studies and Ethnicity at the University of Southern California.

Mary Waters is Professor of Sociology and Department Chair at Harvard University.

Cara Wong is Assistant Professor of Political Science at the University of Michigan.

Janelle Wong is Assistant Professor in the Department of Political Science and the Program in American Studies and Ethnicity at the University of Southern California.

Index

Race, Ethnicity, and Politics